AF352481

Xu Bing and Contemporary Chinese Art

SUNY SERIES IN CHINESE PHILOSOPHY AND CULTURE

Roger T. Ames, *editor*

Xu Bing and Contemporary Chinese Art

Cultural and Philosophical Reflections

Edited by

Hsingyuan Tsao
and Roger T. Ames

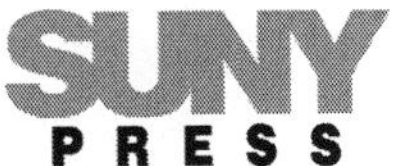

Cover image: *A Book from the Sky*, Xu Bing, 1987–1991;
installation view; courtesy of the artist.

Published by
State University of New York Press
Albany

© 2011 State University of New York

All rights reserved

Printed in the United States of America

No part of this book may be used or reproduced in any manner whatsoever without written permission. No part of this book may be stored in a retrieval system or transmitted in any form or by any means including electronic, electrostatic, magnetic tape, mechanical, photocopying, recording, or otherwise without the prior permission in writing of the publisher.

For information, contact
State University of New York Press
www.sunypress.edu

Production by Diane Ganeles
Marketing by Anne M. Valentine

Library of Congress Cataloging-in-Publication Data

Xu Bing and contemporary Chinese art : cultural and philosophical reflections / edited by Hsingyuan Tsao and Roger T. Ames.
    p. cm. — (SUNY series in Chinese philosophy and culture)
  Includes bibliographical references and index.
    ISBN 978-1-4384-3790-3 (pbk. : alk. paper) — ISBN 978-1-4384-3791-0 (hardcover : alk. paper)
  1. Xu, Bing—Criticism and interpretation.   2. Art, Chinese—20th century—Themes, motives.   3. Art, Chinese—21st century—Themes, motives.   I. Tsao, Hsingyuan.   II. Ames, Roger T.
  N7349.X8X8 2011
  709.51'09051—dc22   2011004148

10 9 8 7 6 5 4 3 2 1

Contents

Illustrations

Acknowledgments

This book project began as an idea for a team-taught graduate seminar while I was teaching at the University of Hawai'i, Manoa, with my colleague Dr. Roger T. Ames. We were interested in how we might define the Chinese tradition-based discourse, if there is any, for Chinese contemporary art. Before the course was offered, however, I accepted a teaching position at the University of British Columbia (UBC) and consequently held the seminar without the important Chinese philosophical interventions I would have anticipated from Roger.

A symposium based on the contents of the seminar was held on the campus of St. John's College of UBC on March 5, 2005. Many thanks to the Joan Carlisle Irving Lecture Series for providing us the opportunity to host the public lectures by acclaimed artist Xu Bing, whose work became a primary focus of the symposium and this volume. I would like to warmly thank our symposium supporters, including Dr. Timothy Brook, principal of St. John's College, who offered us generous financial and intellectual resources; Dr. Darrin Lehman, the associate dean of the Faculty of Arts at UBC for his support and encouragement; Professor Rhodri Winsor-Liscombe, the head of the Department of Art History, Visual Arts, and Theory at UBC; and Ms. Whitney Friesen, the department administrator. My gratitude also goes out to our collaborators, the Vancouver Art Gallery and *Yishu: Magazine for Contemporary Chinese Art*, guided by Mr. Zheng Shengtian and the wonderful staff. I salute the graduate students of our department for their diligent work in producing the poster and organizing all the details of the event: Adam Chu, Susan Chang, Zoe Li, April Liu, Christian Monks, Kazuko Kameda-Madar, Yusuke Suzuki, and Gary Wang.

I particularly appreciate the contributions of Christian Monks and Jean Kares, who copyedited the manuscript before it was sent out for review; Susan Chang and Adam Chu, who compiled the timeline of contemporary art; Zoe Li, who put together a bibliography of writings on Xu Bing for both the symposium and this volume; and April Liu's extremely devoted copyediting work after this volume was accepted by the publisher.

Last, but not least, I want to thank the people of Vancouver for all their support and participation over the course of the symposium.

Hsingyuan Tsao

A Dilemma in Contemporary Chinese Art

An Introduction

HSINGYUAN TSAO & ROGER T. AMES

Is contemporary Chinese art "Chinese" art? Chapters in this collection attempt to address this question by investigating the relationship between ancient Chinese philosophy and the ideas being expressed in contemporary Chinese art at a time when this art becomes increasingly popular in the West. Contemporary Chinese art is in a cultural dilemma. On the one hand, it is not exactly "Chinese" even though it does address the Chinese experience and its issues. And on the other hand, it cannot abandon this "Chinese" identity because it is only by labeling itself "Chinese" that it can gain a place in the international art arena. Today the expression *contemporary art discourse* is almost synonymous with Western contemporary art discourse. Contemporary art has been vetted and evaluated internationally under Western assumptions about modernity and postmodernity. Within this rather narrowly defined cultural space, the relative position of contemporary art from China has been an important issue for artists and art historians. The identity of contemporary Chinese art is often challenged by the competing claims that it is either derivative of Western contemporary art or that it has been defined within the indigenous cultural identity of China and is thus the manifestation of contemporary China.

This dialogue about contemporary Chinese art began as early as 1981 when China was recovering from the Stars Group, an art movement driven by social protest that anticipated the New Wave of 1985. David Hockney visited the Central Academy of Fine Arts in Beijing where a young teacher asked him, "'What national exhibitions are there in England?' Puzzled, David responded with an 'Er . . . ' Then he hazarded: 'Well, the best is the Royal Academy. It's mostly for amateurs.' Another 'er. . . . '"[1]

A thousand years ago in China, the pioneers of literati art set themselves up against the court practitioners, using their amateur art as a media for critiquing government policies. Chinese artists in the 1980s were heirs to this same pattern: they either belonged to the camp under the sway of official socialist ideology and reputable national exhibitions, or they belonged to an independent, nongovernmental supported avant-gardism. It was not that Chinese artists did not try to revitalize the literati tradition, but the mid-1980s New Literati Art Movement deteriorated into a playfulness of ink and brush that was characteristic of literati art in late imperial times. The urge to find a powerful language to strike out against the official control of art was indeed the initial motivation of Chinese artists who looked to Western contemporary visual language as a resource. Moral support for these Chinese artists came from foreign diplomats, visiting scholars, and foreign students residing in China.

In the early 1990s, the contemporary Chinese art movement was forced to go underground and Chinese artists found the West as a new audience for their works. An increasingly active dialogue has emerged between the local (Chinese) and the global (Euro-American) worlds, raising the visibility of China's new art to unprecedented heights. Andrew Solomon's influential essay, "Their Irony, Humor (and Art) Can Save China," published in the *New York Times Sunday Magazine* (1993), made an indelible impact on the view of contemporary Chinese art among a growing Western audience.[2] However, Homi Bhabha has offered an ominous warning about these Chinese artists: "Despite the claims to [what is] a spurious rhetoric of 'internationalism,' the relationship between Chinese artists and the postmodern art world is that they live in 'the nations of others.'"[3]

In this volume, we hoped to investigate this issue of "otherness" from different angles:

1. Are these Chinese artists ideologically "imprisoned" as they depend on the Western social system and discourse for their life and art?

   2. Does the use of Chinese-segmented visual and linguistic marks and traditions "add to" the Anglo-American postmodern discourse "without adding up"[4] to anything itself?

To put it simply, is Chinese contemporary art rooted in the tradition of Chinese culture, or is it yet another excellent example of cultural self-colonization?

In order to investigate these questions, the contributors to this volume have attempted to relate Chinese artistic expression to the structure and function of the Chinese language and to the unadvertised assumptions of Chinese natural cosmology. Many of the world's cosmologies associate language and cosmic creativity, from "in the beginning was the word" to aboriginal Australians who believe that order is created and sustained through song. A major theme in the *Yijing* (*Book of Changes* 易经), a text that grounds the evolution of Confucian and Daoist cosmology, is the fertile and productive relationship between image, language, and meaning. Can we go beyond the more obvious political and social commentaries on contemporary Chinese art to find resonances between some of these artistic ideas and the indigenous sources of Chinese cultural self-understanding? This volume is dedicated to an exploration of how Xu Bing and other artists have navigated between two different cultural sites and established a "third" place from which they are able to appropriate novel Western ideas to address centuries old Chinese cultural issues within a Chinese cultural discourse.

There are at least four reasons for selecting the art of Xu Bing as a central focus for this volume. First and foremost is the nature of Xu Bing's work. *A Book from the Sky*, for example, incorporates over four thousand characters that were fabricated using the theoretical principles of word making in the written Chinese language. They look like Chinese characters but none of the characters could be pronounced in Chinese nor did they possess shared, designated meanings. They are unintelligible to an otherwise literate audience. These characters can be "meaningful" only when "read" outside of normal linguistic practices. As Bei Dao, a contemporary Chinese poet, has said of Xu Bing's characters: "You are nothing but a pictograph that has lost its sound."

The second reason for using Xu Bing's work as an axis of discussion is that both editors, Tsao and Ames, are enamored with Xu Bing's *A Book from the Sky*, believing that it has much to offer as a heuristic for reflecting upon the role of language and meaning-making

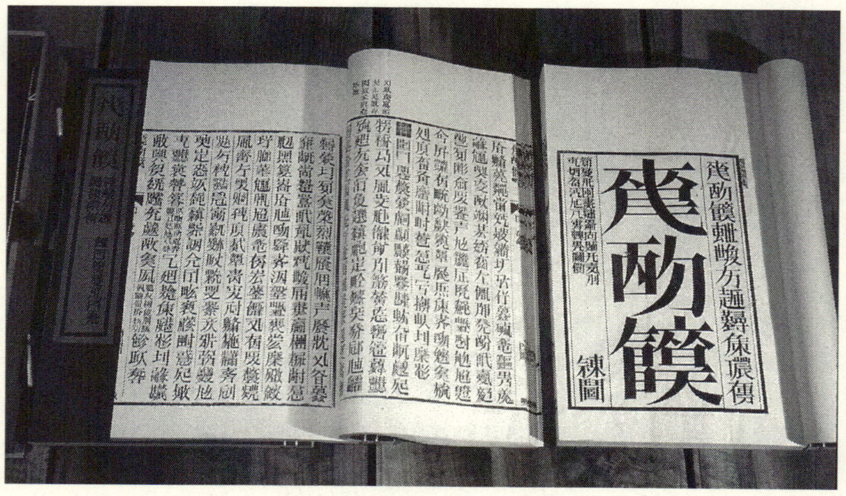

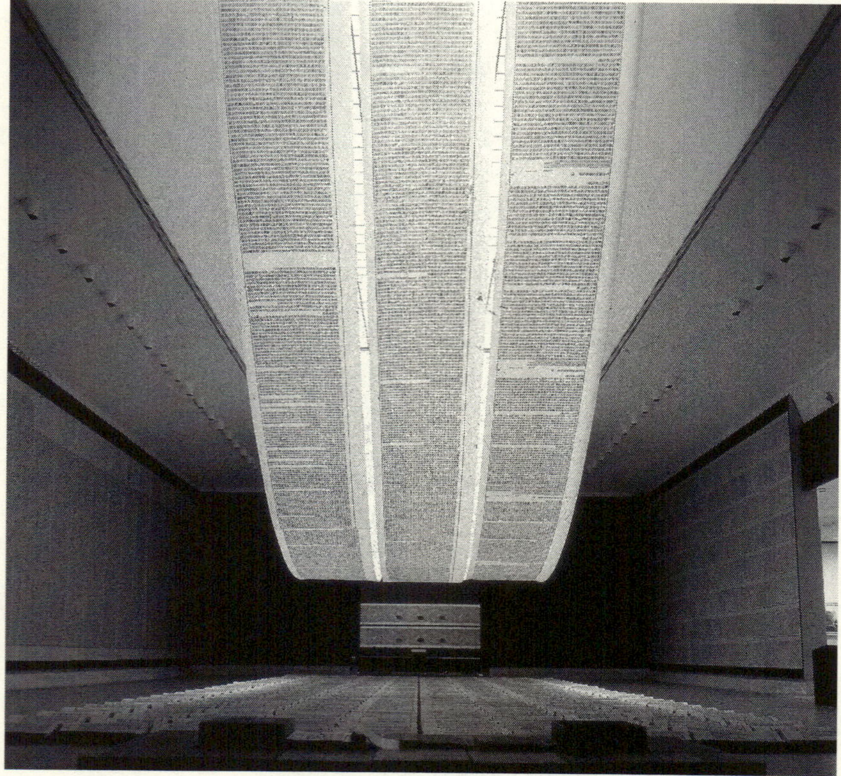

FIGURE I.I. *A Book from the Sky* (*Tian shu* 天书), Xu Bing, 1987–1991. Above: detail of pages from two of the set of four books. Below: Installation view. (Courtesy of the artist.)

in the traditional Chinese cultural discourse. It provides an occasion for bringing into focus commonalities that are broadly shared by philosophy, history, art, and culture, while allowing each of these disciplines to speak from their own unique perspective.

The third, but equally important reason for engaging Xu Bing's oeuvre is that this work allows critics to look at Chinese culture in a panoramic way. Xu Bing's "text" carries the conversation back into the wealth of ancient Chinese culture and forward into China's recent launch into the international contemporary art world. *A Book from the Sky* is a spectacle that requires us to locate contemporary Chinese art within its cultural context, allowing that this work was admittedly crafted under the invisible influence of Western postmodern culture at a time when the Chinese authorities—political and academic—exerted a concentrated effort to prohibit its people from studying the issues of postmodernity.

Finally, both editors are persuaded that there is real aesthetic profundity in Xu Bing's *A Book from the Sky* as a work of art itself. It is a piece that provokes animated theorizing among its readers as in the substance of this volume. At the same time, it resists any reduction to specific abstract explanations. Like all great art, it is bottomless, allowing us in our appreciation only to "get on with it" as opposed to "getting it right."

There are seven chapters in this collection. Tsao Hsingyuan begins the volume by offering the general background needed to contextualize the contemporary art scene in China, illustrating how artists have sought to please different audiences under different circumstances. In "Reading and Misreading: Double Entendre in Locally Oriented Logos," Tsao's primary focus is the audiences for contemporary Chinese art. Tsao suggests that the term "avant-garde" was used to describe contemporary art in China simply because in the 1970s it served the Chinese artist as a way of deploying Western modern art language to challenge the grip of political and authoritarian control through a kind of cultural insurgency. However, after 1989, the audience for contemporary Chinese art shifted from a strained, sometimes shrill polemic with the Chinese authorities to a dialogue with an increasingly appreciative Western audience that had emerged through the international commoditization of their work. Still, Tsao argues, while some Chinese artists have self-consciously divorced themselves from traditional Chinese culture, the diluted relationship between geographical site and cultural experience brought on by globalization has allowed other Chinese artists,

such as Xu Bing, to achieve a kind of "interculturality" by presenting a strong Chinese cultural identity in an international forum.

Such "interculturality" might sound liberating, but Tsao
Hsingyuan, invoking the specter of the global capitalist art world,
rejects any naïve assumption that the cultural specificity and "local-
ness" of Chinese artists such as Xu Bing represent some kind of
Chinese triumph in which these artists have a transformative affect
on world art. Tsao cautions that, on the contrary, these artists are
being absorbed wholesale into the discourses and corporate values
of a global postindustrialist capitalism that is not of their own making, and that in many ways contradicts the substance of their own
traditional Chinese culture.

Roger T. Ames, in "Reading Xu Bing's *A Book from the Sky*:
A Case Study in the Making of Meaning," appeals to the canons
of the Chinese philosophical tradition to bring detail and textual
specificity to some of the more general claims about a persistent
Chinese cultural identity being made by Tsao Hsingyuan. He associates the characters in Xu Bing's *A Book from the Sky* with the "fish
traps" and "rabbit snares" metaphors for catching meaning that we
find in Daoist writings. He argues that language is self-referencing,
and that the meaning of a word is a function of its use within a
language system. The act of ordering the world through language
does not begin from assumptions about a "literal" language that,
in mapping onto a given "reality," enables us to reference things
in the world correctly. Rather, the use of language requires that
we constantly adjust and reinvest words and their meanings with
the practical intention of increasing communal harmony and significance. This is perhaps what Guillaume Apollinaire (1880–1918)
means in claiming that art should be more real than reality. Once
the situated meaning has been "trapped" and expressed in these
particular words, the words are then "emptied" and stand available
for further deployment in capturing and conveying new meanings.

To the extent that *A Book from the Sky* is identifiable as "language" and yet stands empty, we are confronted with linguistic
"ruins" that threaten our faith in the persistence of a shared dogma,
a shared common sense. On the one hand, this is a disturbing,
even startling, experience that undermines our feelings of communal solidarity and our assumed competence within our community, underscoring perhaps a sense of the ultimate precariousness of
the human experience. However, as the reassurance of shared linguistic "objectivity" recedes from sight, we are renewed as unique,

historical, contingent, and provisional beings that struggle with imagination to quite literally make sense of the nonsense. Xu Bing's work forces us to appreciate our own role in the making of meaning, renewing our confidence in our own subjectivity. Indeed, Xu Bing in offering us his empty "traps" is challenging us to capture a new world impressed with new meanings of our own making.

Kuan-Hung Chen shares a common starting point with Ames in his "Seriousness, Playfulness, and a Religious Reading of *A Book from the Sky*," but focuses on the religious implications of Xu Bing's work. Chen argues that *A Book from the Sky* has a profoundly religious import, and with its movement between seriousness and playfulness, allows us to distinguish Xu Bing's inclusive religiousness from the more familiar exclusive paradigm of religion. As a basis for framing his discussion of inclusive and exclusive religiousness, Chen uses John Dewey's distinction between a liberating, unique expression of religiousness and the often oppressive, suffocating strictures and dogma of institutionalized religion.

Exclusive religiousness is based upon a kind of transcendentalism that utterly separates the object of reverence from the supplicant, operating within a clear dualistic paradigm. The problem with applying this model to a reading of Xu Bing's work is that a Western audience familiar with exclusive religiousness but having little or no background in Chinese culture will conclude that there is little religious import in Xu Bing's work. Of course, this response is prompted by the fact that the transcendental ground of exclusive religiousness has little relevance for traditional Chinese philosophical and religious sensibilities. Further, the "One behind the many" model of religiousness with all of its accoutrements of a 'Reality' behind appearance and its single, universal 'Truth' precludes the playfulness that is so evident in *A Book from the Sky*.

Chen appeals to a mantra often invoked by scholars of premodern China to define religiousness—"the continuity between humanity and the divine (*tianren heyi* 天人合一)"—as a basis for arguing for the inclusive nature of the Chinese religious experience. The *qi* 气 cosmology, which serves as the interpretive context of traditional Chinese culture, begins from the wholeness of experience and the unbroken continuity among the unique things and events that constitute it. In the absence of some transcendental ground, religious meaning is made through productive correlations that allow for both persistence and novelty, for continuity and uniqueness, for reverence and a creative playfulness. Indeed, it is only when Xu Bing's *A Book from the Sky* is understood in terms of this inclusive religious sensibility that the audience is able to appreciate both the sophisticated profundity of the work and its openness to creative play.

In his chapter, "Making Natural Languages in Contemporary Chinese Art," Richard Vinograd first defines his terms. "Natural languages" is a broad category of textual rather than spoken language ranging from Chinese characters and trigrams to tattoos and talismans that are perceived as having their source in nature rather than in culture. "Chinese" references the early training and culturally based allusions of these contemporary artists. By using the term "making," Vinograd captures the paradoxes inherent in the contribution of these Chinese artists to the contemporary art world: the seeming artificiality, meaninglessness, and obscurity of the putatively "natural" languages. The specific work of Xu Bing is not an altogether unusual phenomenon in the language-based art that has been an important part of public consciousness during and following the Maoist era.

In several of his projects, such as *Square Word Calligraphy* and *A Book from the Sky*, Xu Bing plays on a tension between the anticipated familiarity expected from a natural language and the frustration or anxiety one feels in encountering its defamiliarized and estranged form. In spite of the magnitude of these installations and the obvious labor that has gone into their construction—Xu Bing's and other artists as well—the role of the spectator is paramount. Whatever meaning or lack of it that such projects are able to communicate, it is not a message from artist to viewer but an encounter between the embedded graphs and the viewer's response, even when the response is one of utter bemusement.

Vinograd rehearses a range of Xu Bing's artworks in which each mode of natural language represents an alternative to our expectations around conventional language. There is a difference between "seeing" and "reading" that places an enormous burden of recognition on the viewer that is required for decoding and decipherment. In all of this, there seems to be a mistrust of conventional language and pessimism about the possibility of meaningful communication. The natural languages are repeatedly referenced in ways that defer the usual expectations of legibility and meaning. Perhaps there is some compensation in the aesthetic deployment of these natural languages, which require further probing to reveal deep and abiding cultural identities.

In her chapter "The Living Word: Xu Bing and the Art of Chan Wordplay," April Liu begins with Xu Bing's professed interest in Chan Buddhism. The strategies for indirect communication that we find in Xu Bing's art find immediate resonance with images of the Chan tradition as a possible cultural resource—associations with the "*gongan* 公案" or nonsensical dialogue form, the frequent use of wordplay and paradox, the use of repetitive, menial tasks as a meditative heuristic, and so on. But Liu poses the challenging question: whose Chan anyway? That is, does Xu Bing appeal to traditional understandings of a decidedly Chinese variation on an antique Indian philosophy and religion, or is he playing to a thin, popular, "Westernized" version of the same?

Liu identifies three moments in Xu Bing's entry into the international art world that we might associate with Chan Buddhism. First, in *A Book from the Sky*, without explicit reference to Chan, Xu Bing attempts to communicate by subverting the expectations of existing cultural and linguistic frameworks through the use of empty signifiers. Second, in his recent prize-winning installation *Where Does the Dust Itself Collect?* Xu Bing includes a direct reference to a familiar Chan poem where its original meaning is itself subverted by complicity in the institutionalized agenda, nationalist politics, and preexisting meanings of the international art world for whom it is displayed. And third, Xu Bing has been associated with popular, commodified representations of Chan sensibilities and a "depthless" romantic imaginaire. Within this context, Xu Bing has been challenged to open up an "alternative space" that acknowledges the Chan infiltration of popular Western culture and problematizes simple East–West, traditional–modern binaries. Still, for Liu, the most important question is not the possibility of success or failure in Xu Bing's subverting a hegemonic Western ideology, but whether or not his Chan-inspired commitment to engaging the viewer can open up alternative ways of communication through visual art.

Kazuko Kameda-Madar, in her chapter "A Study of *Shen Wai Shen* (Body Outside Body) by Xu Bing," explores a work by Xu Bing that literally means "the body outside the body." This installation recontextualizes the way in which Chinese calligraphy has been historically used to transcribe the Japanese and Korean spoken languages; it reflects on how these East Asian languages have been affected by the emergence of recent digital and computer technologies.

Shen Wai Shen was presented in the exhibition at Ginza Graphic Gallery in December 2000 to explore the possibilities of the electronic publishing and book industry among East Asian countries, particularly those regions that share a common heritage of Chinese-based scripts. East Asia is currently struggling to get past persistent historical tensions to achieve some degree of political unification in the face of the growing hegemony of the Euro-American world. To this end, the organizers of the exhibition felt some urgency to seek a solution within the shared artistic, linguistic, and cultural expressions of East Asian countries. They thus invited representative artists from China, Korea, and Japan to produce artworks involving a specific passage from the classical Chinese story *Journey to the West*, an influential text in the heritage of all three cultures.

In order to investigate the political and cultural instability and the linguistic ambiguity of this region from an East Asian perspective, Kameda-Madar observes *Shen Wai Shen* through the lens of Confucian and Buddhist cosmologies, as well as from the vantage point of eighteenth-century Tokugawa-era philosophies. Her approach thus stands in stark contrast to the more common application of Western theories and ideologies that are used to study Xu Bing's work.

In this installation, Xu Bing uses the "body" of "Monkey" (Sun Wukong) as a metaphor for the Chinese writing system. Sun Wukong is known for pulling out hairs from his body, blowing them into the air, and transforming each hair into a duplicate of himself to help fight off various foes. This act of pulling out hairs and replicating himself suggests the long history of spreading the Chinese writing system from China proper to the outlying Sinitic cultures. Thus, these "bodies" are understood as the distinct new writing systems that emerged in East Asia, with each one possessing some unique asset needed to help Monkey battle against the demons.

Shen Wai Shen experiments with the degree to which the three languages that rely on the Chinese-based scripts can communicate. In the installation, as viewers randomly remove sheets of paper on which the story is written, an evolving block of a multilingual text appears. Although the text at any given time frustrates an understanding of the details of the story, the overall content of the passage is comprehensible. Thus, taken together, these languages are paradoxically at once intelligible and unintelligible. For Kameda-Madar, it is her hope that a sociopolitical reconciliation among these East Asian countries based on their overlapping traditions will establish a new allied power that might achieve a balanced and complementary relationship with the Euro-American powers.

Jerome Silbergeld broadens the scope of the volume by locating Xu Bing among a cadre of contemporary Chinese artists. In his chapter, "The Space Between: Cross-Cultural Encounters in Contemporary Chinese Art," Silbergeld discusses the works of four artists who work in different media: Xu Bing, Lin Zhi, Zhang Hongtu, and Jiang Wen.

Silbergeld rehearses the various different kinds of "inbetweeness" found within word and image, content and context, China and non-China, and so on. As one among several artists, certain works by Xu Bing are addressed: *A Book from the Sky*, *Square Word Calligraphy*, *Reading Landscape*, and *Monkeys Grasp for the Moon*. Silbergeld proceeds from the observation that "the space between cultures, native and adopted, is frequently dark, uncomfortable, or unexplored." Appealing to Homi Bhabha's theory of liminal space and Rey Chow's rejection of "absolute difference," Silbergeld pursues a careful reading of representative artworks of these four artists to conclude that all "have developed signature styles based on borrowings from China and the West, transforming these into something neither East nor West, not just Chinese, not not Chinese. Their art creates and operates in a world of its own."

But what does this all add up to? Silbergeld is not persuaded that these artists are necessarily going to have some transformative impact on their adopted worlds. Indeed, he leaves us with the open question: "Art is shaped by society—that can be measured in the art itself. But how does one measure whether art, in turn, changes society?"

This volume tries to provide a theoretical space to reflect on the meaning of contemporary Chinese art. Even though scholars such as Edward Said, Homi Bhabha, and Rey Chow have complicated perceptions of the relationship between the West and the Other, they have not yet changed the binary intellectual perspectives that constantly haunt the efforts at a productive conversation between the East and the West. Proceeding from Heidegger's claim that language is our cultural being, perhaps the key point of Xu Bing's *A Book from the Sky* is to establish a space where the putative language, word, or script cannot be claimed by any specific culture, a space where the East and the West cannot be easily separated.

In his famous dialogue with a Japanese philosopher, Heidegger remarks, "Some time ago I called language, clumsily enough, the house of Being. If man by virtue of his language dwells within the claim and call of Being, then we Europeans presumably dwell in an entirely different house than East Asian men."[5] Allowing, as with Heidegger, that in our own times these cultural differences persist, we can also claim that contemporary Chinese art is indeed "Chinese" art, and that it serves the dual function of championing the quest for artistic freedom precious to all cultures, and at the same time asking for an understanding and tolerance of the values that it represents from a sometimes reluctant West.

NOTES

1. Stephen Spender, *China Diary* (New York: Harry N. Abrams, Inc., 1982), 31.
2. *The Sunday Magazine* of the *New York Times* 19 (1993), 42–72.
3. Homi Bhabha, *The Location of Culture* (New York: Routledge, 2002), 30.
4. Ibid.
5. Martin Heidegger, *On the Way to Language* (New York: Harper Collins Publishers, 1982), 1.

CHAPTER ONE

Reading and Misreading

Double Entendre in Locally Oriented Logos

HSINGYUAN TSAO

Is contemporary Chinese art part of contemporary Chinese culture or part of a Western-centered global culture in this era of globalization?[1] In the past two decades, prestigious museums and galleries such as the Whitney Biennial, the Venice Biennale, the Museum of Modern Art in New York, the Pompidou Center in Paris, and the Guggenheim Museum have featured works by Chinese artists. Scholars and artists alike from both China and the West (Euro-America) celebrate an ever-booming art industry that now has added a new member to the club. Some Chinese believe that the display of works of artists from China in these exhibitions symbolizes China's entrance into the world arena of contemporary art—"China going to the world."[2] This celebration of "world-going" assumes that "'the emerging global culture transcends national boundaries'; or, as prominent writers in the West such as Huntington bluntly state, if a culture can help improve the economic development and living standards of other nations, that culture should be shared by all human societies and be called 'a shared culture of the human race.'"[3] While certain Chinese hold this naïve, apolitical view, the West celebrates the inclusion of art with a strong Chinese appearance as the greatly expanded "global [context] of our time."[4] From a more colonial perspective, this situation proves that Chinese artists work for "the nations of others,"[5] a version of self-colonization.

In this chapter, I attempt to offer a different reading of the situation through a reexamination of the process of China's initial efforts of "world-going" as a means of renewing its culture. In particular, I want to discuss how Chinese artists have applied and still apply their managed selection of Western discourse, rhetoric, and semantic elements in art making (and presenting) as a means of protesting the political control of art in their still officially socialist homeland. As they encounter and participate in the culture of global capitalism they are playing an important role in the ongoing cultural decentralizing or deterritorializing process of the late twentieth and early twenty-first centuries. This decentralization of culture has diversified and diluted the relationship between geographical place and cultural experience, allowing the realization of interculturality with strong Chinese cultural presence in the international art scene; and, further, advocates art "work that attempts to frame the framer as he or she frames the other."[6] The process of recontextualizing a local cultural iconography in a diversified global environment is more dependent than ever on the network of relationships that closely influence the artists' daily life experiences.

This process of interculturality is particularly evident when the works of Chinese artists interact with the changing cultural background of their audience. The past two to three decades of China's foray into contemporary art can be seen as comprising two distinct periods based on the different audiences expected for their works: before 1989 the dialogue was mostly an internal attempt at negotiation within a China-defined geo-cultural space. After 1989, cutting-edge artists from China crossed geo-cultural boundaries and faced mainly audiences whose cultural experiences are non-Chinese. Their works, based on both Chinese and Western contemporary art discourse, share both Chinese and Western visual elements that are neither Chinese nor Western, because they result from the artists' borrowing of different cultural presentations, displays, and cultural symbols. For example, Cai Guoqiang's (蔡国强) trademark traditional brush and ink calligraphy is replaced by traces of burnt gunpowder on paper; rubbings of the flat surfaces of architectural structures are reassembled into installations in Xu Bing's (徐冰) *Ghosts Pounding the Wall* (鬼打墙); Chinese characters transformed into unreadable logos are now considered postmodern art as in Xu Bing's *A Book from the Sky* (天书, Figure I.1). In addition to all this, scientific and information technologies have been brought into the traditional realm of Chinese art, transforming them from a local cultural practice to newer forms of art. Xu Bing's *What's Your Name* changes Chinese script into pictorial elements to rearrange syllabic units in phonetic languages, or the Romanization of nonphonetic languages. For the first time, with the help of a computer, Chinese calligraphy-like words can be written and read in all languages.

Since the 1990s, contemporary Chinese art, which is very innovative both visually and culturally, has been functioning outside China's home cultural discourse and markets. Chinese artists often live and work outside China, outside Chinese cultural expectations, and in the nations of others. Thus their art has come to be considered part of the postmodern Western cultural environment, where Chinese artists are allowed to participate in global Western culture; yet the price Chinese artists must pay is a compromised cultural position. In their own country, outside of a small circle of artists, these worldly, famous artists are almost unknown. Although the Chinese government has somewhat loosened its control over what artists may produce, it has successfully confined this new art within a very small, closely defined area. However, at least some contemporary Chinese artists, in one way or another, manage to participate in the postindustrial, capitalist institutions of art—museums, the market, academia, and the media—outside China. Still, they do not function as the traditionally defined, ethnic "Others" within the Anglo-American worlds that use their works to address the political struggle of these "ethnic Others." Works by Ken Lum or Gu Xiong, for example, more typically address issues that Asian Americans and Asian Canadians are concerned with, not Chinese issues.

I will draw on a series of works to argue that Chinese contemporary art began with the zealous subverting of socialist cultural control, and that this subversion, encouraged by the Western world throughout the 1980s, ended with the students' movement in Tiananmen Square in 1989. Shocked by the slaughter of student protesters calling for freedom and an end to government corruption, and by the government's suppression and persecution of the movement, in the early 1990s Western art critics welcomed Chinese avant-garde artists as an embodiment of the hope that might bring change to China.[7]

The first point to be made is that there are two distinct periods in the contemporary Chinese art movement, the first distinguished by the artists' use of Western artistic discourse, and the second by the intended audience—those for whom the art was made. These two periods are fundamentally different. In the first period, China was far from being part of the world art market as Chinese contemporary art interested few people in the West. To put it simply, the artists then were using the language of Western modern art to reach an internal audience, hoping to change not just the art created in China, but also the polity and society—their use of the localized Western language was aimed at an internal audience in hopes of changing the art world *in* China. However, after Tiananmen Square, China was in the international spotlight and its artists, especially after the banning of contemporary art in China (no exhibitions of such art were allowed for more than a year, between 1989 and 1991) aroused a new level of interest in Chinese contemporary art where some Westerners believed that the new art might stimulate major social and political change to China.

The second period starts in the aftermath of the 1989 student movement with the government's ban of the few leading newspapers and journals devoted to debating contemporary issues, and a great wave of emigration to the United States. Many artists began a life of cultural exile, trying to make their way in the Western countries that had helped them to escape the political pressures of post-1989 China. Their works entered Western mainstream galleries and museums as never before; they also began to address international issues, or issues that were relevant in the culture they now inhabited. This participation in the Western art world and use of the Western discourse on culture and politics allowed them entrée into the Western cultural arena. This discourse was the same discourse that had long imposed a rigid European rule that inflicted cultural oppression on others: Europe's cultural authority betrayed through its rejection of other "languages." The use of non-European languages in such a situation provides previously colonized subjects an unprecedented opportunity to resist the oppression and, via their native language, to overcome the imposed cultural context. Thus, Chinese artists now participate in the international art market while at the same time advancing cultural pluralism in the West. These artists bring with them the visual linguistic references of the Chinese native. Through their use of such visual references, Chinese artists such as Xu Bing have created a distinct, if "liminal," position from which a third cultural space can be established. My theoretical assumption is that the international art world, with the participation of speakers of many languages, consists of a network of "texts" to which all readers have equal access, choosing the linguistic path speaking through art that is most familiar to them. As J. D. Botler suggests, "in that simple fact (or theoretical assumption) the reader's relationship to the text changes radically. A text, as a network, has no univocal sense; it is a multiplicity without the imposition of a principle of domination."[8] Instead of considering the relationship between contemporary Chinese art and the globalization of art production and consumption as "discursive division between the first and third world," I suggest that the use of Chinese visual references—the logos—in Chinese art in recent decades has dramatically changed Chinese self-esteem, and ended the heretofore reinforced dominant position of Anglo-American cultural discourse; or at least undermined it, without intentionally doing so.[9]

The cultural tension between Chinese artists and the West began as a challenge-and-response reaction when China confronted the Europeans in the nineteenth century and suffered defeat in the Opium War. China's artists learned that the best solution to the problem of empowering China in relation to the West was one that had a long history in China even before it first confronted the West.[10] The problem of empowering China in relationship to others was older and more serious than its confrontation with Western armed might. Chinese critical discourse is focused primarily on applying general "formulations derived from the Western mode of theorizing to the resolution of practical issues in China."[11] Using the Western model of theorizing social and artistic issues to subvert the West's own imperious discourse gained intellectuals great success. One example was the rise of oil painting to a cultural position as important as that of traditional Chinese painting, if not of greater importance. However, during this period of learning from the West, the Chinese notion of the *ti/yong* dichotomy (*ti*, 体, the essence of a thing; *yong*, 用, its application)—which held that the two were aspects of a single phenomenon, just as Aristotle had held that substance and appearance were indivisible—in fact became separated. Chinese learning (that is, Confucian learning) could remain the *ti*, while Western learning would be the *yong* or application.

In the nearly thirty years since 1976, when the Cultural Revolution ended, art in China has gone through several stages in its pursuit of modernity and postmodernity. This period saw movement from subversion of socialist cultural and political control in the late 1970s, to participation in the New Wave and "cultural fever" movements in the 1980s, to the politically cynical and politically charged popular art and final joining of the international art activities of the late 1990s and end of the century. In the 1990s, the cultural relationship between China and the West gradually changed from one of a Chinese mimicking of Western visual language to one of constructing a cultural hybrid that can finally play a major role in the international art world. Just as economic success in recent decades has allowed China to proclaim a Chinese-style road to modernization, so too was successful art recognized as a means of building an image of China as a modern country. The art produced inside China is a hybrid that combines contemporary art approaches only at the level of presentation, and not at the level of problematizing social or cultural issues.

THE STARS GROUP (1979)

I characterize the Stars Group's mission as the subversion of socialism through the use of a localized Western vocabulary, rather than a mere mimicking of Western artistic language. Many Chinese critics and viewers have criticized the Stars Group as lacking in originality and only closely imitating early Western modernism.[12] Even worse, few realized that for these artists, the mimicking of early twentieth-century Western modern art styles, borrowed from Western liberalism but packaged as art, was a powerful weapon to critique and even subvert the socialist cultural policies of the late 1970s.[13] It is no secret that the Stars Group wrapped their political discontent in the cloak of Western modern art, but should they be associated with the society where they lived or the society they imitated?[14] The Stars Group was not a cultural negotiation between two cultures, but one that used Western modernism—the early modern art style—to oppose Socialist Realism, the officially sanctioned Chinese art of the time. When we situate our investigation within the context of the latter seventies, we realize that the Stars's pursuit of freedom was a response to the government's new policy. In 1977, just after Mao's death, the fall of the Gang of Four, and the return of Deng Xiaoping to power, China's newspapers began to proclaim the need for democracy. The *People's Daily*, reborn with a completely new voice, declared that if China's socialist bureaucracy remained unchecked by elections and other democratic institutions, it might again run amok and degenerate into "feudal fascism." That June, unbelievably, the government instigated a campaign that asserted that China's socialist state would no longer function for China if it were no more than merely "copying straight from Marx, Lenin, and Chairman Mao."[15]

By February 1978, a new constitution had been adopted; Article 45 guaranteed "freedom of speech, correspondence, the press, demonstrations, and the freedom to strike."[16] In response to the government's call to reform China, people began to take advantage of this relaxation of political controls and in concert with the late 1970s democracy movement, such as the famous Democracy Wall at Xidan, a group of artists made their historic move. On October 1, 1979, a chilly and gloomy day, a group of young people in Beijing went into the streets with banners in their hands and signs on their shoulders to demonstrate for freedom of art. For the first time, the culturally and politically oppressed people wanted their voice to be part of the cultural discourse of late twentieth-century China.[17] Articulating their demands in an art style that imitated the early modern art of the West, but in a substantially localized version, these artists criticized "crawling behind Abstract Art; it is simply raping the art." This was a period when most Chinese equated abstract art with the avant-garde, and believed abstract art to be radical and virtually undecipherable. Meanwhile, the majority of those who viewed the Stars's exhibition supported the use of early modern art as a way to launch the attack on the socialist control of cultural production.[18]

The sparks set off by this group of artists blazed throughout China; their unyielding cultural confrontation with the "oppressors" inspired and changed the cultural landscape of the country. At the same time, their use of the vocabulary of modern art and their use of such slogans as "Seeking Freedom of Expression" touched the hearts of some Westerners, and these people helped the artists' message to reach the West.[19] The late 1970s pursuit of freedom prepared thousands of Chinese artists to embrace different cultural discourses—in particular, that of the West—as a means of gradually subverting the socialist system. This movement occurred at a time when China had just escaped the turmoil of the Cultural Revolution: a time when the West did not expect to see the advent of avant-garde art in China; and a time when neither Chinese audiences nor artists were confident about just how far to test the government's tolerance. As a result, artists' use of Western visual language triggered debates over whether art in China should be more Westernized or return to a more traditional mode.

The Westerners in Beijing who observed the Stars's movement believed that in mimicking the West, the Stars were using the Western social model to change China, but did not remember that in the West avant-garde art had failed miserably at stimulating social transformation.[20] In fact, the term "avant-garde" had become something of a comical concept in the West, leaving the Chinese contemporary art movement as the last real avant-garde. From the point of view of the Chinese people at the time, such art was not for "camouflage,"[21] or to blend into Western society, or a mode of disguise used by both predators and prey for survival in a shared environment. On the contrary, the Stars's imitation of the West within the cultural context of the aftermath of the Cultural Revolution was an act of *anti*-mimicry that allowed the artists to distance themselves and subvert the politically controlled cultural environment of the late 1970s. The Stars's mimicry of a modern art style that stood for freedom and modernity, for liberty and democracy within the context of Maoist socialism, was intended to serve as a protest and demonstration of their own cultural and ideological orientation. Most Stars members had suffered during the Cultural Revolution; their works acted against the cultural and ideological control of the period. Their art, Western in appearance, was a Chinese response to the historical circumstance of Maoist and immediate post-Mao China.

The Cultural Revolution and its dramatic demise threw China into a cultural limbo; it ended so abruptly that there was no transition period. The rethinking of the horrific years that had consumed thousands, or even millions, of people's lives was quickly and strictly prohibited in response to the rise of the Stars movement that used literature, art, film, and other media to condemn the Cultural Revolution that had wounded people in the most brutal way.

Socialist Realist art and its extreme version, the politically controlled art expressions that developed during the Cultural Revolution in the mid-1960s, was the main visual environment and pool of cultural resources for artists who played important roles in the avant-garde movement during the 1980s. Although these artists were young during the ten years of the Cultural Revolution (1966–1976), some were already enlisted in the nationwide propaganda effort of writing and illustrating posters. At the end of the 1970s, when the grandiose revolutionary stage collapsed, to people's surprise, oil painting, calligraphy, and traditional ink painting, instead of being mere distant echoes, were energized in new ways and elevated to a much higher level. With skills well honed in depicting exaggerated revolutionary images, these artists had at least two options when the Cultural Revolution ended: follow current trends, i.e., pursue a milder version of the Cultural Revolution art style, or convert to something new and fresh. The avant-garde artist chose to transcend the tradition of pursuing a social mission that developed when early modern Western art was introduced to China.

This was a period of restoring and revising the disrupted mission of modernization of the early twentieth century. It recalled the dim memory of the art movement that occurred in China in the early twentieth century—a movement that involved such artists as Liu Haisu (刘海粟, 1895–1992) who declared his belief in the social mission of art in *The Trader of Art*, published in 1925: that artists should be heroic builders of history.[22] Other organizations, such as the Storm Society (决澜社), established in 1932, were brought back to jog the collective memory. The manifesto of the Storm Society was powerful: "In China, twentieth-century art should take on a new complexion: Let's rise, with our storm-like passion, iron-willed to build a world of line, color and form."[23] And it was the Stars Group who rediscovered the language and political power within the modern art movement, revitalizing the power of art in the context of loosened cultural control and the excitement of tasting "new" art forms and styles, as well as the social freedom that allowed society to tolerate what they were doing. It would not be an exaggeration to say that Chinese avant-garde art, as embodied by the Stars, began with those who rebelled, in one way or another, against the cultural forms that had been established under the communist regime and further developed during the Cultural Revolution. Chinese artists either adopted a Western vocabulary and struggled for an exit from cultural limbo, or returned to their traditional roots. Divisive as it might be, the Cultural Revolution had become the central focus of people's memories and inspirations. For the next decade, artists either fought to get out of the Cultural Revolution's shadow, or critiqued it by using the language of Western art. Borrowing the language and ideas of the West was nothing new to the Post-Cultural Revolution era; it was a practice begun in the nineteenth century that continued throughout the twentieth century as a means to empower China: using Western ideas, technology, and even borrowed discourses to change China.[24] According to János Mátyás Kovács, "External cultures have frequently been lured into the . . . Communist countries by unsatisfied demand, not forced on the 'innocent natives' as the smart colonization thesis would assert. . . . Why mistake invitation for capitulation?"[25] The two different readings of the artists' use of Western visual references have existed ever since the Stars movement, despite the fact that the Stars had no intention of being co-opted by the Western market at the time.

"NEITHER-NOR": SCRIPTS AS LOGO

The period 1979–1985 was one in which China's New Wave artists detached themselves from Chinese socialist cultural ideology, even though the pre-1985 art movement was in many ways still influenced by the Grand Socialist Narrative. Such developments as the Present Generation Painting Exhibition (同代人油画展), first held in Beijing in 1980, was influential for displaying works that had broken free of the official art molds and for being organized by and featuring a group of young artists who were well trained in prestigious art academies. Some works in this exhibition particularly expressed the artists' deep concern for their detachment from Chinese tradition and their hope that true talents might be recognized and utilized in the society. Differing from the Stars artists who came mainly from outside the mainstream Chinese art world, artists of the Present Generation were already well-known painters of government-run art academies and artists' associations such as the Beijing Art Academy (北京画院), the Yunnan Provincial Artists' Association (云南美协), or the Central Academy of Fine Arts. This exhibition set the precedent for the next generation of young artists with academic backgrounds—children of the establishment who rejected the legacy that produced them. Like the Stars but differing from the Present Generation artists, this next generation, who played major roles in the New Wave of 1985, was not sympathetic to Chinese cultural tradition. Most of them even refused to identify themselves with that tradition. Works of art of the culturally bustling 1980s imitated the Western visual language not only as a way to negotiate with the government, but also in order to fundamentally question the validity of Chinese culture and call for real change. The New Wave emerged when "a strong pro-West trend clearly took shape during the 1980s, culminating in the six-part TV documentary *River Elegy*, which was aired in 1988–1989."[26] Living amid this pro-West trend, China's artists strove to negotiate a series of artistic breakthroughs and to take their place in the new post-Mao cultural environment— a freer time in the pursuit for modernity. Discontented with the social reality and frustrated with the slow pace of social change, artists of the 1980s, such as Huang Yongping's "Xiamen Dada" Group (厦门达达), imitated or appropriated conceptual art, as did Zhang

Peili (张培力) with his series of paintings and installations of rubber gloves. The coherent, yet vacant, social ideology established over the decades after 1949 was diluted by the colorful, kaleidoscope-like cultural changes of the 1980s. These changes split China's art into two major camps: officially sponsored and nonofficial art, including art sponsored by people from other countries but produced mainly in China. By the late 1980s and early 1990s, whether voluntarily like the Stars Group or due to economic and artistic needs, many artists chose to live at the margins of society, becoming cultural exiles within their own country.

While some artists chose to detach themselves from the Chinese traditional culture (as had the Stars and many other artists of the 85 New Wave), beginning in the mid-1980s artists like Xu Bing, Wu Shanzhuan (吳山專), and Gu Wenda (谷文达) distanced themselves from this trend of Chinese cultural detachment. Here I must point out that the term "Chinese tradition" was, at the time, used as a euphemism for Chinese revolutionary or socialist tradition. Artists like Gu Wenda, who was very well trained in Chinese classical culture, calligraphy, and painting, can serve to help us to understand what was meant by "detaching from tradition." That distancing neither subverted nor challenged the Marxist ideology that legitimized the Chinese Communist Party's rule over China. For the artists of the 1980s, as for many intellectuals, "the best strategy . . . [was] not [to] openly challenge the party-state but [to] achieve more intellectual space and freedom. This means importing Western theories and research paradigms and using them to critique the contemporary society and culture."[27] Two works by these artists can serve to clearly illustrate from which tradition they wanted to detach themselves: Gu Wenda's *Do We Have to Examine the Word Jing Written by Three Men and Two Women?* (Figure 1.1) and Wang Guangyi's *Mao Zedong—Red Grids Number 1* (Figure 1.2). These works draw visual references directly from, and subvert notions promoted in, the Cultural Revolution—that is, the tradition of Revolutionary culture.

Along with many of his generation, Xu Bing had no systematic school education, even though books and words attracted him more than anything else. Indeed, most of his childhood was spent in the midst of battles of words—the "big character" posters or *dazibao* (大字报, Figure 1.3) of the Cultural Revolution.

Even though quantities of books were destroyed or put into storage, some people still had limited access to books, although most people were not so lucky. According to Xu Bing:

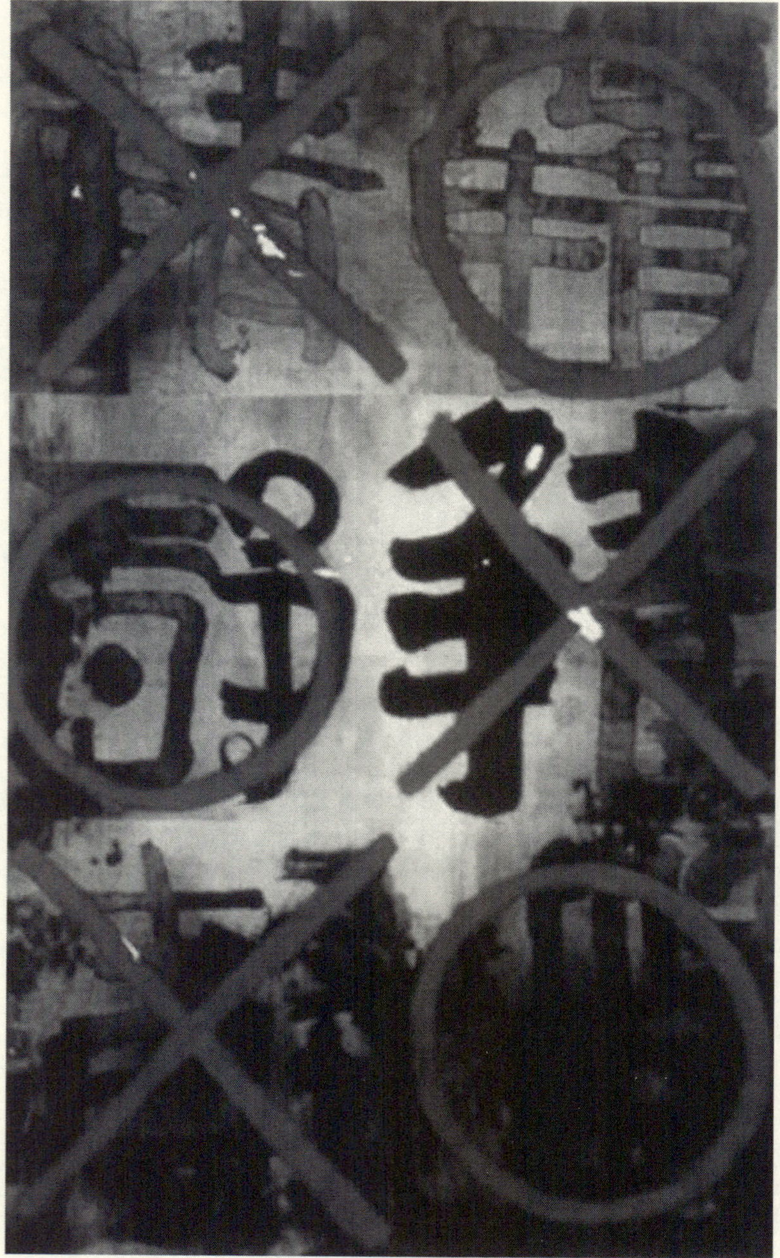

FIGURE I.I. *Do We Have to Examine the Word Jing Written by Three Men and Two Women?* Gu Wenda, ink on paper, 1985. (Courtesy of the artist, photo: Tsao Hsingyuan.)

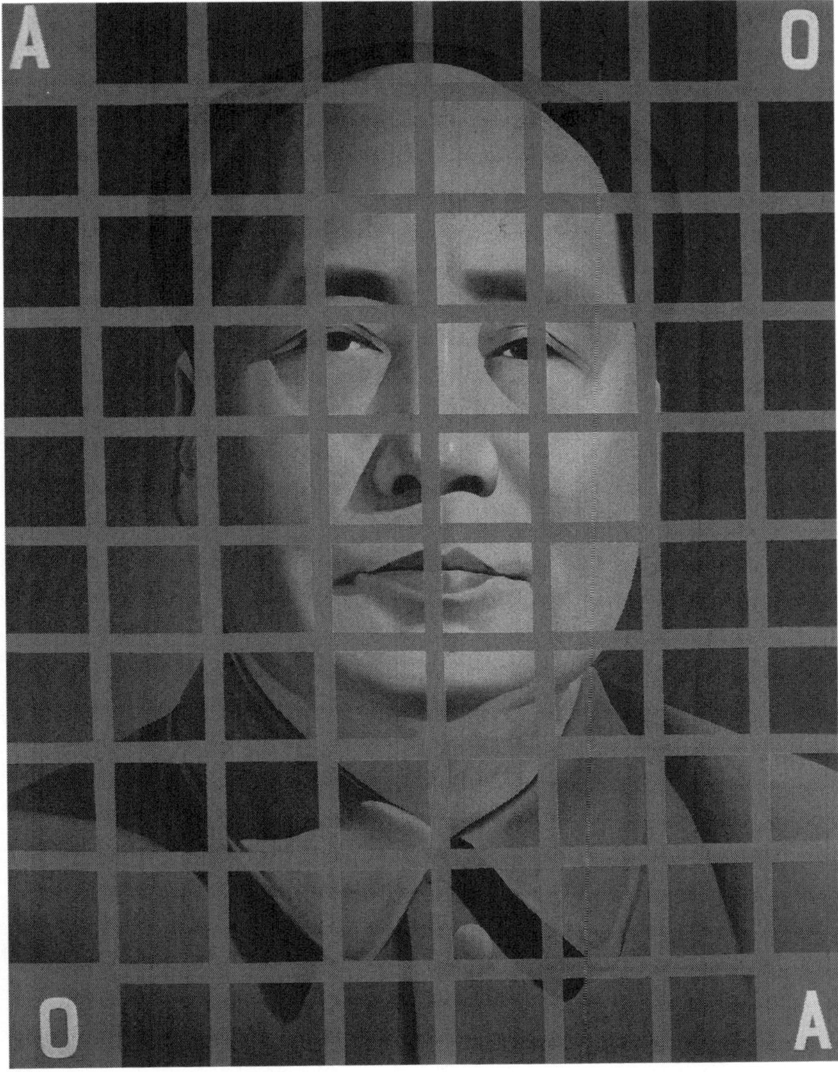

FIGURE I.2. *Mao Zedong—Red Grids Number 1*, Wang Guangyi, oil on canvas, 1986. (Courtesy of the artist.)

My parents worked in a university campus—my father was in the department of history and my mother worked in the department of library sciences—and I became familiar with all sorts of books at a very early age. But books seemed strange to me then because I couldn't read them—I was too young. And when I finally could

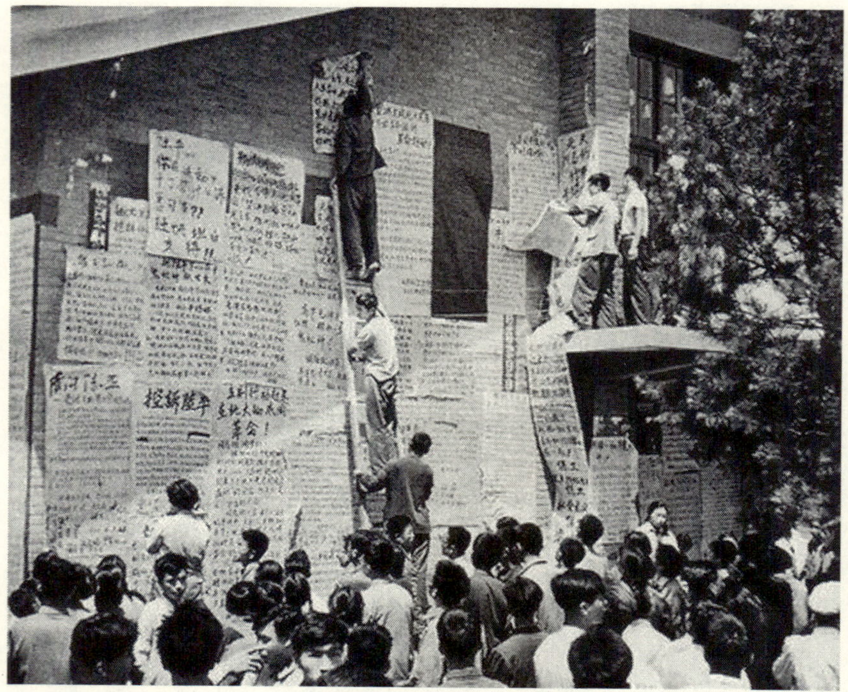

FIGURE I.3. Big character posters (*dazibao* 大字报), photo from the Cultural Revolution, 1967.

read them, I was not allowed to read them. These were the years when we could no longer read whatever we chose to. We read *Mao's Little Red Book*.[28]

To make the situation worse, Xu Bing finished nine years of schooling without really learning anything. He was sent to the countryside to be "reeducated" by the peasants, because he was then considered, by Cultural Revolution standards, a young intellectual who had lost contact with the reality of society.

This was not simply a period of detachment, and it was not the artists' choice to truly pull themselves away from China's cultural tradition. Even as they used Western vocabulary to destabilize current cultural policies, artists such as Gu Wenda and Xu Bing continued sifting through Chinese history and literature in order to find their own cultural roots. The attempt to find those traditional roots might not even have begun without their traumatic experience of the Cultural Revolution, as Xu Bing has often remarked.[29] Growing up during those years of turmoil, this generation may have lacked a stable school environment, but there was never a lack of words "in your face" when the entire nation was papered with both big and small character posters dissecting various social and cultural issues. For many people who experienced the Cultural Revolution far away from books and culture in the countryside, life during this period is almost beyond imagining: books and words seemed powerful and yet remote to Xu Bing and many others of his generation. Streets, walls—virtually every flat surface—were covered with *dazibao* and slogan posters with even bigger characters, the *dabiaoyu* (大标语). The messages conveyed via these displayed words were often contradictory: the same people could be the worst of enemies one day, the best of comrades the next, although the progression was more often the reverse. Too many extravagant words were used, too many grand ideas delivered; in the end, their sheer weight numbed the readers and anesthetized the nation. In the late 1960s the notion spread that China should be turned into a "great red ocean of slogans" (红海洋). When submerged deeply in a red sea of words, however, there was little anybody cared to read. It was at this time that hand-copied novels became popular and many people were jailed for disseminating thrillers or romance books such as *Meihua Dang* (The Black Club Party) or *Shaonü zhi Xin* (Young Girls' Hearts). The strict prohibition against these books alienated yet another group of people. Wu Shanzhuan, who grew up in the successive battles of words but without any books to read, best expresses the disjuncture, displacement, absurdity, and visual bombardment of the poster words in his work *Red Humor*.

USING TRADITION TO SUBVERT THE TRADITION

The years 1985 and 1986 must be considered a time of "cultural insurgency." As early as 1983, Gu Wenda painted a long horizontal hand scroll, seven meters wide and nearly one and a half meters high, entitled *Diagram of the Supreme Ultimate*. The entire far right end of the painting is devoted to hexagrams written on three square pillars that are almost the height of the work itself, while the rest of the painting is submerged in a group of absurd, unreadable images. The painting apparently draws on Western surrealism but also evokes attempts by Chinese traditional culture to come to terms with the mysterious and irrational. In 1985, Gu Wenda, one of the first academic avant-garde artists to surface, enraged many conservative art critics who considered his works illogical and chaotic. As one critic wrote, "Entering the display hall, what I saw was chaotic ink splashes, characters written backwards, cursive and blocky printing styles intermixed and displaced, all conveying a 'spirit,' 'time,' and 'space' that are far from [our] reality and perversely mimicking 'religion' to lure the viewers into a haze. Some people describe [this work] as 'the funeral of a homo neuroticus!' At the very least, there is some distance between our experience in exhibitions and this viewing."[30]

Influenced, in terms of visual and behavioral experience, by the Cultural Revolution, Gu Wenda used various styles to disassemble, reassemble, displace, and reverse characters as a way of questioning the meaning of words written in different contexts. Borrowing directly from the Cultural Revolution, he used red ink relentlessly to cross out many of the characters. Crossing out a person's name with red ink has been conventionally used in China to indicate that the person in question has been condemned to death. During the Cultural Revolution, this name crossing was more commonly used to discredit people condemned as enemies of the society or of a particular political movement. Gu Wenda's crossing out of certain characters was also intended to apply to the Cultural Revolution itself, negating the common practices of the time—an act of a "double-crossing," or double negation. His thorough training in calligraphy and Chinese philosophy gave him the skills to mimic, mock, and challenge the significance of words when they were used to excess in many contradictory situations. Disjuncture, gaps, and chaos destabilized the conventional ways of understanding written language as a vehicle to convey meaning through words—to decipher meaning based on words.

RED HUMOR: MEMORY OF THE RED HORROR

Wu Shanzhuan, who was born in 1960, is another Hangzhou artist who was too young to participate in or really understand the Cultural Revolution, yet remembers the "red ocean" of propaganda symbols. Wu's most famous work, *Red Humor* (1985), causes every Chinese viewer to tremble, no matter what part the Cultural Revolution played in his or her experience. Wu uses nothing but red, white, and black to write unrelated, disordered, and sometimes absurd messages in large and small characters. He confesses that the reason for using the great quantity of red stems from his memory: "an artist cannot escape from his memory and [survive] as a human." According to Wu's memory, the Cultural Revolution consumed more red pigment than the rest of Chinese history combined.[31]

Wu was one of the first artists to attempt to use disassembled and reassembled characters; his abuse of characters derives from his vivid memories of the "red ocean" during his childhood. His understanding of the relationship between word and meaning is conveyed in his famous discourse on Chinese art and culture:

> [W]e believe that our works aroused some humorous feelings among the viewers. The key [to understanding this] is that we use Chinese characters as pure aesthetic elements to be finished on canvas, but the viewers realize that [these constructions] express a conceptual language. The humor rests in the fact that the 'characters' are at the same time considered as pure aesthetic elements; they are meaningful although they do not convey the concepts that Chinese written language would normally [convey].[32]

Wu Shanzhuan's questioning of the relationship between meaning and words has its roots in the ancient text *Book of Changes*: "Writing cannot exhaust words, and words cannot exhaust meanings (书不尽言, 言不尽意)."[33] However, meaning is the goal when utilizing words; once meaning is achieved, one need take no notice of the words (得意忘言). This is like a fisherman ignoring his weir once the fish are caught (得魚而忘荃); or a hunter ignoring his horse once the rabbit has been caught (得兔而忘蹄).[34] This idea was further developed in the practice of metaphilosophy that flourished during the fourth century. The philosopher Wang Bi (226–249) carried the debate of the relationship between words and meaning further: "There is nothing better at conveying meaning than an image, and nothing better at conveying an image than words (尽意莫若象,尽象莫若言)."[35]

For conceptual art, what matters is not the subject matter or content, not style or format, not even the media and technique of presentation; rather, it is the articulation of an individual artist's cultural experiences and ideas. "Meaning comes before the brush strokes" is a common aesthetic belief among Chinese artists. The famous socialist art critic Wang Zhaowen (王朝闻) reiterates this idea in his book *One Counts as Ten* (一 以当十), emphasizing the relationship between image and meaning.[36] In many ways, the meaning, *yi*, is actually the reader's interpretation of the words, the viewer's interpretation of the image, or the significance beyond the words. In the context of Chinese culture, the concept of meaning beyond words and image is a discourse of interpretation, which seeks to link a message or thought that is communicated through text with the intention with which the message is conveyed. Thus both the conveying and the interpretation of meaning are the end, while the words or physical representations—including format, style, and image—are the means.

MIRRORS TO EXAMINE THE WORLD

The most successful work describing the confused status of words in this generation is Xu Bing's *A Book from the Sky*. In this piece, Xu Bing took on the highly didactic mission of turning the Chinese writing system—the most familiar visual material for any Chinese person—into a collection of alien-looking artifacts, in an attempt to interrogate the very means of communication. As a well-trained woodblock printmaker, Xu Bing devoted himself to making and carving words that no one understands, and may consider himself as reenacting the invention of Chinese characters by the legendary Cang Jie. Such reenactments were characteristic of mainstream traditional Chinese culture but had become obsolete by the time Xu Bing was working. For *A Book from the Sky*, Xu Bing invented over four thousand characters in the twelfth-century style that coincided with the beginning of printing, another Chinese invention. None of the characters is readable or decipherable. Confronting this work, viewers who read Chinese characters experience a sort of double vision: the past and the present. The past is used to reference the present, while the present is based on subverting both past and present. It is this duality that gives the work its power. The original title was *Xishi jian* (析世鉴), *Mirror for Examining the World*, which mimics the title of a book of history by Sima Guang (司马光, a renowned Northern Song scholar-official), *Comprehensive Mirror for Aid in Governing* (资治通鉴), compiled between 1065 and 1084. The work also recalls three collections of short stories compiled by Feng Menglong (冯梦龙 1574–1646): *Yushi Mingyan* (illustrious words to instruct the world), *Jingshi Tongyan* (comprehensive words to admonish the world), and *Xingshi Hengyan* (lasting words to awaken the world). Mostly cast as love stories, Feng's three books aimed to enlighten the world through the wisdom of the stories.

For his part, Sima Guang used both primary and secondary documents to recount and comment on Chinese history by arranging the data into a comprehensive chronology. Xu Bing, however, personally invented four thousand characters in the style common in the Northern Song, carved them into wooden blocks, and hand-printed and hand-bound four volumes that can be read with neither sound nor meaning. In describing the work, Xu Bing says: "In *A Book from the Sky*, I was using traditional culture to reinterpret and subvert culture . . . the sincere and formal grandeur of the work comes out of China's high and weighty cultural tradition, but then at the center you find a joke."

However, for viewers, no matter whether or not they have knowledge of the Cultural Revolution, the disorder, the violent strokes, and the strong red and black colors in Wu Shanzhuan's work do not evoke humor but instead usually induce a reaction of horror; the work *Red Humor* is a comment on the absurdity of a horrific period. Until the Cultural Revolution can be openly studied in China, Wu Shanzhuan must use the word "humor" to mask its terrible memories. Since the work does not stop at critiquing the horrific time itself, but also touches on the prohibition of serious study and analysis of the period, perhaps it would be better called *Red Absurdity*.

Similarly, instead of humor, I find frustration and a strong sense of social mission in Xu Bing's *A Book from the Sky*. What he refers to as a "joke" is his discovery of a social paradox: a means of communication losing its communicative function through its capacity for estrangement, or "alienation" in Marxist terms. Xu Bing's effort reflects the controversy of the mid to late 1980s over modernity. Whereas most scholars search for aesthetic rationality, Xu Bing, like a few other cutting-edge artists, began to face the serious challenge of pursuing modernity or postmodernity. His situation is best compared to modernist writers as described by Xu Zidong, who speaks of their unceasing efforts in the search for the foundation of national culture and the psychological crisis resulting from their experience of the loss of Han culture, calling them "the genuine modernists of our literature."[37]

In *A Book from the Sky*, history—or what Xu Bing considered "traditional culture"—consists only of visual references: font styles, bookbinding method, and means of display, which are removed from their historical context. Xu Bing's characters, though retaining the old forms and made in the same way, are transformed into

"pure" image, or simulacrum. Early installations of this work reso-
nated with the tradition of word-worship; they echoed the tradition of word display—the engraving of granite slabs or steles; the
preservation of the written word through multiple rubbings of such
steles; the relocation of steles to secure places; and the assumption
of a status akin to that of an altar by collections of steles. In Xu
Bing's work it all ends at the visual surface, without any access to
any meaning. If it is an altar, it is one that destabilizes the relationship between image and meaning.

While following the principles of Chinese character making, Xu
Bing's invented words are not readable. Even though all of them are
made up of the appropriate strokes, only whole component parts of
a genuine character convey the phonetic and "radical"—which are
often pictograms—to carry information and indications of meaning. When these component parts and strokes are assembled in an
unconventional way, meaning and sound are lost, while the images,
the "characters," remain. Thus, this work mocks this monument
to national identity; it reestablishes a new identity that is grand
and heroic but also absurd, thereby carrying profound meaning.
Using references from both Chinese and recent traditions, this
new identity speaks of a Chinese culture caught up in a twentieth-
century cultural confusion, one in which localized visual cultures
were imported mostly from Europe and the former Soviet Union.
This mixed identity was not recognized at the time the works were
first exhibited. One pseudo-Marxist art theorist who studied in the
Soviet Union at the end of Stalin's era harshly criticized Xu Bing's
effort this way:

> I have always felt that when people do something they must have
> a clear goal, for themselves, for others, for the people, for all man-
> kind; to have no purpose at all is absurd and dissolute. If I am
> asked to evaluate *A Book from the Sky*, I can only say that it gathers
> together the formalistic, abstract, subjective, irrational, anti-art,
> anti-traditional . . . qualities of the New Wave of fine arts, and
> ushers the Chinese New Wave towards a ridiculous impasse.

What this theorist did not understand was the deep cultural
roots on which Xu Bing's works are based in attempting to delin-
eate the idea of our modernity.[38] Within about ten years, Xu Bing's
pilgrimage in quest of Chinese identity resulted in a transformed
postmodern identity that rose from the ashes of the old—a cultural

phoenix that "makes more universal statements . . . and seeks to create a viable alternative to the older art."[39] *A Book from the Sky* is now an icon, an emblematic piece that stands for the very position of Chinese art in the international art world. Ironically, even as authoritative Chinese socialist art critics were denouncing Xu Bing's work, critics from the West were not only embracing it, but also claiming that works of this kind "are part of the global context of our time."[40]

Word making and remaking have always been politically charged. The power to control words means the power to control people's thinking and ideas. The tyrant emperor of the third century BCE, Qin Shi Huang, standardized the writing system at the same time that he unified China, forcing all the states he conquered to adopt the Qin written script as a symbol of cohesive cultural orientation and identity. He or his bureaucrats amalgamated the locally diverse written logos into a single "universal" one, the hegemonic Qin script, thereby privileging it as the centralized written language. By forcibly imposing this centralized writing scheme as the standard, Qin Shi Huang unwittingly established a cultural system that has lasted more than two thousand years. The logographic images of the ideogram-based Chinese writing system are now recognized internationally, even if not understood. One can only imagine what the world of Chinese culture might be today if the variant scripts of the Qin era had not been unified. Just as there are a number of European languages today that share Romanic roots, the Chu, Qi, Yan, and Zhao scripts could have become separate, Huaxia-based languages.

Although a number of dynasties and rulers made minor modifications to the Chinese written script over the past two thousand years, the most fundamental change in the writing system was the simplification of written script in the early 1950s, undertaken with the aim of facilitating the acquisition of literacy by the masses. By adopting a substantial number of simplified characters—many of which were not created from scratch but had been in popular use since the time of the Six Dynasties—the communist regime also acquired absolute power to control both ideology and its interpretation. The systematically renewed word images symbolized a new cultural identity, one that attempted to include the masses.

If the remaking of words was meant to serve a more powerful system of communication or a wider audience, Xu Bing's "words" frustrated viewers' conventional communication expectations.

Because these "words" were no longer oriented toward localized information, and because they were equally meaningless to all viewers, whether or not they could read Chinese, they transformed a local communicative system into a global noncommunicating system. By blocking word recognition, these "pictograms" can no longer be considered "Chinese words" but mere logograms that only seem to belong to Chinese culture, based on their similarity to actual characters. Britta Erickson entitled her book on Xu Bing's works *The Art of Xu Bing: Words without Meaning, Meaning without Words.*[41] This title inspires me to question whether such pictograms are actually words or logos. For logos to be called words they must convey meaning; but meaning, as we all know, can be conveyed by either word or picture. This situation is more like a basic form of the disjunctive syllogism: either (A) a word conveys meaning, or (B) a word does not convey meaning. This implies that if A is true, B is false, and if B is true, A is false; A and B cannot both be true. We must choose whether these images are words that have no meaning or are not words, but rather groups of symbols from which meaning can be extricated. Every true word is established through an "agreement" reached through history and custom, and becomes a shared practice of people who we identify as having the same culture. Meaning is always interpreted on the basis of this mutual understanding and practice.

As discussed earlier, the concept of meaning is a discourse of interpretation within the context of Chinese culture, a discourse in which the understanding of a message or thought that is communicated through text/words intended to convey the message or thought. Xu Bing's "words" (whether they be logos or pictograms) are intended to convey no fixed message, and each can be interpreted in myriad ways. That is, the relationship between the meaning, *yi*, and the image, *xiang*, can never be established. However, the number of interpretations that can be derived from these images, either through an attempted reading of the component parts—that is, through their misreading—is not only meaningful, but is infinite. Although the Chinese discourse of word interpretation suggests that books cannot exhaust words, and words cannot exhaust meanings, Xu Bing's word-images are derived from but also transcend the traditional bounds of word-image and meaning. *A Book from the Sky* tells the story of a nation that has an ever-changing identity, with which it is forever coping. The work lies within the context of a Chinese discourse of interpretation: the relationship of meaning, image, and words—a third-century aesthetic development of an earlier philosophical proposition.

Behind the work, behind the relationship of meaning and word-image, is a Daoist-like perseverance and tenacity; and beyond all is a renewal of the classic Chinese aesthetic sense. Perfection of skill in the carving of the characters and in the processes of printing and bookbinding renders the mode of production meditative, full of aesthetic sensibility, and in tune with the values of modern art. The display of Xu Bing's works closely resembles the atmosphere in the Forest of Stele Museum in Xi'an, and the annual airings of the painted scroll collections in both the Central Academy of Arts and its affiliated Professional Middle School, where there are hundreds, even thousands, of scrolls in storage. However, for me the installation of Xu Bing's *A Book from the Sky* is *particularly* reminiscent of the airing of scroll paintings, in terms of the ceremonial atmosphere and the reverence of the viewers. Students of the academy must have special permission to enter the large, well-ventilated classrooms where the paintings are hanging, and the impressive quality and quantity of works is more overwhelmingly breathtaking than the installations we usually see in exhibitions.

To sum up, works by Wu Shanzhuan, Gu Wenda, Xu Bing, and other artists of the New Wave since the 1980s have participated in a Chinese discourse in response to China's social problems, while drawing from the Western art of the postindustrial period. Their works speak of the artists' fragmented memories, particularly their traumatic memories of the Cultural Revolution, as well as of visual hybridity and relativism, playfulness and parody of certain aspects of Chinese culture and politics. When it came to an ideological stance, the targets of the works were always aspects of communist governance of China in the Mao era or earlier. With this body of work that has been promoted outside China, we begin to realize that China's postmodern art represents the way that we, people outside China, view China.

ARTISTS AS ETHNOGRAPHERS: ART IN THE CONTEXT OF THE WESTERN

Many Chinese artists came to live in the United States after the mid-1980s. By the early 1990s, some of them had become popular and even famous. Such artists and their works engaged in the postmodern discourse of identity, pluralism, and self-representation

and involved themselves in—and stimulated—the use of ethnographic methods in researching their culture for appropriate materials to use. However, once these artists started working outside
China they were moved to address broader issues that went beyond
local cultural concerns. After the 1990s, the former avant-garde
artists who played a major role in the 1980s dispersed into two
groups, and each group gained new blood. One group stayed in
China, continuing to work with more internationally oriented cultural issues and at the same time bringing elements of their ethnic
culture into the market for New International Art. "Since 1989
and the government attacks on intellectual culture, the Avant-garde
Movement in China has weakened. With the increasing emphasis
on the immediate economic benefits of any activity, both official
and popular culture has common priorities that are significantly
different from those of the intellectuals."[42] These artists travel to
other countries for exhibitions, but return to China and the cultural foundations that legitimize them. While they may be of the
"Third World," they participate in the capitalist social discourse
and manifest the "discursive division between the first and third
world."[43] As in other spheres, within these markets, Homi Bhabha
states, "vicious circuits of surplus value link First World capital and
Third World labor markets through the chain of the international
division of labor and national comprador classes."[44] In this reading,
these artists are third world exploited labor.

Residing within Anglo-American and European societies, the
second group is not the traditional "ethnic other," such as the
second- or third-generation Asian Americans whose works often
address the ethnic Other's political struggle, for example, the racial
problem in the United States. In the spectrum of works identified
with "the Other" in the West, this "Other" group from contemporary China is uninterested in displaying their abjection or representing the condition of abjection.[45] While some of them express a
passion for signs and forms, others are distinguished by their social
and cultural critique of the trans-socialist China, a state that is neither fully socialist nor capitalist, or sometimes by the traditional
China in their memories and knowledge. These artists neither identify themselves with Mainland China nor with the older generations of overseas Chinese. Most of them have avoided, or at least
failed to address, current Chinese problems, even if on the surface
their art deals with Chinese political issues—particularly in the eyes
of those who equate socialism with Stalinism.

This second group is important in the West, however; riding the wave of postcolonialism, they make up the majority of displaced artists and their activities worldwide. While the first group continues to address Chinese local cultural issues in the face of the ever-increasing social pressures on them in China itself, they progressively move toward cooperation with the new international art market, producing works that are more harmless in subject matter and stimulating in style and physical presentation than are marketable in the West. The artists of the second group, overseas sojourners, are now the main force of global capitalist art in the postcolonial world, using their art in response (and resistance) to colonialism.

CLASSROOM SQUARE CHARACTERS

Since he moved to New York, Xu Bing's works have undergone a fundamental change. While he continues to question written words, his newly crafted characters have transformed a local perspective into a global one. In his pursuit of art in his new location, Xu Bing continues to use the traditional form of Chinese characters, but also attempts to depict the cultural relationship between Western culture and that of China. Now that he has lived in New York for some time, his relationship with the West is not the same as it was when he lived in China. In *Classroom Square Characters*, he can no longer ignore his non-Chinese-speaking audience. Repositioning his cultural relationship with his new environment was both urgent and necessary. His work using "New English Calligraphy," which he invented, renders the Latin alphabet in the shape and style of Chinese calligraphy in a way that is meaningful and understandable to the English-speaking viewer—a result of his cultural readjustment. His work is ever more playful. Upon entering the gallery, the viewer encounters a classroom-like space with all the accoutrements for calligraphy writing, in particular a "traditional-looking" book of model calligraphy consisting of rubbings of words incised in stone. But these words, which share the style of Yan Zhenqing of the Tang Dynasty (618–907 CE), are New English letter/characters. There are also exercise books for viewers to use in practicing these, and a blackboard of instructions for brush holding and stroke making written with white chalk. In one corner of the classroom a television set delivers a lecture on calligraphy. The language used in the work is, of course, English; but the visual presentation follows a strictly Chinese traditional approach to the practice of calligraphy.

A famous diagram that explains the art of stroke making in calligraphy (Figure 1.4), attributed to Yan Zhenqing but possibly dating from an earlier time, was transplanted by Xu Bing into his "New Calligraphy" in order to explain stroke making in English. Although this work also exemplifies the forced fissure in the inseparable relationship of words and meanings, the use of a classic Chinese calligraphy approach in English text writing displaces both languages to create something unfamiliar to both cultures. To further complicate the experience, Xu Bing sometimes quotes Mao Zedong's *Little Red Book* in texts written in this new type of calligraphy.

In constructing this work, Xu Bing has gone beyond, but not abandoned, the traditional weighty burden carried by Chinese intellectuals. His *Classroom Square Characters* is a good example of interculturality; it captures his understanding of the constantly changing relationship between him, the world around him, and the lives of the "Other." It is not an artwork of overlapping subjects possessing two different forms of knowledge and experience of the West and the "Other"; rather it "involves a repositioning of the self both intellectually and at the level of 'felt' reality, the apprehension of relationships and material reality and their impact

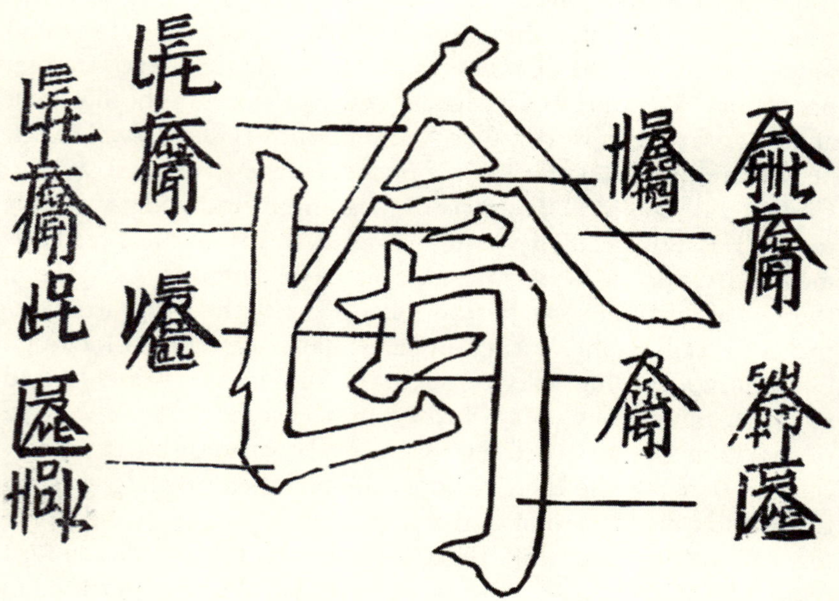

FIGURE I.4. Xu Bing's diagram on naming the strokes. (Courtesy of the artist.)

on us as thinking, feeling beings."[46] Xu Bing engages in ethnographic practices in his art making, giving rise to multiple voices in his works.

WHEN DIFFERENCE BECOMES IDENTITY: A CONCLUSION

Fredric Jameson has pointed out that economy is culture in a time of globalization. In what Ernst Mandel calls a purer stage of capitalism—our own—the distinction between economics and culture has disappeared and "[c]ommodification today is also aestheticization"[47]

Karl Marx noticed 150 years ago that the world market imparts a cosmopolitan character to production and consumption in every country.[48] Similarly, global capitalism deploys and depends on the discourse of differences in strategy making. Within the context of global space, everybody is located in a transcultural position: even while self and Other encounter each other, both are simultaneously displaced.

Within the economic context of globalization, works of Gu Wenda, Wu Shanzhuan, and Xu Bing are part of a global capitalist art; although Wu works from China, his market, too, is outside China. The dynamic new waves of Chinese art in the contemporary global capitalist art market are the result of the expansion of Western global strategy, which, in turn, is "part of the global context of our time."[49] Or, "to put it another way, cultural globalization is the process in which we can observe both the universalization of Western modernity and the emergence of alternative modernities."[50] To the Others, "the West-centered, challenge-response paradigm of global-local interactions may not be universally applicable. The Chinese case demonstrates a new type of cultural globalization: a managed process . . . [in which Chinese artists] actively claim ownership of the emerging global culture."[51] In many ways, they have forced mainstream Western art to compromise with Western culture by incorporating Chinese visual and linguistic features. Their works and the visual traditions articulated in those works "add to" the Anglo-American postmodern discourse, while also "summing up"[52] and recasting what "Western" means.

More than a half century ago, Walter Benjamin posited the relationship between artistic authority and cultural politics by suggesting that artists who work with ideological patronage were passive Others.[53] In the global capitalist art world, the ethnographic turn in, or the discourse about, contemporary art provides an international, cultural space that allows Chinese artists entry. Their identity is transformed or split by entering the transnational art industry space, but the recontextualization of cultural iconography within the global capitalist art arena allows the Chinese people to "come see themselves once again at the center of a world."[54]

This chapter has discussed examples of art from China of the past two decades. The claim is that a Chinese model of cultural hybridization has established a new story line that narrates at least two versions of postmodernity and two versions of the relationship between local and global: that of the West and that of China. Or, said in another way, difference becomes identity in the art world in the era of global capitalism. The artists discussed have been accepted in the West as a part of difference, not as a part of influence. Sadly, we have yet to see how these transcultural artists, namely, Gu Wenda, Wu Shanzhuan, and Xu Bing, may actually influence the international art world. Although they continue to provide diversity in the international art market, their contribution is not much more than an addition to the late capitalist global portrait of a postindustrial world. This situation will not change before the discourse, system of critique, and the market have all adjusted to the rising fame of these artists. What is even more problematic is that as part of the global game with transcultural players, they do not fit into any locally oriented cultural schema centered on China—whether it be in terms of the discourse, the value system, or the market. Ironically, the ambiguity inherent in locally oriented logos sends a complex message to Chinese audiences that allow them to misread the situation as a *Chinese triumph*.

NOTES

1. It is difficult to define the parameters of contemporary Chinese art. At the very least we should distinguish two different types. Since 2000, the Chinese government has recognized that the idea of contemporary Chinese art can help build the image of a "contemporary China," and it has organized many exhibitions of what can be seen as contemporary Chinese art in various world metropolises. As early as 1989, nonofficial exhibitions organized by galleries, university museums, and other museums outside China provided an alternative definition of contemporary Chinese art. In this chapter, the definition used is based on the latter, as defined by art critics and scholars outside China.

2. Peter Berger and Samuel P. Huntington, *Many Globalizations: Cultural Diversity in the Contemporary World* (Oxford and New York: Oxford University Press, 2002), 33.

3. Berger and Huntington, *Many Globalizations*, 34.

4. David G. Wilkins, Bernard Schultz, and Katheryn M. Linduff, *Art Past Art Present*, 4th ed. (Upper Saddle River, NJ: Prentice Hall, 2001), 585.

5. Homi Bhabha, *The Location of Culture* (New York: Routledge, 2002), 139.

6. Hal Foster, "The Artist as Ethnographer," in *The Return of the Real* (Cambridge: MIT Press, 1996), 203.

7. Andrew Solomon, "Irony, and Art Will Change China," *New York Times Sunday Magazine*, December 19, 1993.

8. Jay David Bolter, *Writing Space: The Computer, Hypertext and the History of Writing* (Mahwah, NJ: Lawrence Erlbaum Associates, 1991), 25.

9. These words from Spivak are quoted in Bhabha, *The Location of Culture*, 20.

10. In his essay, "Where Do Correct Thoughts Come From?," Timothy Cheek articulates, from a different perspective, how, in the past hundred years, China looked for theoretical authority to various Western leading scholars of culture and political studies.

11. Timothy Cheek quotes Dr. Gloria Davies, "Anticipating Community, Producing Dissent: The Politics of Recent Chinese Intellectual Praxis," *China Review* 2, no. 2 (Fall 2002): 2–3. See also "Where Do Correct Ideas Come From? Xu Jilin and the Search for a Theory of Practice among Contemporary Chinese Intellectuals," University of British Columbia. Article draft for the China Studies Group, Centre for Chinese Research, IAR/UBC, August 2004, 1.

12. Wu Hung, *Transience: Chinese Experimental Art at the End of the Twentieth Century* (Chicago: The David and Alfred Smart Museum of Art, The University of Chicago), 176.

13. Michael Sullivan, "Art and Reality in Twentieth Century Chinese Painting," in *Twentieth-Century Chinese Painting*, ed. Kao Mayching (Hong Kong: Oxford University Press, 1990), 18.

14. See Chang Tsong-zung, ed., *Xingxing shinian* (The Stars: Ten Years) (Hong Kong: Hanart TZ Gallery, 1989); exhibition catalogue. For a concise overview of the development of Chinese contemporary art as a project of modernity and its relationship with the West (including the Stars), see Gao Minglu, "Toward a Transnational Modernity," in *Inside Out*, ed. Gao Minglu (Berkeley and Los Angeles: University of California Press, 1998), 15–22.

15. Orville Schell and David Shambaugh, *The China Reader: The Reform Era* (Toronto and New York: Vintage, 1999), 157.

16. Ibid., 158.

17. Demonstration of the Star Group. The name of this group has been variously translated as "Star Group," or the "Stars." Both are mistranslations. The name refers to an ancient phrase Mao Zedong borrowed as a theme for a letter to Lin Biao to persuade Lin that although the numbers of Red Army soldiers were small, they are like sparks, *xingxing* 星星 (literally "star star"), that could set the prairie ablaze. Hence, I always want to call this group the "Sparks."

18. See Chang; for a discussion of the impact of the Stars exhibitions, see Wu Hung, 17–18.

19. *Newsweek*, October 15, 1979.

20. Norman Bryson, "The Post-Ideological Avant-Garde," in *Inside Out*, ed. Gao Minglu (Berkeley and Los Angeles: University of California Press, 1998), 51–52.

21. Jacques Lacan, *The Line and Light* (Oxford: Oxford University Press, 1989), 103.

22. Zhao Li and Yu Ding, eds., *1542–2000: Documenting Chinese Oil Painting*. (Changsha: Hunan Art Press, 2002), 482.

23. The original Chinese is as follows: " . . . . . . 二十世纪的中国艺坛, 也应当现出一种新兴 的气象了: 让我们起来吧!用狂飘一般的激情, 铁一般 的理智, 来制造我们色、线、形交错的世界吧!" See ibid.

24. In Peter G. Rowe and Seng Kuan, *Architectural Encounters with Essence and Form in Modern China* (Cambridge, MA: MIT Press, 2002), the discussion on *Ti yong bian* (体用辩) is important for our understanding of the culture of twentieth-century China. The choice of using the Western early modern art style is also related to the fact that in the early twentieth century, two major groups of artists returning from Europe had a strong impact on China's art education. Xu Beihong, who learned directly from the Classicism that became the dominant force in delivering the communist ideal, was representative of one; the other group, led by Liu Haishu, attempted to promote Western modern art theory as similar to the theory of the traditional-type Chinese art literati. The debate between Xu and Liu art resulted in Xu's belief in realism being adopted as official art, while Liu's effort was criticized as indulging in petty bourgeoisie pursuit of the little pleasures of life—just as the literati artists were criticized during this time. The Stars, who adhered to the style promoted by Liu, were condemned by the authorities over the past three decades when they rebelled against the norms of art at this later time.

25. János Mátyás Kovács, "Rival Temptations and Passive Resistance: Cultural Globalization in Hungary," In *Many Globalizations: Cultural Diversity in the Contemporary World*, ed. Peter Berger, 146–182 (Oxford: Oxford University Press, 2002), 167.

26. Ibid., 25.

27. Ibid.

28. Britta Erickson, *The Art of Xu Bing: Words without Meaning, Meaning without Words* (Seattle and London: University of Washington Press, 2001), 14. This story of Xu Bing reminds me of a childhood experience of my own. During the first part of the Cultural Revolution we lived not very far from a huge house that was turned into a storehouse for things that were confiscated during that time. One day, my brothers came home with the secret that this huge house was filled with books—hardcover books—and that these books might soon be sent to a paper factory. At night, they went back to the house to ask the old, illiterate guard to let them in so they could read some of those good books. Soon my brothers came out in great disappointment—all the stored books were in Braille.

29. Unpublished interview with Xu Bing, October 2000, Portland State University.

30. *Chinese Art Weekly* (*Zhongguo Meishu Bao* 中国美术报), 1986, 33.

31. Wu Shanzhuan, "About the Red Humor," *Meishu Sichao* (*Art Waves*) 1 (1987): 23.

32. Ibid.

33. See *Yijing* [*Zhouyi*] 44/xishang/12. Cf. Richard Wilhelm and Cary F. Baynes, *I Ching or Book of Changes* (Princeton, NJ: Princeton University Press, 1967), 322.

34. *Zhuangzi* (Peking: Harvard-Yenching Institute Sinological Index Series Supplement 20, 1947), 75/26/48–9.

35. See Wang Bi, *Zhouyi Lueli* (1965), 10b–11b.

36. See Wang Zhaowen, *One Is Equal to Ten* (一 以当十) (Beijing: Zhaohua Meishu Press, 1956).

37. Xu Zitong, "Xungen wenxuezhongde Jia Pingwa he Ah Cheng" [Jia Pingwa and Ah Cheng in Root-Searching Literature], *Bulletin of Chinese Studies* 3 (1996): 81–91.

38. Yang Chengying, "Xu Bing de Yishu: Behind the Success," *Zhongguo Meishu Bao* 22 (1989).

39. Wilkins, et al., op. cit., 585.

40. Ibid.

41. Erickson, op. cit., 7.

42. Wilkins, Schultz, and Linduff, *Art Past Art Present*, 585.

43. Bhabha, *The Location of Culture*, 20.

44. Ibid.

45. With a few exceptions, such as Liu Hung, professor of Visual Art at Mills College, California, whose work *Fortune Cookies* addressed the traditional Asian-American social issues.

46. M. Byram, *Cultural Studies in Foreign Language Education* (Clevedon, UK: Multilingual Matters, 1989), 6, 42.

47. Fredric Jameson, "Globalization and Political Strategy," *New Left Review* 4 (July–August 2000): 49–68.

48. Karl Marx and Friedrich Engels, *Manifesto of the Communist Party* (Signet Classics, 1998).
49. Wilkins, Schultz, and Linduff, *Art Past Art Present*, 585.
50. Berger and Huntington, *Many Globalizations*, 301.
51. Ibid., 44.
52. Bhabha, *The Location of Culture*, 161.
53. Walter Benjamin, *Reflections*, ed. Peter Demetz, trans. Edmund Jephcott. (New York: Harcourt Brace Jovanovich, 1978), 220–238.
54. Berger and Huntington, *Many Globalizations*, 300.

CHAPTER TWO

Reading Xu Bing's
A Book from the Sky

A Case Study in the Making of Meaning

ROGER T. AMES

INTRODUCTION

I am not concerned here to speculate on authorial intent—what Xu Bing's *A Book from the Sky* (*Tianshu* 天書, Figure I.1) might mean to him as the artist of this installation.[1] And there are better informed interpreters available to evaluate the many different, often insightful, sociological and political interpretations of this work. Among such scholars are those who would read this installation as a critique of the meaningless babble (and sometimes Babel) of the ossified Maoist political ideology eventuating ultimately in a Cultural Revolution that tried to smother the living history of Chinese culture. There are other scholars who see in it a putative expression of the very absurdity of life in contemporary China in which nonsense has become the common sense. And then there are also those scholars who interpret it as an indictment of the suffocating politics of the art establishment that vilified *A Book from the Sky* in its 1987 debut. We must agree with such readings at least to the extent of allowing that the particular social and political context is integral to the art itself, and that such interpretations are most illuminating.

Again, I am not an art historian who might be able to make profitable associations between *A Book from the Sky* and other examples of "conceptual art"—a genre of art that promises a message we might not immediately understand, but that invites an open-ended range of speculation about meaning. The poised yet silent pianist in the Carnegie Hall performance of John Cage's *4 Minutes and 33 Seconds* and Christo and Jeanne-Claude's saffron *Christo's Gates* that have fluttered in Central Park are provocative in just this way, with the not unlikely possibility that the ultimate message is the work of art itself.

I do, however, want to take a stand and dispute any suggestion that Xu Bing can be explained as playing largely to a foreign audience without significant recourse to his own Chinese cultural tradition. Specifically I want to extrapolate off of a familiar postcolonialist discourse that might suggest contemporary artists such as Xu Bing live in the nations of others and participate in the Anglo-European postmodern discourse without adding up to anything in and of themselves. These critics ask: Are such Chinese artists ideologically imprisoned as they depend on Western values and discourse for their art? Is this contemporary art really rooted in Chinese culture, or is it yet another excellent example of cultural self-colonization?[2]

LOCATING XU BING'S *A BOOK FROM THE SKY* WITHIN CHINESE CULTURE

What I have to offer here is a phenomenological description of my own response to Xu Bing's art—what the "new art" of *A Book from the Sky* means to me as a student of Chinese philosophy when I attempt to locate it within the formative cosmological assumptions of Chinese culture. I want to argue that for me at least, Xu Bing's *A Book from the Sky* certainly evokes some associations that are decidedly Western—James Joyce's enigmatic *Finnegans Wake*, for example, comes immediately to mind, as do the "Ukiyo-e" paintings of Vincent Van Gogh with his impression of Chinese characters on the picture frames.

But Xu Bing's work also stimulates a much richer reflection that is located squarely within a familiar Chinese cultural discourse and a demonstrably Chinese understanding of the way in which language works in the production of meaning. I want to suggest that, in contrast to this decidedly Chinese understanding about where meaning comes from, there are persistent cosmological assumptions about language and meaning that have predominated within the Western philosophical narrative, and that such assumptions would provoke a fundamentally different reading of *A Book from the Sky*.

At the outset we must allow that *A Book from the Sky* is multivalent, and will not be reduced to some single authoritative interpretation. In fact, Xu Bing's own title for this work was originally "A Mirror to Interpret the World 析世監," which he himself changed when an appreciative member of the audience suggested that it meant *A Book from the Sky (tianshu* 天書) to him. Hans-Georg Gadamer addresses this multivalence when he asserts:

> [T]he work of art distinguishes itself in that one never completely understands it. . . . An artwork is never exhausted. It never becomes empty.[3]

But Gadamer in respecting the bottomlessness of aesthetic appreciation also wants to separate himself from the reception-aesthetics of Robert Jauss and the deconstructionism of Jacques Derrida in setting real limits that we must appeal to when insisting on the cultural identity of *A Book from the Sky.* Gadamer continues:

> It is a mistake, I think, to try to make this endless multiplicity a denial of the unshakable identity of the work. . . . The work, the text we read, is not something we dream up.[4]

If interpretation is inexhaustible, then by what criteria do we judge the quality of any particular reading? The answer I think is ultimately the "value added" to the work by the interpretation.

Appreciation is certainly a recognition of the quality, significance, and magnitude of the artwork in itself. Such an appreciation is an appropriate admiration for the creative energy invested in it, so pronounced and powerful in the spectacle of *A Book from the Sky.* And such recognition entails a sensitivity and responsiveness to the artwork that establishes a special relationship with the observer. But this burgeoning capacity for appreciation can go well beyond the private enjoyment that would begin and end in a single experience. Indeed, as a communal phenomenon, this aesthetic appreciation spills over to become "value-added"—quite literally increasing the meaning of the transformed cultural cosmos in which this relationship occurs. I want to suggest that when viewed from within the Chinese cosmological tradition, an appreciation of *tianshu* is not only different, but different in magnitude, having the potential to take on a much greater meaning—arguably even a deep religious significance.

Indeed, there is a profoundly serious philosophical problem prompted by Xu Bing's *A Book from the Sky*: Where does meaning come from? An attempt to answer this question will provide us with the occasion to distinguish Chinese cosmology from our own persistent ontological assumptions about language and about creativity itself. But before embarking on this philosophical excursus, I want first to engage in a thought experiment with *A Book from the Sky* and reflect on a more fanciful response that the culturally informed observer might have at a less deliberate and more immediate level.

However opaque the text in *A Book from the Sky* might appear, there are familiar formal continuities with contemporary Chinese written culture that give it a logic and coherence—for example, there are the individual, self-contained graphs themselves as a distinctive style of writing, a finite, yet sufficient vocabulary of some four thousand characters (about the same number as recognized by an educated Chinese person), the proportional redundancy of the characters, the physical structure and organization of a stitched book with title page, table of contents, front matter, columns, and folio and verso pagination, the inclusion of interlinear commentary in smaller characters, the familiar carved calligraphic brushstrokes of twelfth-century woodblock printing, and so on. And even more suggestive of their legibility, in the construction of *A Book from the Sky* "characters," many of the 214 standard "radicals" or "signifiers" are used that tell us that the meaning of this particular character has some reference to "earth 土" or "silk thread 糸," to "cutting 刀" or "handling 手," and so on. The promise of textual prophecy—of the text speaking its message—lies in the degree to which it evokes a familiar sense of language and arouses an anticipation of meaning in the observer. At this level, the promise and the disappointment must be more meaningful to someone who is literate in the Chinese language than someone who is not.

The not unfamiliar title of the new art, *A Book from the Sky* 天書, reiterates this promise that the text is meaningful, with the character *shu* 書 denoting first "writing," and derivatively a "written document" or "book," and *tian* 天 meaning "sky," "the numinous," "deified ancestral heroes," and by extension, the "inherited cultural legacy." The art historian Wu Hung has argued that colloquially, *tianshu* 天書 in this context would mean "nonsense writing"— "abstruse or illegible writing that makes no sense to its reader."[5] But certainly *A Book from the Sky*, while not producing the "sense" or meaning that the "reader" would expect, is not to be understood as the nonsense of a merely unintelligible scribble.

A CULTURAL THOUGHT EXPERIMENT

To begin with, writing in the Chinese tradition from earliest times has had a palpable and immediate religious association. And, *tian* 天 itself has a numinous, fabulous reference that might evoke an oracular, "inspired," even sacred feeling perhaps associated most directly with Daoist talismanic practices. Indeed, *A Book from the Sky* or *Tianshu* 天書 itself is a familiar expression in Daoist scriptures as the first of the eight kinds (*balei* 八類) of esoteric writing. *Tianshu* 天書 in this context is "a style of complex writing that in prizing the mysterious and concealing what is most real, befuddles the eyes." The other seven styles include *shenshu* 神書 as another name for "cloud seal writing," *dishu* 地書 as images of the phoenix and dragon, *neishu* 內書 as what is spit up by turtles, dragons, fish, and birds, *waishu* 外書 as what is borne on scales of fish or reptiles, shells, fur, and feathers, *guishu* 鬼書 as weird graphic forms intelligible only to nonhumans, *zhongxiashu* 中夏書 cursive cloud forms, and *rongyishu* 戎夷書 , which is a written form of a kind with insects and beasts and presumably the barbarians associated with them.[6]

Indeed, within this inherited Chinese cultural legacy, an encounter with an inaccessible, esoteric "text" of one kind or another—a "nonsense writing" that resists our reading and understanding—is not an altogether unfamiliar experience.

For example, in recent years, there has been the recovery of a "woman's language"—*nushu* 女書—from the remote Jiangyong prefecture in Hunan province containing between one thousand to fifteen hundred "characters." These graphs are in fact phonetic syllables that provide pronunciation and then meaning by virtue of context, with some of the script modeled on recognizable Chinese characters. They have been used to transcribe the local Chengguan vernacular language (*chengguan tuhua* 城関土話).

Further, such local writings, although in this case decidedly Chinese, recall the many minority languages and scripts that lay on the periphery of a Chinese cultural consciousness—some derived from Chinese script such as the Khitan of Mongolia, the Xixia and the Jurchen, and other scripts of independent origin such as the Tibetan, Uighur, and the Manchu. And sometimes in this cultural world, indeed often, the periphery moved to the center. We must not forget that "foreigners" occupied the dragon throne for almost one of China's two imperial millennia.

Thinking further of unintelligible texts, for many if not most Chinese readers, without extensive training many of the Buddhist sutras and Daoist treatises we have inherited from the tradition remain impenetrable, constructed of characters that at best suggest sounds rather than meaning—the transliteration of a foreign or an esoteric language into strings of sometimes familiar sometimes exotic "cloud seal" characters (*yunzhuan* 雲篆) that still remain syntactically and semantically meaningless.

Even the *Zhouyi* 周易—the primary divination manual portion of the *Book of Changes* (*Yijing* 易經)—is yet another example of an opaque mantic text that provides columns of characters, hexagrams, and numerical associations that at best reveal sounds without much grammatical or semantic information.

We might be prompted to think of *A Book from the Sky* (*Tianshu* 天書) as "historical" by the fact that there is enough continuity with our current sense of the written language that we can identify it as such. At the same time it evokes an antique primordiality in that its intelligibility suggests that the novelty attending an always continuing present has outrun its linguistic reference. What once was a determinate, rational language has become residual, and we are left with an obsolete vocabulary that would speak if it could of a lost world before the birthing of our present linguistic epoch—of a profoundly literate civilization that we no longer have the cultural competence to know.

If we were to think speculatively and more historically, one possible association one might have with *A Book from the Sky* is these characters are some long-lost language of the mysterious Xia dynasty or some earlier proto-Chinese culture that, having vanished from sight in the morning mists of history, are still at least formally continuous with an always emergent Chinese literate culture. After all, subsequent to the Xia is the Shang dynasty from which we have only in the last century inherited the language of the oracle bones—the *jiaguwen* 甲骨文—written on the physical medium of bovid scapula and turtle plastron that in form are less familiar than the books in *A Book from the Sky*. These oracle bones contain a rich although largely incomprehensible vocabulary of some three thousand characters that are unintelligible to most people. Indeed, only trained paleographers are able to read some of them, while even this expert group with a century of painstaking detective work behind them has only been able to decipher about one thousand of the three thousand characters. And again from the Western Zhou we have the *jinwen* 金文—commemorative inscriptions on bronze vessels written in a seal script that is at best identifiably a written form, but largely impenetrable except to the learned few.

The recent, hugely exciting archaeological excavations over the past generation are recovering even much later texts that are still incomprehensible to most modern "readers" at the level of word, image, and meaning. These texts, like Xu Bing's *A Book from the Sky*, invite an "archaeology" of meaning. The 1993 Guodian *Daodejing*, for example, dating to about 300 BCE from a world still impressed by the footprints of Alexander the Great, is comprised of seventy-one bamboo strips that allow for little more than tentative guesses at a few characters by all but the experts. And these recovered texts present us with yet further dimensions of complexity. Only the *Daodejing* among these recovered texts is presently extant with a few other documents known only by title from court bibliographies. The two versions of *Wuxingpian* 五行篇—one from Mawangdui dating from 168 BCE and the other from Guodian dating from 300 BCE—belong to this category as discoveries of a previously known text that has long been lost. Most of the documents, such as *Xingzimingchu* 性自命出, which also appears in a variant version called *Xingqing* 性情, are entirely new to us. That is, in these archaeological finds we have redactions of texts recovered from tombs located in different parts of contemporary China dating from different centuries where the general population of a literate China cannot "read" them at all. And once the experts have decoded them and have enabled us to "read" the characters, we still struggle with only limited success to recover the images and even less to find the profundity of meaning that clearly made them canonical in their own time and place.

When we are confronted by Xu Bing's "nonsense" text, a playful and fanciful response is thus to seek for the security of a specific, culturally revealing context—to make the text familiar and friendly by locating it historically as some archaic or esoteric form of transmission. Of course, this attempt to seek context is going to be one source of difference that indeed "adds up to something" when entertained from within a Chinese cultural sensibility.

But when we "read" Xu Bing's *A Book from the Sky* as an invitation to search for meaning, it shuts down our usual expectations and redirects the inquiry to another level. The unyielding recalcitrance of the "language" takes us beyond any of these rather desperate contextualizing speculations, and forces upon us profoundly philosophical questions: Where does meaning come from? How is meaning made? And how does language convey this meaning? How do we construct our *imaginaire*?

I want to suggest that the answer to these important questions will require us to distinguish Chinese cosmological commitments about the source of creativity from assumptions that have persisted within the Western philosophical narrative. After all, ontological concerns that have given us an entrenched reality and appearance distinction and a corollary distinction between literal and metaphorical language have little relevance for Chinese cosmology.

WHERE DOES MEANING COME FROM?
CREATIO IN SITU AND CREATIVE ADVANCE

I begin by taking my own "commentary" as a clear object lesson in what Xu Bing's provocative artistic expression can hope to accomplish within its own Chinese worldview—that is, it is a heuristic for the further production of meaning. Indeed, I will argue that one distinctive feature of Chinese process *qi* 氣 cosmology is the continuing "emergence" of determinate order—a hermeneutical assumption about how meaning is made that will not allow for any severe distinction between "text" and the productiveness of interpretation. Stated simply, the production of meaning is radically situated, emerging from the changing relations within our world of experience in our continuing present. "Emergence" is a *creatio in situ* assumption about creative advance, and is captured early in the Chinese tradition in the expression *tiyong* 體用—"the mutuality of reforming and functioning." The earliest extant occurrence of this *tiyong* expression is by the commentator (and philosopher) Wang Bi 王弼 (226–249) in his interpretation of Chapter 38 of the *Daodejing* 道德經, but subsequently *tiyong* becomes a ubiquitous explanatory expression in subsequent Confucian, Daoist, and Buddhist philosophical reflection. Simply put, in Chinese cosmology, *all* creativity is construed as situated and radically embedded—a collaborative co-creativity. Creating oneself and creating one's world is a coterminous and mutually entailing process.

Perhaps the clearest canonical statement of this notion of emergent co-creativity is *Zhongyong* 25 in its explanation of *cheng* 誠—a familiar term usually translated as "sincerity" or "integrity," but herein used with a less familiar cosmological application about the production of meaning. Immediately relevant to our reflection on the "language" of *A Book from the Sky*, the etymology of the character *cheng* 誠 itself suggests "realizing or completing (*cheng* 成)" through "discourse (*yan* 言)." This cosmological application of *cheng* has prompted us along with other commentators to consider "creativity" as an appropriate extension of "sincerity" and "integrity" in rendering it in this important passage:[7]

> Creativity (*cheng* 誠) is self-realizing (*zicheng* 自成), and its way (*dao* 道) is self-advancing (*zidao* 自道). "Creativity" references anything (*wu* 物) taken from its beginning to its end, and without this creativity, there are no things or events. It is thus that, for exemplary persons (*junzi* 君子), it is creativity that is prized. But creativity is not simply the self-realizing of one's own person; it is what realizes other things as well. Realizing oneself is becoming consummate in one's conduct (*ren* 仁); realizing other things is exercising wisdom in realizing one's world (*zhi* 知).[8] It is achieved excellence (*de* 德) in one's natural tendencies (*xing* 性) and is the way of integrating what is more internal and what is more external.[9] Thus, when and wherever one applies such excellence, the result is fitting.

Following Zhu Xi 朱熹 in taking the *Zhongyong* as a linear and coherent text, I would observe its early sections begin rather tentatively with expressed concern over the continuing failure of human beings to forge their way in the world. Indeed, an exasperated Confucius laments, "This proper way, alas, is not being traveled at all!"[10] But once under way, the pace of the *Zhongyong* then accelerates with increasing speed toward an "Ode to Joy" crescendo in the last several sections in which the text quite literally breaks into song in celebration of the human capacity to create meaning and to realize its world, describing the consummatory human being as fully "a co-creator with the heavens and the earth" in shaping the order of the cosmos (可以與天地參矣 and 配天). In the Chinese cosmology expressed here, the lived world is the bottomless unfolding of an emergent, contingent world according to the rhythm of its own internal creative processes without any fixed pattern or guiding hand save that of creative human intelligence. Indeed, the absence of any creator "God" in this cosmology lifts the bar rather significantly on the degree of creativity expected from the human collaborator.

PROCREATION IN CHINESE COSMOLOGY

Xu Bing's *A Book from the Sky* prompts us to think of procreation itself as another example of the relationally situated creation of meaning. The contemporary philosopher Pang Pu 龐朴 provides us with another way of illustrating the centrality of the *creatio in situ*, transformative *tiyong* sensibility in Chinese cosmology. In explaining the notion of "procreation *sheng* 生," Pang Pu makes an illuminating distinction. "*Paisheng* 派生" is authoring, birthing, originating in the sense that one thing creates something as an independent existent, like a hen producing an egg or an oak tree producing an acorn. "*Huasheng* 化生," on the other hand, is one thing transforming into something else, like summer becoming autumn, or a caterpillar becoming a butterfly. In the *paisheng* "derivation" sensibility, the egg goes on to become another hen, and the acorn to become another oak tree, whereas in the *huasheng* "transmutation" sensibility, most eggs become omelets and most acorns become squirrels.

It is a *creatio ex nihilo* variation on the *paisheng* derivation sensibility that has predominated in our own persistent, very Aristotelian cosmological assumptions—the hen reproduces its own essence, or in the human case, the child has its own soul as an essential identity independent of the parent. And the logic of knowing is being able to identify and categorize the progeny.

In Chinese cosmology, on the other hand, these two senses of "procreating" qualify each other. Importantly, in Chinese cosmology the putative discreteness and independence entailed by *paisheng* is qualified by the processual and contextual assumptions of *huasheng*, and the processual continuity of *huasheng* is punctuated as unique "events" by the consummatory nature of *paisheng*.

This understanding of procreation can be expressed concretely by appeal to the metaphor of family pervasive within the Chinese cosmological order, where neither uniqueness nor continuity will yield to the other. The notion of intrinsic relationality that on the one hand allows for the uniqueness and distinctiveness of each particular member of the family (I am this particular matrix of familial relations) also accounts for the continuity that obtains among them (I have a genealogical relationship with my parents and my siblings). This constitutive relationality disqualifies part-whole analysis and requires instead a gestalt shift to focus-field thinking in which "part" and "totality" are two nonanalytic foregrounding and backgrounding perspectives on the same phenomenon. The identity of the family is focused and revealed through each of its members, and each of its members is a particular expression of the meaning of the family.

Again, the putative goodness of any particular person is a relational virtuosity rather than some essential characteristic or quality. Goodness is not the purity of one's individual soul, but emerges first and foremost as a focal achievement in one's aggregating conduct in one's roles as this daughter and this sibling and this wife, and then derivatively and abstractly, it is interpreted as a personal quality.

In pursuing this distinction between "derivation" and "transformation," Pang Pu is alerting us to a further refinement in our understanding of where meaning comes from—that is, of the relationship between what comes before and what follows in the ongoing process. While teleologically we might be inclined to understand the progenitor/progeny genealogy as a series in which there is quite literally an "essential" independence of the latter from the former, early Chinese cosmology on reflection is clearly a combination of both *paisheng* and *huasheng*, taking the progenitor as giving way to *this* unique progeny, but at the same time, as proliferating and living on within its progeny. In Confucianism, there is a stronger sense of the genealogical continuity where the progeny is to be understood as the foregrounding of this unique person in a continuing flow of procreation—a unique and particular current in a particular stream.

A "proper" name might by definition be "one's own" name (*paisheng*), but in a Chinese world one's complex of names is profoundly relational and processual (*huasheng*). One's family surname is the first and continuing source of identity, while one's given name (*ming* 名) proliferates with assumed style names (*zi* 字), sobriquets (*hao* 號), and a web of specific family designations of "uncle number two" and "auntie number three" (*ershu* 二叔 and *sanzhou* 三妯) and professional titles of "teacher" and "director" (*laoshi* 老師 and *zhuren* 主任) even in the course of one's lifetime, and posthumous titles (*shi* 謚) after it—a reflection of the unfolding contribution one has been able to make to family and community over time.

This contrast between the *ex nihilo* and *in situ* senses of creativity that predominate within the Western and Chinese philosophical narratives is immediately apparent in the exaggerated originality ascribed to our independent philosophers, from Plato to Whitehead as they turn on the merry-go-round of systematic philosophy, and

in the overstated orthodoxy of the Chinese commentarial tradition—in fact, the ongoing transformation of Confucianism—as it
passes through the hands of Mencius and Xunzi, and is bequeathed
to Tang Junyi 唐君毅 in the present day.

Having said this, the "emergent" sense of creativity that Xu
Bing's installation prompts us to reflect upon is not entirely unfamiliar in our recent philosophical narrative. But as the Italian philosopher Gianni Vattimo observes, the Anglo-European world has
come relatively late to its current hermeneutical awareness of how
the commentary as well as the text is a significant source of meaning:

> By the productiveness of interpretation, I mean that interpreta-
> tion is not only an attempt to grasp the original meaning of the
> text (for example the authorial intention) and to reproduce it as
> literally as possible but also to add something essential to the text
> (to understand it better than its author, the adage resonating in
> eighteenth century hermeneutics). . . . [T]he European culture of
> late modernity "discovered" the productiveness of interpretation
> or—which is the same—the nonepiphenomenality, instrumental-
> ity, or secondariness of the commentary.[11]

Gadamer's "fusion of horizons" is only a fairly recent philosophical cliché. In fact, I want to argue that the Chinese cosmology in which the factic life experience is processual, "never stopping
night or day,"[12] places it historically in rather stark contrast to the
"logocentrism" of the pre-Darwinian Anglo-European philosophical narrative that has inspired the internal critique to which Vattimo
alludes. To use Heidegger's language, our narrative begins from
"theo-ontological" rather than cosmological questions—the search
for some permanent and certain reality, a *logos*, that grounds and
causally explains appearances with only a secondary interest in a pre-
scription for how changing things can hang together most productively. In this search for a unifying "reality," one specific aspect of
the human religious, philosophical, physical, and volitional experience—God, rationality, matter, or will—has often been lifted out of
the always fluid process and then privileged as causal and originative.

This isolation of some determinative principle is the pervasive
methodological problem that John Dewey has called "*the* philosophical fallacy": "the abstracting of some one element from the
organism which gives it meaning, and setting it up as absolute,"
and then proceeding to revere this one element "as the cause and

ground of all reality and knowledge."[13] This isolated and privileged aspect is then treated as the determinative One behind the many making our changing world a *uni*-verse governed by some unchanging *logos* that serves as the proper object of knowledge. In rejecting *the* philosophical fallacy in all of its different iterations, Dewey is attempting to recover process and particularity.

Until the philosophic revolution beginning slowly with Darwin and gaining real cultural ascendancy only over the past generation or so, we have been importantly a "logocentric" tradition. Logocentrism with respect to language is the assumption that a literal language of presence can be recovered in an "archaeology" of a text—the search for primitive origins or beginnings. On the analogy of the *Logos* as expressed in the scriptures, a search is undertaken for the objective authorial intent as a source of meaning that stands quite independent of the reader or the text's changing context, where interpretation is merely derivative and instrumental. The Platonic and Aristotelian quest for essential definitions—what-it-is-to-be-things-of-this-kind—as the true objects of knowledge, and the primary understanding of etymology as the search for the original—indeed, the "true (*etumos*)"—meaning of a word is closely linked to the traditional importance of *creatio ex nihilo* in our assumptions about the ultimate source of meaning. The putative search for the "literal" meaning behind the metaphorical or interpretive is itself a search for origins, for the reality behind appearances, a quest for certainty. Indeed, "in the beginning was the Word, the *Logos*."

In spite of the much advertised revolution against "*the* philosophical fallacy" that is being waged within the contemporary Anglo-European discipline of philosophy in recent years, such logocentric presuppositions about the source of meaning have over the centuries been sedimented into a self-understanding that we have only just begun to dredge. To use an analogy to suggest how entrenched and persistent our logocentric assumptions remain, we might reflect on our understanding of an individual person. With our enlightened scientific sensibilities, we might claim to have largely given up on the notion of an immortal human "soul," but we are still very much wedded to persisting default assumptions about the integrity of our discrete and essential individuality that developed out of this way of thinking. A focus-field, relational conception of person that this same contemporary science would recommend is still counterintuitive for most of us, and would be defeated by most appeals to common sense.

In the most general of terms, our own cosmological sensibilities emerge out of a narrative in which a *creatio ex nihilo* understanding of creativity has predominated—a commitment in understanding creativity that translates into the cultural importance of novelty, originality, and authorship. In John Hope Mason's recently published monograph, *The Value of Creativity*, this British philosopher argues that "creativity" became a desirable value (such as heroism, honor, piety, and various kinds of virtue) only relatively recently in the mid-nineteenth century when developments in science and technology fostered human independence, a free-market economy encouraged innovation, and ameliorative "progress" became an expectation.

According to Hope Mason, the notion of creativity has a complex history that has construed it in at least two radically different ways, a history that continues to condition the way in which we understand and use the term today. In the most general and certainly not exclusive terms, one persistent tradition is neo-Platonic: creativity is associated with the Creator God, and connotes moral goodness, harmony, and spirituality. The word of God speaks a world into being and " . . . it was good." As *Psalms* 24 insists:

> The earth is the Lord's and the fulness thereof
> It is He that has made us and not we ourselves.

In a transcendent and perfect God, we have the complete identity between creativity and morality.[14]

The second tradition is Promethean, where creativity is daringly original, but at the same time, it is amoral if not even immoral, dangerous, disruptive, and conflicted: the product of a struggle between the justice of Zeus and the Titan pioneer of human civilization, Prometheus. Hope Mason would see Kant, Coleridge, Carlyle, and Arnold as exemplars of the neo-Platonic valorization of creativity, and would read Machiavelli's Prince, Goethe's Faust, Milton's Satan, the monster of Mary Shelley's "Victor" Frankenstein, and Nietzsche's Übermensch as at once assaults on the neo-Platonic sensibility and as variations on a Promethean theme.[15]

Interestingly, the idea of creativity according to both the neo-Platonic and Promethean models emphasizes novelty and originality. Such creativity issues from the imagination of a single, *creatio ex nihilo* source. Either creativity is the prerogative of a God and God alone, or it is the product of a wandering Promethean hero who is audacious, self-willed, fiercely independent, incapable of compromise, and prone to isolation and madness, the epitome of a solitary pride that is a challenge to divine order. This being the case, human creativity and human morality are incompatible in both the neo-Platonic and the Promethean traditions. In the former where God has a monopoly on both creativity and morality, the emphasis falls on obedience, and human creativity as hubris is immoral. In the latter, where Jove too has a monopoly on justice, his divinely sponsored morality stands in tension with the expression of a self-assertive human freedom and creativity.[16]

If we reflect informally for a moment on our own commonsense use and valorization of the word "creativity" in ordinary language, it would seem that those connotations that made it almost antithetical to moral responsibility up until the Industrial Revolution are still very much freighted in the way in which we think and speak. The notion of "creativity" is usually invoked comfortably with reference to the more exuberant occupations of the arts and literature, that is, with respect to the entertaining occupations of producing artifice and harmless fiction. But when we turn to our responsibilities for the serious business of the day—morality, theology, science, and even "business" itself—"creativity" becomes suspect.

For example, if I were to learn that a colleague is morally "creative," I might properly stand in admiration of his rakish charms, but I would also be concerned about his having anything but a passing acquaintance with my comely wife or my innocent children.[17] If my friend is known to be theologically "creative," John Paul II and I are both going to be worried about the ultimate disposition for his immortal soul. If our cloning colleague is described publicly as having been "creative" in his experiments with glowing mice, his multimillion-dollar federal grants are going to be at risk. And if my financial advisor has been "creative" in those suggestions that have made me unseemly rich and the IRS has found out about it, I am likely to be audited if not jailed first. In the discipline of philosophy itself one can argue that Gadamerian "play" is philosophically intriguing because it challenges the Aristotelian seriousness that we have traditionally invested in philosophy. Indeed, what is perceived as Richard Rorty's Cheshire cat–like, grinning assault on our discipline at the end of his career banished him beyond the walls of philosophy to Stanford's Department of Comparative Literature, and earned him all but excommunication from our professional society.

Further, while we tend to associate "creativity" with our Bohemian artistic adventures, we do not seem to construe such areas of the human experience as causal or linear, and thus ineluctable in the same way as the serious business of being human. Compare, for example, our sense of art history to other historiographies: Christian, Marxist, Hegelian, Scientific. The strong commitment to teleology and necessity that is assumed in our commonsense understanding of the human experience drives cosmic progress without need for an appeal to any real human creativity. Our unstated Kantian responsibility is to "discover" natural laws and particularly moral imperatives, and to do our best to act in accordance with them.

Let me try to bring the contrast between this familiar *creatio ex nihilo* sense of creativity and the Chinese commitment to *creatio in situ* that is prompted by a reflection on Xu Bing's *A Book from the Sky* into clearer focus by appealing to the *Yijing* 易經—the *Book of Changes*—that has held pride of place as the first among the classics defining of Chinese culture. It is this open-ended classic with its centuries of appended commentaries rather than "the word of God (*logos*)" that has set the terms of art for Chinese cosmology. Willard Peterson, in analyzing this profound yet frustratingly obscure document, insists that it "has been for some two thousand years one of the most important statements in the Chinese tradition on knowing how the cosmos works and how humans might relate to that working. Especially from the Sung [Song] through the Ch'ing [Qing] period, the 'Great Commentary' (*Ta chuan* [*Dazhuan*] 大傳), as it was called, provided the locus classicus for vocabulary and concepts in nearly every major abstract discussion of the physical world and man's place in it."[18]

Edward Shaughnessy, in his recent retranslation of the *Dazhuan*, echoes Peterson's evaluation of its importance in observing that "the worldview of its *Xici* or *Appended Statements* Commentary—integrating man and nature through the medium of the *Yijing*—is arguably the most sophisticated (it is certainly the most subtle) statement of the correlative thought that has been so fundamental to all of China's philosophical systems."[19] Shaughnessy is not exaggerating when he says that "indeed, so central has the *Yijing* been to Chinese thought over these two millennia that a history of its exegetical traditions would require almost a history of Chinese thought."[20]

This *Great Commentary* in telling the story of its own origins provides us insight into how this tradition from early on has conceived the relationship between language and meaning that is at issue in the Xu Bing installation. The *Yijing* explains how a human responsiveness to context has enchanted the cosmos. The remote ancestors Fu Xi 伏羲 and Shen Nong 神農 established a rhythm in the human experience that enabled them to chime in to the cadence of the "flux" and "continuity" (*biantong* 變通) that they perceived as persistent characteristics of the world around them. Inspired by the efficacy of their insights into the workings of the cosmos, they then represented their interpretation of life in the world in a hexagramic language of images, models, and patterns for the benefit of generations yet to come. Importantly, these antique sages were engaged in a project of self-understanding and self-articulation rather than some disinterested interrogation of nature. By their efforts at *ars contextualis*—the art of effectively contextualizing the experience of the human being within the processes of nature in an effort to optimize the creative possibilities of the cosmos—Fu Xi and Shen Nong cultivated a thick continuity between nurture and nature expressed in the evocative images that constitute the *Yijing*. This continuity between the human experience and the natural forum in which it occurs—between petroglyphs and the striations in stone, for example—is later made explicit in the various expressions that describe the relations between humanity and nature such as 天人合一, 天人相應, 天人感應. This continuity between nature and nurture is reflected in the fact that the same vocabulary is used to express the creative advance in both the human and the natural ecologies: for example, "the way of things (*dao* 道)," "vital energies (*qi* 氣)," "inscribed culture (*wen* 文)," "patterns (*li* 理)," "*yinyang* 陰陽," and the perpetual interface between "flux and continuity (*biantong* 變通)" itself. There is no initial and originative *Logos*. Language and its significance emerges *pari passu* with a world that is continually being spoken into being. The process of making meaning, inspired by our imagination, becomes our reality, our *imaginaire*.

Building on this auspicious beginning, the sage kings who descended from Fu Xi and Shen Nong—the Yellow Emperor, Yao, and Shun—continued to construct technologies, modes of transportation, social institutions, and customs that were inspired by particular hexagrams, each of the hexagrams providing a dynamic image of some natural process:

> The sages had the capacity to see the way the world operates, and perceiving the way things come together and commune, they put into practice their statutes and codes of propriety.[21]

Importantly, it is this gradual process of structuring and ritualiz-
ing the human experience thus remembered in and inspired by the
Great Commentary that has enchanted life in the world, and in so
doing, continues to produce its spirituality:

> In comprehending the flux and flow of the world around them,
> the sage kings were able to save the people from exhausting
> themselves. With their spirituality, they transformed the people,
> and enabled them to find what was most fitting for them.[22]

The productive symbiosis that can be achieved between the human
and the natural worlds is practical inspiration for effective human
living. This ongoing production of human culture has transformed
bird tracks and the markings on the backs of turtles into awe-
inspiring calligraphy and the *Book of Songs* 詩經. It has elevated
feeding into fine dining and elegant tea ceremony, and stirred raw
sense data into heights of aesthetic expression. It has uplifted random copulation into love and family, made noise into the magic of
sublime music, and inspired inchoate interpersonal relations into
the flourishing community and the profound religious sensibilities
that such human communion fosters.

In addition to enabling human beings to live moral and aesthetic lives, this understanding of the processes of change and
productivity revealed by the *Yijing* allows them access to the very
mysteries of the cosmos:

> The Master asked rhetorically, "Does not the person who under-
> stands the course of flux and transformation in fact understand
> the workings of the spiritual?"[23]

Importantly, the enchanted, spiritual dimension of the human
experience (*shen* 神) does not belong to another world. On the contrary, spirituality is the inexhaustible product of human efficacy and
refinement in this one:

> The *Yijing* is the sage's means of probing what is profound to
> its very limits, and examining thoroughly what is still incipient
> (*ji* 幾). It is only through this profundity that the sages can dis-
> cern the purposes of the world; it is only through the incipient
> that they can consummate the business of the world; it is only

through the spiritual they can be quick without haste and can arrive without even going.[24]

In the course of time, such high expectations of the human experience have produced an atheistic religiousness that elevates the *cultivated* human experience into what Tu Wei-ming has called "anthropocosmic" proportions.[25] Human beings, without reference to limiting assumptions about religious transcendentalism and supernaturalism, have become a source of profound meaning in their own world—the only world. Cosmic creativity is fully a collaboration between human beings and their own environing context, a cosmology that is consistent with what John Berthrong calls "the world-dependent nature of divine reality."[26] Indeed, it is the cosmic import of human co-creativity that moves the *Zhongyong* to its religious crescendo:

> Only those in the world of utmost creativity (*zhicheng* 至誠) are able to separate out and braid together the many threads on the great loom of the world. Only they set the great root of the world and realize the transforming and nourishing processes of heaven and earth.
>
> How could there be anything on which they depend?
> So earnest, they are consummate (*ren* 仁);
> So profound, they are a bottomless abyss (*yuan* 淵);
> So pervasive, they are *tian* (*tian* 天).
> Only those whose own capacities of discernment and sagely wisdom extend to the powers of *tian* could possibly understand them.[27]

Borrowing an expression from the *Yijing*, Tang Junyi has described this processual flow of experience without initial beginning or end as "the notion of ceaseless procreation 生生不已觀."[28] Experience is persistent, historicist, and naturalistic in the sense of having no appeal to any metaphysical or supernatural source. Meaning is emergent in the transactions among the unique things that constitute the world.

The phenomenological world in classical China is an endless flow, evidencing its formal character only as "trans-*form*-ation." In fact, the *Great Commentary* says explicitly that "spirituality is without squareness and change is without body 神無方而易無體."[29] Interpreting this passage, Willard Peterson suggests, "To have no 'squareness' is to be not susceptible of being differentiated into parts and to be not adequately delimited by any conceptual bounds."[30] "Things" are in fact a processive and hence always a provisional flux of "events," where the shifting dispositioning of these events is interactive and mutually shaping.[31]

When we locate Xu Bing's *A Book from the Sky* within these underlying cosmological assumptions about the radically situated nature of creativity, we have to realize that in this early and persistent Chinese cosmology, language and people are the outside and inside of the same thing, where meaning is made through productive associations. Turning explicitly to the way in which language functions, the *Great Commentary* insists that persons are created discursively. The identity of a person, while seemingly localized by "body" and "home," is in fact defined by patterns of deference established and fostered through effective discourses that certainly include body and gesture, but also the written and spoken language, music, ritualized roles and relationships, food, and so on. Gadamer observes:

> The "use" of words is not a "using" at all. Rather language is a medium, an element: language is the element in which we live, as fishes live in water. . . . In the exchange of words, the thing meant becomes more and more present. A language is truly a "natural language" when it binds us together in this way.[32]

The Chinese processual cosmology grounded in the *Yijing* would perhaps take this understanding of language one step further and claim that, more than a medium, "language" in its broadest sense is constitutive of who we are as irreducibly relational people. Indeed, the medium and the message are one and the same.

The evolving pattern of personal names discussed in the preceding pages is one manifestation of this discursively created identity. If we pursue the question: "What does relationality mean?" we must allow that these various modalities of discourse are certainly pivotal—that is, a relationship is largely a "relating to" or "giving an account of oneself." We create each other linguistically.

The efficacy of what the exemplary person says not only influences the immediate community, but also has a profound and lasting affect on the world broadly. The exemplary person as the source of effective speech and action has to be understood both relationally and contextually as catalytic within a configuration of circumstances that precipitates a certain course of events:

If what the exemplary person says even while remaining at home is felicitous, those in distant quarters will respond to it; how much more so those near at hand. If what is said is not felicitous, those in distant quarters will oppose it; how much more so those near at hand. What is said comes from one's person but has an effect on the people; actions arise near at hand but are seen from a distance. Words and actions are the hinge and trigger of the exemplary person. The operations of hinge and trigger control honor and disgrace. It is with words and actions that the exemplary person moves the heavens and the earth.[33]

Wang Bi in his "Elucidating the Images (*mingxiang* 明象)" commentary on the *Yijing* provides a hermeneutical explanation for the relationship between image (*xiang* 象), language (*yan* 言), and meaning (*yi* 意) in the human quest to make this life significant. He gives an account of how the antique sages "figured out" the world around them, and then conjured up a set of sixty-four "figures" or images (*xiang* 象) that captured their own interpretive "configuration" for life lived in this world—their best understanding of our natural and cultural ecologies. In doing this, the sages were not seeking to "discover" or to "explain" the "ontological" ground of the human experience. Rather they sought to provide a contingent, explanatory vocabulary for the cultivation of an open-ended and continuing cultural adventure. They began from the basic assumption that culture is an ongoing evolving process that entails both novelty and persistence, both crises and continuities, both transformation and resistance.

Image thus understood is the interpretation and presentation rather than representation of a configured world at the concrete and historical levels—our constructed and projected *imaginaire*. The evocative, conjured image as such assumes considerably more rhetorical explanatory force than would any logical account[34] because it is not intended to give a rational account of some given reality, but rather has incitatory force in its capacity to activate our affective and linguistic resources in shaping our world. An image is a broadly sensory (that is, visual, auditory, tactile, olfactory) presentation of a perceptual, imaginative, and, to some degree, recollected experience. The form of the perception, memory, or imagination may be distinct from the mode of its presentation. For example, the olfactory or visual experience of a rose may be imaged in the words of the poet. The word-picture as experienced by the celebrant of the poem, and not (necessarily) the private experience of the poet, makes the image socially accessible and efficacious. The most productive manner of discussing images, therefore, is in terms of their communally experienceable character. Only such images have direct efficacy.[35] Willard Peterson in fact argues that the term *xiang*, generally translated "image" or "model" in the *Yijing*, ought to be rendered "figure" in the collaborative sense of "to give or to bring into shape."[36] The act of conjuring is participatory and aspirational, becoming a communal negotiation of realizing a desired world.

There is a conversation reported in the *Yijing* between Confucius and his protégées:

> The Master said: "The written word cannot do justice to speech, and speech cannot do justice to meaning."[37]
>
> "If this is the case, then is the meaning of the Sages beyond our grasp?"
>
> The Master replied: "The Sages constructed 'images' to give a full account of their meaning, set up the hexagrams to give a full account of what is natural and what is contrived, wrote their judgments on the images and hexagrams in order to say completely what they had to say, introduced the presumption of change and continuity as a way to take full advantage of any situation, and elaborated upon and embellished all this to do justice to its profundity."[38]

The invention and ramification of images or metaphors is one of the fundamental ways through which a culture interprets its world.[39] In Wang Bi's commentary, there is an attempt to explain the relationship between image, word, and meaning. Wang Bi begins by defining the role of word and image in constituting meaning:

> An image expresses meaning; words clarify the image. To do full justice to meaning, nothing is as good as an image; to do full justice to an image, nothing is as good as words. Because words arise from images, we can explore the words as a window on the image. And because the image arises from meaning, we can explore the image as a window on meaning. Meaning is given full account with an image, and the image is articulated in words. Hence, words are whereby we clarify the image. In getting the image, we forget the words. The image is whereby we hold on to meaning. In getting the meaning, we forget the image. It is

like the snare serving to capture the rabbit; in snaring the rabbit, we forget the snare. Or like the fishtrap serving to catch the fish; in catching the fish, we forget the trap. As such, words are the "snare" for the image. And the image is the "trap" for meaning. For this reason, holding on to the words is not getting the image; holding on to the image is not getting the meaning.[40]

Wang Bi ends here by indicating both the heuristic function and the limitations of words and images. Word and image are triggers rather than repositories of meaning; in fact, if they are interpreted as repositories, they can obstruct the process of meaning-making. On the other hand, we cannot catch rabbits and fish without snares and traps, and we cannot capture meaning without the effective deployment of words and images. This is what the *Zhuangzi* means when it insists on having a further word with the person who has forgotten words:

The reason for fishtraps is to catch fish, but having caught the fish, you forget the fishtrap. The reason for rabbit snares is to snare rabbits, but having caught the rabbit, you forget the snare. The reason for words is to capture meaning, but having grasped the meaning, you forget the words. Where can I find a person who has forgotten the words so that I can have a word with him.[41]

Imaging is analogical in the sense that it requires a movement between a generalized situation made intelligible in word and image, and the meaning-productive detail of one's own particular circumstances. Imaging as such has performative force. Meaning is not simply given; it is reflexively appropriated and projected. As such, while it is appropriated, it is also "made up" and "made one's own."

In the *Yijing*, the meaning of a general situation is captured in an image, and the image is explained in words. The words constitute the most abstract level of discourse and, as such, have the least degree of meaning for one's particular situation. Words, however, have the power to evoke an image, which in stirring one's imagination, enables one to focus the situation for oneself. What was general becomes increasingly particular; what was abstract becomes increasingly concrete; what was vague becomes increasingly focused and meaningful. By virtue of its relative explicitness, the image displaces the words, and as the image is explored as a repository and stimulus of significance for one's own circumstances, the lines of the image begin to fade. The image gives way to meaning. In being deepened and made more determinate, more meaningful for one-self, the image loses its more general character and becomes increasingly indistinct. The image retreats as the particular situation is focused and inscribed.

Wang Bi's most important insight here is the fluidity of the process, and the insubstantiality of any foundational claims. There is an inexhaustibly isomorphic relationship obtaining among these levels of discourse that allows us to privilege each level in turn.

Words and images in their stipulated forms are reasonably clear, but are equivocal in their application to particular situations. The meaning of a particular event, on the other hand, is clear as an immediate experience, and yet in its particular detail, is resistant to conceptual and explanatory clarity. Hence, in moving from words to meaning, the impoverished vagueness of generality, which we often term "clarity," gives way to the rich vagueness of particularity.

Wang Bi's next step is to turn the circle in the alternative direction. Now, instead of images and words expressing meaning, they inscribe it. Meaning gives rise to new images and words, which in turn give rise to new meaning:

> Given that an image arises from the meaning, in holding on to the image, what you are holding on to is not really the image. Given that words arise from the image, in holding onto the words, what you are holding on to is not really the words. As such, to forget the image is to get the meaning; to forget the words is to get the image. Getting the meaning lies in forgetting the image; getting the image lies in forgetting the words.[42]

The intimacy of word, image, and meaning challenges any severe disjunction between reality and appearance, between reasoning and imagination, between determinacy and indeterminacy. There is an unbroken line between meaning as what is real, image as the presentation and inscription of what is real, and words as the constitutive articulation of what is real. Words as articulations of the image do not identify and describe an independent reality, but both inscribe and participate in it. That which is known and the act of realizing come into being together.

In the Chinese tradition, without a notion of *objectivity* derived from a reality/appearance, One-behind-the-many ontology, there can only be the flux of passing circumstances. Without the stable, institutional order that *objectivity* guarantees, temporarily persistent objects dissolve into the flux and flow: the changefulness of their surround. Indeed, they are not objects, but *events*, continuous with all other events. What are perceived as persistent "things" that sustain an identity across time from birth, maturation, and eventual decline are in fact loci of relative yet transitory stability within a manifold of continual change. The identity of anything thus conceived, though enduring, is analogical: an integrity sustained through a range of dynamic associations.

The sages thus conceived of the images that both capture and inspire this world as a heuristic for the always natal, procreative project of reconceiving this world. It is a deobjectified, defactualized discourse—the language of process—and to speak and hear that language is to experience the flow of things. Wang Bi explains how meaning arises through the continuing, creative process of *ars contextualis*—the art of constructing a virtuosic life discursively—in his very early version of what we now are tentatively exploring as the hermeneutical circle.

It is within these cosmological assumptions about language and human co-creativity expressed in the *Yijing* that we have to locate *A Book from the Sky*. At an intellectual level, *A Book from the Sky* certainly presents us with the question that we have rehearsed in the preceding pages: Where does meaning come from? And in so doing, *A Book from the Sky* has enabled us to make an important distinction between the *creatio ex nihilo* sensibility of some single, independent, originative, and determinative authority that has had such broad play within the Western philosophical narrative, and the *creatio in situ* (*tiyong, biantong, paisheng/huasheng*) sense of emergent, participatory meaning so familiar and persistent within Chinese cosmology.

When considered from the *creatio in situ* perspective, *A Book from the Sky*, in initially resisting understanding, interrupts the ecology of meaning-making and self-articulation. While frustrating our search for immediate linguistic meaning, *A Book from the Sky* presents us with the incipient, the inchoate, the yet indeterminate—a still dark yet promising hint of meaning that forces a confrontation with our own unique imaginative powers of commentary and interpretation.

The *Daodejing* 56 tells us:

Those who really understand it do not talk about it,
And those who talk about it do not really understand it.

What does this saying say? The *Zhuangzi* can serve as commentary here. In the *Zhuangzi*'s description of what it calls "tipping goblet" words (*zhiyan* 卮言), we find this contrast between the putatively "full" language of reference and authority and the "empty" language that always requires refilling. Language is constituted primarily by premise-dependent disputational words (*yuyan* 寓言) and the weighty, conversation-stopping words of orthodoxy and authority (*chongyan* 重言). *Zhiyan* are words whose function invokes the image of a goblet that empties out automatically when filled to the brim, and then again rights itself to offer the opportunity be filled once again. According to the *Zhuangzi*:

> Words that have premises occupy some 90% of our speech, and weighty, repeatable sayings occupy 70% of that. "Tipping goblet" words are new every time, and achieve a productive coherence on the revolving wheel of nature.
>
> The 90% of words that have premises appeal to something beyond themselves for justification. It is like the father who will not act as the matchmaker for his own son because the praises of someone other than the father are more persuasive than his own. The onus thus falls on someone other than oneself. People accept only what accords with their own premises, and reject what does not—they give affirmation to what accords with their premises and take exception when it is otherwise.
>
> Canonical sayings that occupy 70% of such speech are conversation-stoppers, so they must come from our seniors. But where such persons are merely ahead of us in years but do not have the comprehensive know-how and discrimination we expect from elders, they are not ahead at all. Indeed, a person who does not have access to our precursors has no cultural legacy, and without it, is simply called old and useless.
>
> The "tipping goblet" words that are new every time and achieve a productive coherence on the revolving wheel of nature can be relied upon to meet the ceaseless changes in life and to realize one's full complement of years. There is parity in not speaking. . . . Thus there is the saying: "Do not say anything." If in speaking you do not say anything, then in a lifetime of speaking you have yet to say anything, and in a lifetime of not saying anything you have never failed to speak up.
>
> From one perspective something is permissible, and yet from another it is not; from one perspective something is so, and yet

from another it is not so. What makes something so? Declaring it so makes it so. What makes it not so? Declaring it not so makes it not so. What makes it permissible? Declaring it permissible makes something permissible. What makes it not permissible? Declaring it not permissible makes it not permissible. Everything as a matter of course has that which is so about it, and that which is permissible about it. There is nothing that is not so and that is not permissible. If it were not for "tipping goblet" words that are new every time and that achieve a productive coherence on the revolving wheel of nature, who could endure for long?[43]

Zhiyan is language understood as responsive to context and thus always appropriate: a living, emergent vocabulary that is constantly being reinvested and reauthorized as the cultural conversation continues. The *Zhuangzi* is declaring the speciousness of any "literal" metanarrative that would promise to give us access to some foundational truth—what is identified here specifically as referential language that has premises (*yuyan* 寓言) and that is freighted with the authority of repeatable, canonical sayings (*chongyan* 重言). Indeed, this chapter of the *Zhuangzi* is often construed as a commentary on statements made about language in the "Inner Chapters":

Saying is not just exhaling breath; it is supposed to be saying something. The problem is that, since what is said is not fixed, in the final analysis are we saying something or have we in fact said nothing at all? People surmise that language is different from the twittering of fledgling birds, but in fact is there really any way of making this distinction?[44]

Without fixed reference, all we have is language as a currency for productively renegotiating situations as they arise—what Richard Rorty calls our possibility to generate infinite "redescriptions" (or perhaps better, "represcriptions") so that the conversation might continue. Silence is not an option—it is an inverse obstinacy to literal language. What we need is to speak up and say nothing— that is, to say no "thing" as an object of fixed reference. That in a lifetime of such speaking, one can claim to have said nothing is consistent with *Daodejing* 78, which states "appropriate language seems contradictory 正言若反." Indeed, through the *Zhuangzi's zhiyan* all language becomes art—it becomes poetry in which the text emerges in its full autonomy. In Gadamer's words, "here language just stands for itself, it brings itself to stand before us."[45] What Gadamer means, I think, is that poetry is presentation, and cannot be treated instrumentally and reductively as representation.

For the *Zhuangzi* it is the flexibility of this kind of language that enables us to survive. The *zhi* or tipping goblet is the fishtrap or rabbit snare that provisions the table for every meal. Xu Bing's "characters" are such "tipping goblet" words that, in standing invitingly empty before us, declare the impermanence and ultimate emptiness of any invested authority while at the same promising us an inexhaustible flow of adaptable, always provisional meaning.

In the new *Daodejing* that was recovered at Guodian in 1993, there is an additional piece of text—in fact, the earliest statement we have on early Chinese cosmology—that is being called *Taiyi shengshui* 太一生水: "The Ancestral One Gives Birth to Water." In addition to reiterating the collaborative, situated nature of co-creativity that we explored earlier, it asks the question: Why use the obscure name *dao* instead of a familiar vocabulary that everyone already knows?

As for *dao*, it is just another style name for the same things— the familiar vocabulary of the heavens and the earth. But what may I ask, is its proper name? *Dao* is used to accommodate creative advance. The different names for the heavens and the earth—both their original name and their style names—are well-established. It is just that in trying to venture beyond these categories, we do not think that such names are fitting.

We use *dao*—discourse that has neither squareness nor body— rather than the language we all know and rely upon in our dis- course in order to confront the limits of our world and to reach beyond accepted concepts and categories, to think outside the box. Invoking *dao* liberates metaphor from common sense, and wonder from familiarity. We are challenged to begin again.

If in viewing *A Book from the Sky* we allow that the process of meaning-making is made possible by the productive indeter- minacy of image and language, with only the dawn or twilight of meaning available, we are overwhelmed by the weight of that indeterminacy. We might not be able to read the graphs them- selves, but in spite of our frustration we presuppose access to the unmarked conjunctions and transitions that animate the Chinese language, and these fluid transitions and conjunctions give us the "and" of additional significance.

Language thus conceived as context- and relation-dependent and, at the same time, open and indeterminate has the potential to liberate and animate our own aesthetic responsibility as co-creators—to release our unmediated, authentic experience of temporality, our *gongfu* 功夫. The encounter with *A Book from the Sky* presents us with an opportunity for recovering the personal aesthetic experience by bringing into question "literalism" and the culture of the book. The "meaningless" text forces us, in the absence of the normal contextualizing relations of "community," "reference," "dogma," and "science" that is usually freighted in a shared language, to acknowledge in a continuing present our own vital lived historicity, our factic life. It forces what Gianni Vattimo calls a "weakening of thinking"—a thinking without the oppressive, aggregating historical narrative presumed in the everyday use of language.

On the one hand, this abrupt awareness can be frustrating if not frightening. We are, in real degree, confronted with a feeling of cultural dyslexia if not amnesia. To the extent that the text is identifiable as "language" and yet stands empty, it is a disintegrating encounter with linguistic "ruins" that threatens our faith and feeling of security in the persistence of a shared common sense. It is an experience that undermines our sense of communal solidarity and our assumed competence, underscoring the ultimate precariousness of the human experience.

On the other hand, this stimulating encounter has the potential to renew our confidence in our own creative and penetrating subjectivity. In the receding objectivity and orthodoxy, we are renewed as unique, historical, contingent, and provisional beings who struggle with imagination to quite literally make sense of the nonsense. Reassuring objective definition and true description gives way to the authentic experience of temporality—existential language as the source of our song and our poetry. Indeed, it is this "authentic temporality," our historicity, that is the mystery and inspiration of art. As a response to the life-threatening, suffocating weight of objectivity, life itself is nothing more or less than making a difference.

But at the same time, we must not overstate the indeterminacy. We must remember that this confrontation with our "lived historicity" is not pure, raw, and vacant, as Sartre would have us believe. It is a specious present still located within a most particular historical continuity that will not be denied. Indeed, it is this historical continuity that, in the absence of conventional meaning, is at once our most primordial identity and our remaining resource for real spontaneity—a liberated virtuosity that certainly exhorts us to think outside the box, but inevitably, from inside *this* box. What is at stake in the liberation of our historicity is the renewed possibility of the aesthetic and religious quality of experience itself. The weakening of erstwhile commanding values and definitive doctrines that perpetuate a hierarchical center allows for the renewal of our creative possibilities through a proliferation of our own existential narratives. The world becomes ever more beautiful and spiritual through the ongoing embellishment of the tradition as we add the meanings of our own significant, inspired lives.

NOTES

1. I do, however, think it would be naïve to think that we can separate in any final way the artist and the connoisseur, where in the aesthetic project that artist is anticipating appreciation, and the connoisseur is searching for the creative act. See John Dewey, "Having an Experience," in *The Philosophy of John Dewey*, ed. John J. McDermott (Chicago: University of Chicago Press, 1973).

2. I am thinking here of the work of Homi Bhabha in his *The Location of Culture*.

3. Dave Ramsey Steele, ed., *Genius in Their Own Words* (Chicago: Open Court, 2002), 222.

4. Ibid.

5. Wu Hung, "A 'Ghost Rebellion': Notes on Xu Bing's 'Nonsense Writing' and Other Works," *Public Culture* 6, no. 2 (Winter 1994): 411.

6. See "Shuosanyuanbahui liushu zhi fa 說三元八會六書之法" in *Sandongjingjiaobu* 三洞經教部 in the *Daozang* 道藏雲笈七籤卷之七.

7. See Roger T. Ames and David L. Hall, *Focusing the Familiar: A Translation and Philosophical Interpretation of the* Zhongyong (Honolulu: University of Hawai'i Press, 2001), 30–35, for our justification for translating *cheng* as "creativity" along with the commentarial evidence that supports such a rendering. Commentators late and soon have repeatedly defined *cheng* as "ceaselessness" and "continuity itself," and ZhuXi glosses it as "what is true and real." Wing-tsit Chan, in *A Source Book of Chinese Philosophy* (Princeton, NJ: Princeton University Press, 1963), 96, puts these two aspects of *cheng* together, insisting that *cheng* is "an active force that is always transforming things and completing things, drawing man and Heaven together in the same current." Tu Wei-ming, in *Centrality and Commonality: An Essay on Confucian Religiousness* (Albany: State University of New York Press, 1989), 81–82, concludes explicitly that *cheng* "can be conceived as a form of creativity" and that it "is simultaneously a self-subsistent and self-fulfilling process of creation that produces life unceasingly."

8. This passage is reminiscent of *Analects* 6.23:

    > The Master said, "The wise (*zhi* 知) enjoy water; those consummate in their conduct (*ren* 仁) enjoy mountains. The wise are active; consummate persons are still. The wise find enjoyment; consummate persons are long-enduring."

    Wisdom entails appropriateness to context (see *Analects* 6.22). Thus, in realizing oneself, one necessarily brings realization to one's situation.

9. Importantly, the internal/external *neiwai* 内外 distinction is a correlative notion like *yinyang* 陰陽, and hence means "more or less." Character and conduct cannot be treated as exclusive demarcations.

10. *Zhongyong* 5 道其不行矣夫.

11. Gianni Vattimo, *After Christianity*, trans. Luca D'Isanto (New York: Columbia University Press, 2002), 62–63.

12. *Analects* 9.17 逝者如斯夫, 不舍晝夜.

13. John Dewey, *Early Works, 1892–98*, 5 vols., ed. Jo Ann Boydston (Carbondale: Southern Illinois University, 1969–1972), 1:162. A.N. Whitehead's "misplaced concreteness" is a variation on this same complaint about introducing ontological disparity by investing the abstract with an exclusive claim on reality. See Whitehead, *Process and Reality: An Essay in Cosmology*, Donald Sherbourne corrected edition (New York: Free Press, 1979), 10.

14. Indeed, the virgin birth is a repetition of the *creatio ex nihilo* model, "preserving the unity, purity, and spirituality of God." John Hope Mason, *The Value of Creativity: The Origins and Emergence of a Modern Belief* (Aldershot: Ashgate, 2003), 26.

15. A good example of this assault is Nietzsche's attack on what he takes to be a hypocritical Wagner. The frequent comparisons made between Zhuangzi and Nietzsche need to be qualified by contrasting models of human realization. The agonistic tone of Nietzsche casts the Uebermensch as Herculean: the celebration of extraordinary deeds as a product of struggle. The more accommodating tenor of Zhuangzi entails "齊物論": "the standing together of things." Zhuangzi presents the "authentic person (*zhenren* 真人)" as someone who rejects all forms of coercion and who pursues virtuosity collaboratively in the ordinary affairs of the day.

16. Hope Mason, *The Value of Creativity*, 30.

17. I am almost afraid to mention that in fact there is a chapter in Eliot Deutsch's *Persons and Valuable Worlds: A Global Philosophy* (Honolulu: University of Hawai'i Press, 2002) entitled "A Creative Morality." Not unexpectedly, Deutsch in his aesthetic turn is quite self-consciously challenging traditional ways of thinking about morality.

18. Willard J. Peterson, "Making Connections: 'Commentary on the Attached Verbalizations' of the *Book of Change*," *Harvard Journal of Asiatic Studies* 42, no. 1: 67.

19. Edward L. Shaughnessy, trans., *I Ching: The Classic of Changes* (New York: Ballantine, 1997), 1.

20. Ibid.

21. *Great Commentary* A6. Translations are my own.

22. Ibid., B2.

23. Ibid., A9.

24. Ibid., A9.

25. See Tu Wei-ming, "Chinese Philosophy: A Synopsis," in *A Companion to World Philosophies*, ed. Eliot Deutsch and Ron Bontekoe, 6–7 (Oxford: Blackwell, 1997).

26. John H. Berthrong, *Concerning Creativity: A Comparison of Chu Hsi, Whitehead, and Neville* (Albany: State University of New York Press, 1998), 1.

27. Ames and Hall, *Focusing the Familiar*, 113.

28. Tang Junyi, *Complete Works Vol. 11* (Taipei: Xuesheng shuju, 1988), 20–22.

29. *Great Commentary* A4.

30. Peterson, "Making Connections," 103.

31. In fact, at least as early as the Ming dynasty, the Chinese expression for "thing," *dongxi* 東西, is literally "east-west," underscoring the relational and contextual understanding that attends Chinese phenomonological perceptions.

32. Steele, *Genius in Their Own Words*, 196.

33. *Great Commentary* A6.

34. In fact, just as *kosmos* in its classical Greek usage means an elegant as well as an ordered world, so *logos* means *oratio* as well as *ratio*, the rhetorical as well as the rational, the "word" itself as well as the reasoned explanation. That is, the aesthetic and rhetorical side of cosmology tends to go underadvertised in the more rationalistic interpretations of the classical Greek tradition.

35. It is perhaps significant that the basic meaning of *xiang* 象, the term used for "image," is "elephant." Although we have archaeological evidence that elephants once existed in northern China and that ivory carving as a contemporary Chinese art form was already highly developed as far back as the Shang dynasty, an analysis of this evidence suggests that the elephant, like the whale and the rhinoceros, were rare species imported from outside of China, which, because of their novelty, were used primarily for display. Thus a creature known but rarely seen came to be used to denote the presentational act of "conjuring" or "imaging." See J. Norman and T. Mei, "The Austroasiatics in Ancient South China: Some Lexical Evidence," *Monumenta Serica* 32 (1976): 274–301.

36. See Peterson, "Making Connections," 67–116, especially 80–81.

37. The character *yi* 意 is translated variously as "concept," "thought/s," and "ideas." *Yi* is glossed in the *Shuowen* lexicon as "intended meaning,

purpose" (*zhi* 志), reflecting its performative connotation. It is in this sense of "to design" that I understand it.

38. See the *Yijing* [*Chou-i*] 44/*xishang*/12. Cf. Richard Wilhelm and Cary F. Baynes, *I Ching or Book of Changes* (Princeton, NJ: Princeton University Press, 1967), 322.

39. For discussions of the importance of metaphor in this way, see George Lakoff and Mark Johnson, *Metaphors We Live By* (Chicago: University of Chicago Press, 1980), and more recently, George Lakoff, *Woman, Fire, and Dangerous Things: What Categories Reveal about the Mind* (Chicago: University of Chicago Press, 1987). See also Stephen Pepper's classic treatment of metaphors underlying our metaphysical traditions, *World Hypotheses: A Study in Evidence* (Berkeley: University of California Press, 1967) and his later extension of this work in *Concept and Quality: A World Hypothesis* (La Salle, IL: Open Court, 1967). For accounts of metaphor associated with postanalytic pragmatism, see Donald Davidson, "What Metaphors Mean," in *Inquiries into Truth and Interpretation* (New York: Oxford University Press, 1984) and "A Nice Derangement of Epitaphs" in *Truth, Language, and History* (New York and Oxford, 1986).

40. See Wang Bi, *Zhouyi Lueli* (1965), 10b–11b.

41. *Zhuangzi* (Peking: Harvard-Yenching Institute Sinological Index Series Supplement 20, 1947), 75/26/48–9.

42. Ibid.

43. Ibid., 27.

44. Ibid., 4/2/23–4.

45. Steele, *Genius in Their Own Words*, 217.

CHAPTER THREE

Seriousness, Playfulness, and a Religious Reading of *Tianshu*

KUAN-HUNG CHEN

INTRODUCTION

In this chapter, I intend to explore the religious dimensions of *Tianshu* (known as *A Book from the Sky*, 1987–1991, Figure I.1; hereafter, *Tianshu* 天書) and its relationship to seriousness and playfulness. Since Xu Bing's immigration to the United States in 1991, discussions about the religious dimensions of *Tianshu* are generally absent from curatorial descriptions and scholarly investigations of the work. Reading *Tianshu* as a religious text would thus seem to be a new suggestion.[1] However, it is evident that the religious elements of *Tianshu* have significantly stimulated the energetic responses it received beginning with its initial appearance. During its first exhibition in Beijing, it was reported that "the exhibition evoked sensations similar to those felt in a temple or in a hall of mourning" and that "some people felt breathless or frightened."[2] Not long after the work went public, the current title, *Tianshu*, was appended. While *shu* refers to writing or texts, *tian* was employed to characterize its numinous quality.[3] Hence, the problem at stake is not *whether* there is a religious reading of *Tianshu* but *how* to appropriately interpret such readings.

There is yet another characteristic of *Tianshu* that is not directly related to its religious dimensions yet immediately problematizes them: the interplay between its seriousness and playfulness. While viewers can sense the incredible discipline and labor with which Xu Bing approached the work, *Tianshu* is also perceived as wordplay, a pun—which makes the expression of seriousness almost absurd.[4]

One may not encounter much difficulty in associating the serious with the religious; but how can playfulness be accommodated as well? This question seems to challenge any attempt to interpret *Tianshu* as a religious text at a fundamental level. A "commonsensical" and certainly persistent response is to disassociate the playful from the religious. Nevertheless, I shall take an uncommon approach and argue that the playful has a lot to do with the religious.

In the following sections of this chapter, I shall first provide a theoretical framework that sets up the backbone of my inquiry. I will appeal to the Deweyan distinction between "the religious" and "religion" and further distinguish two possible yet incompatible readings based on either an inclusive or exclusive sense of religiousness. I intend to use Rudolf Otto's theory of religious absolutism as a salient example of exclusive religiousness and argue that while it is unthinkable to link religiousness and playfulness together in an exclusive sense of religiousness, it is much less problematic for playfulness to find its place within an inclusive framework of religiousness. *Tianshu* and its religiousness, I proffer, belong to the latter paradigm. Secondly, I shall contextualize *Tianshu* in the Chinese religio-philosophical tradition from which it emerges in order to demonstrate how seriousness and playfulness can be altogether accommodated in a religiously inclusive model. I will pay close attention to the characteristics of Chinese religio-philosophical traditions that are distinctively inclusive, including the resonant features of *qi* cosmology. Thirdly, I shall identify three concepts—noncoercive action, readiness for awakening, and leaving off speaking—that are deeply rooted in Chinese religious sensibility to articulate the profundity of the dynamic interplay between the seriousness and playfulness of *Tianshu*. Finally, I would like to draw three implications deduced from the previous investigations by referencing Chinese religio-philosophical discourse that may constructively situate *Tianshu* within the current international and transcultural arena. These are: reinstating playfulness, reframing seriousness and playfulness, and reconstructing meaningfulness and religiousness.

RELIGIOUS READINGS OF *TIANSHU*: AN OVERVIEW

Religion, the Religious, and Religiousness

Before looking closely at what could be meant by qualifying *Tianshu* as a religious text, several pivotal distinctions have to be made in order to prevent the current inquiry from slipping into murky water. Due to the ambiguity that the term "religious" conveys, clarifications of a working definition are of central importance prior to introducing two possible readings of *Tianshu* as a religious text.

John Dewey, one of the preeminent founders of American Pragmatism, makes a significant distinction between religion, *a* religion, and the religious. For Dewey "religion" is a substantive noun and a "strictly collective term" that signifies various bodies of beliefs and practices situated in different social and cultural conditions.[5] It is in this sense that Dewey rejects any claim concerning the universality of religion except for the fact that "all the peoples we know anything about have *a* religion."[6] Hence, there is no religion in the singular sense but a multitude of religions that reflect different worldviews, doctrines, and practices in various forms of institutional organizations or systems of belief.

On the contrary, the adjective "religious" indicates a certain phase or quality of experience that is not necessarily associated with any religion:

> [It] denotes nothing in the way of a specifiable entity, either institutional or as a system of belief . . . For it does not denote anything that can exist by itself or that can be organized into a particular and distinctive form of existence. It denotes attitudes that may be taken toward every object and every proposed end or ideal.[7]

Dewey argues forcefully against assertions that religious experience and attitude are the ultimate ground of religion, or conversely, that religions are the ultimate basis of religious experience and attitude. Instead, a religion is built upon certain *interpretations* of the religious experience that are not inherent in the experience itself.[8] An experience of religious ecstasy can be interpreted as the blessings of deities, the outcome of good karma, or the result of an unusual release of dopamine in the brain. Since there is arguably no inherent connection between the interpretations and the experience, it is important to make a distinction between them. The religious experience does not presuppose the existence of religions and vice versa. The religious experience, emancipated from the frame of religion, is concerned with "the *effect* produced" rather than "the manner and the cause of its production."[9] Many biblical theologians hold that religions result in generic and enduring transformations in attitude from which religious experience emerges. Such a statement presupposes a kind of reality that makes religious experience possible. In other words, the reality is already there; people just experience that reality. When theologians and scholars fail to find such a reality in the physical world that is shown to be purposeless and devoid of human or religious values, they often "metaphysicalize" it, making another (religious) world more real than this one. Nevertheless, Dewey wants to turn the statement around and claim that "whenever this change [i.e., religious transformation] takes place there is a definitely religious attitude."[10] Religious attitudes for Dewey should be generically open by definition. What makes religious experience and attitude distinctive is their unifying effect and impact on people's lives in ever-changing conditions. It follows that the religious experience is entirely concerned with the situated interactions between humans and nature.

Dewey defines the term "religiousness" as the common quality amongst various kinds of religious experience and attitude, emphasizing its function of "bringing about better, deeper and enduring adjustment in life."[11] If Dewey's distinction between religion and the religious is warranted, then what characterizes religious experience and attitude is not only their openness but also their inclusiveness. Along this line I intend to further identify and distinguish between an exclusive and inclusive view of religiousness. I will also demonstrate the limitations of an exclusively religious reading of *Tianshu* exemplified by Otto's theory of religious absolutism.

Exclusive and Inclusive Religiousness

There is a significant contrast between either a supernatural or human-centered way of thinking of religiousness and religious experiences. The former is usually, if not always, aligned with religious exclusiveness, while the latter is usually associated with inclusive religiousness. Conventionally, especially within the biblical traditions, it is unthinkable to disassociate religiousness from supernatural beings and events. As a consequence, religious experience must be exclusively characterized in terms of engagement with supernatural beings or forces. A salient as well as sophisticated work of this *doxa* is Otto's classic *The Idea of the Holy*. Otto qualifies religious experience as an encounter with the *numen*, which is a category of "interpretation and valuation *peculiar to* the sphere of religion."[12] We thus have a distinction between the religious and the nonreligious, the sacred and the secular. Religious experience, by definition, cannot occur in the sphere of nonreligion.

Otto further introduces the notion of "creature-feeling," which is not only attendant to an experience of the numinous, but also denotes one's absolute separation from something "wholly other." At least two things will simultaneously occur in circumstances of encountering the *numen*: first, the persons having the experience will be totally overwhelmed and arguably lost in the experience; second, these individuals will place ultimate value upon the *numen* while at the same time devaluing and depreciating themselves as absolute nothingness.[13] These are genuine feelings of authentic religious awe.

Focusing on the framework in which Otto analyzes the religious experience, it is important to point out that he is operating within a dualistic framework. There is a distinctive line between the creator/created, the sacred/secular, the valued/devalued, the dominating/dominated, the transcendent/dependent; and thus between religious experience and other kinds of experience that are intrinsically and qualitatively different, and between religion and nonreligion.

Such a framework will inevitably lead to statements of exclusiveness (e.g., religious experience is exclusively associated with some supernatural event). I shall term this kind of religious sensibility "exclusive religiousness." Within exclusive religiousness there is a clear-cut distinction between the supernatural and nature: they are different in *kind*, not simply in degree. An important implication for reading *Tianshu* from this viewpoint is that its message, whatever it may be, corresponds to something supernatural that is at the same time the source of meaning. It thus makes little sense for humans to participate in the creative meaning-making process; what people need to do is to listen, rather than speak.

An alternative to exclusive religiousness is "inclusive religiousness." Such a framework suggests that religious experience does not have to occur under certain conditions, focusing instead on the interpenetrating and nondualistic nature of experience. Literally every experience could be religious. Here the main task of humans is to optimize, make sense of, and appreciate the fullness of experience. Even though there are still events that may be qualified as supernatural, they differ in *degree* rather than in kind from natural events. In the absence of an ultimate meaning-giver, human participation is thus located in the center of the process of perceiving the seemingly obscure and nonsensical. From this perspective, making sense of *Tianshu* may open a door to a religious journey.

Tianshu *as a Religious Text*

Tianshu can be read as a religious text, in the sense of both exclusive and inclusive religiousness. Through the lens of exclusive religiousness, *Tianshu* indeed possesses certain mystical, magical, and even numinous qualities. As mentioned in the opening paragraph, among the reactions of *Tianshu*'s first audience were feelings of breathlessness, fright, and what one might experience in a temple or a hall of mourning. These are traits that may urge people to ponder whether a viewing of *Tianshu* is associated with encountering the *numen*. Otto identifies three direct methods in art that represent the numinous: emptiness (or void), silence, and darkness. All three qualities are relevant to *Tianshu*.

In terms of emptiness (or void), *Tianshu* has long been recognized as a book devoid of semantic meaning. Such emptiness may be conceptually compatible with the factor of void in Chinese architecture and painting that Otto regards as an insight into the expression of the *numen* distinctively developed in Oriental art. Otto states that "void is . . . a negation that does away with every 'this' and 'here,' in order that 'wholly other' may become actual."[14] To put it another way, "in fact the 'void' of the eastern, like the 'nothing' of the western mystic is a numinous ideogram of the 'wholly other.'"[15]

Tianshu is not only semantically empty, but also vocally silent. Usually people report an experience similar to hearing words even when they are reading silently. However, *Tianshu* is a book that refuses to be read. Even though the best-trained experts of Chinese phonology may come up with several possible pronunciations, the uneasy silence is only emphasized to a more profound degree. Facing such a silent book, there seems to be few choices for reaction except for maintaining silence, which, according to Otto, is "a spontaneous reaction to the feeling of the actual *numen praesens*."[16]

Darkness is the last feature that needs to be discussed here. Even though Xu Bing seems to have no particular interest in manipulating the lighting aside from highlighting the scrolls hung on the ceiling and certain parts of the texts on the walls and floor, there is inevitably a certain contrast between the highlighted sections and areas of semidarkness, which may be seen as the starting point of a mystical effect.[17] Uniting with the sublimity—which is not only observable in *Tianshu* as an installation, but also in the exhibition hall—the darkness "has always spoken eloquently to the soul," Otto states.[18]

Although such a reading of *Tianshu* may be accepted according to the principle of hermeneutical generosity, it is certainly not unquestionable. First and foremost, there is no equivalent account of seemingly religious awe from audiences who cannot read Chinese. Instead, the non-Chinese-reading audience misses the central experience of the Chinese audience. Such a sharp division amongst audience members implies that either the emotional responses of the Chinese audience are not concerned with authentic religious awe or that those religious feelings must be somewhat culturally specific. If the first line of reasoning is followed, one will soon conclude that Chinese people are essentially nonreligious and must follow some mysterious logic that sets them apart from the rest of the human race, which is absurd. If one follows the second line of reasoning, then Otto's position of religious absolutism will be significantly weakened. If religious feelings were culturally specific, the *numen* must fall into the category of *a posteriori* rather than *a priori*. In other words, encountering the *numen* is a phenomenon that should be recognized as one possible result rather than the cause and essence of religious experience. There is no one and only *numen* that transcends and underlies all cultures; instead, there are many culturally constructed *numen*s that may not be homogeneous. If this is so, then the following consideration has to be dealt with seriously.

Second, reading *Tianshu* in terms of exclusive religiousness is inconsistent with the Chinese religious and philosophical sensibilities that, as I will demonstrate in greater detail in the following, are characteristically inclusive. For instance, in the Chinese tradition, it would be a mistake to view the concepts of the deity and the human as mutually exclusive. On the contrary, they are different only in degree, not in kind. Another example is the Chinese *qi* cosmology, which plays a pivotal role in most, if not all, Chinese thinking systems. It presents a worldview within which all events and things are interconnected. There is literally nothing, not even the most sacred and numinous experience, that transcends others in a strict sense. Thus, reading *Tianshu* as a religious text in an exclusive sense is incompatible with the various traditions from which the work emerges.

Finally, an exclusively religious reading of *Tianshu* has great difficulty in accommodating the playful aspects of this work. According to Otto, the numinous experience—marked by overwhelming, devaluing, and depreciating characteristics—is irreducibly a zero-fun game. However, as aforementioned, *Tianshu* has long been associated with wordplay in the Chinese tradition. The playful and delightful features of *Tianshu*, which have equal claim with its seriousness, cannot be appropriately addressed in an exclusively religious framework. Interpreting *Tianshu* through an exclusive framework of religiousness is limited by its lack of cultural sensibility and compatibility, as well as explanatory efficacy. Insisting upon this interpretation will most likely lead to hermeneutic closure. Hence, there is sufficient reason to switch to an inclusive framework that is culturally sensitive and compatible, as well as leading to hermeneutic openness. Sourcing the cultural traditions from which *Tianshu* emerges is a suitable place to begin because it introduces another viewpoint from which one may read *Tianshu* effectively. In doing so, I have no intention of asserting that the Chinese cultural discourse has a monopoly on interpreting *Tianshu*; however, a proper understanding of Chinese religio-philosophical narratives could generate meaningful discussion and provide a vocabulary for effectively articulating the religious implications of *Tianshu* in our transcultural world.

TEXT AND CONTEXT (I): CHINESE RELIGIO-PHILOSOPHICAL BACKGROUND OF *TIANSHU*

A Tradition of Inclusive Religiousness

In contrast to the framework of exclusive religiousness, Chinese religious tradition is profoundly inclusive. Addressing the meaning of animal designs on Shang and Zhou bronzes, distinguished anthropologist and archaeologist K.C. Chang makes a convincing case that the idea of human-centered "communicating/going through (*tong* 通)" is of central importance in the pre-Qin texts, especially in terms of the relationship between the human and spiritual realms that are not strictly divided:

The animal designs on Shang and Chou [Zhou] bronzes are iconographically meaningful: they are images of the various animals that served as the helpers of shamans and shamanesses in the task of communication between heaven and earth, the spirit and the living.[19]

In fact, myth serves as the very beginning of Chinese taxonomy. Texts such as *Classic of Mountains and Seas* (*Shanhaijing* 山海經) are actually guidebooks to assist religio-political elites in identifying the spiritual beings that cohabit *this* world. There is literally no "other world" and no such thing as a "wholly other" as Otto has defined. If religious experience had been defined exclusively as encountering the wholly Other in ancient China, the effort devoted to writing these guidebooks would have been pointless.

A Confucian way to reframe such a religious sensibility is the expression of "continuity between *tian* and humans (*tianrenheyi* 天人合一)." Commenting on the Confucian text *Zhongyong* (中庸), Tu Wei-ming states:

> The development, or the unfolding, of this humanistic vision in *Chung-yung* [*Zhongyong*] seems to suggest a simple transition from the individual person to the human community and finally to nature . . . In an ultimate sense, human beings, in order to manifest their humanity, must themselves fully participate in the creative process of the cosmos. They do not create *ex nihilo*, yet they are capable of assisting the transforming and nourishing process of heaven [*tian*] and earth.[20]

What has to be stressed here is the fact that this kind of sensibility is not exclusively Confucian. It is shared by other institutional religions as well as philosophical schools. For example, there are numerous relevant expressions, such as "heaven [*tian*] and earth were born together with me, and the myriad things and I are one"[21] in the *Zhuangzi*, one of the Daoist canons. Speaking of pre-Buddhist China, Peter Hershock observes:

> Because humans, ghosts, spirits, and gods were all understood and treated as equally "nature"—none, that is, being understood in the Western sense as supernatural or beyond nature—they were also seen as part of an overarching cosmic society throughout which the same basic principles and laws applied.[22]

Buddhism, to some extent, shares this profoundly inclusive religious sensibility, in the sense that enlightenment (*wu* 悟, realization of Buddhahood) is to see the interdependence of all things. One of the most religious moments in a Buddhist's life is to see the inclusive nature of the whole world.

The large body of historical texts demonstrates how Chinese people have been operating within an inclusive framework of religiousness for millennia. It is not surprising that the Chinese term for "god-the numinous-spirituality (*shen* 神)" is co-defined with "human-extension (*shen* 神)."[23] In this framework, being religious is a process of refinement and cultivation of a sincere attitude towards everything, not just the exclusively "religious." *Tianshu* is in this sense religious not because it represents the *numen*—the "wholly other"—but because it signifies an unfolding process that extends from the enormous effort invested in its making to its public reception.

A Tradition of Cosmological Continuity

Qi 氣 is an idea that was introduced to Euro-American cultures relatively early and is now familiar to many; yet it still remains largely inaccessible because of the very different worldview for which it stands. The importance of *qi* can never be overstated. There is arguably no other notion (including Buddhist metaphysics) that could parallel the idea of *qi* in terms of its influence on shaping the ways that Chinese people have perceived the world. The Chinese character *qi* appeared in the very earliest texts, such as Shang oracle bones and the Zhou bronze inscriptions dated no later than the eleventh century BCE.[24] Around the fourth century BCE, the notion of prevasive *qi* had pervaded the major, if not all, schools of thought including Confucianism, Daoism, Mohism, and Legalism. By the time of the *Huainanzi* (淮南子, second century BCE), *qi* was the multivalent energy-matter-fluid "out of which all phenomena in the universe were constructed, both physical and psychological."[25] Generally speaking, *qi*—the key idea through which ancient Chinese grasped the world—encompasses the sense that everything is intrinsically correlated and is constantly changing and changed.[26] In short, the world is in flux.

The English renderings of *qi* are confusing for many people living under the influence of a persistently dualistic worldview; that is, a worldview that asserts that matter (the physical) is clear and distinctive from mind (the mental) and feeling (the psychological). According to Stephen F. Teiser, *pneuma* emphasizes the etymological sense of *qi* as vapor, breath, or stream; "psychophysical stuff" is based on the understanding that *qi* involves phenomena of both the psychological and the physical; "vital energy" accentuates the potential for life inherent in certain forms of *qi*; and "material energy" refers to the fact that *qi* is applied to both matter and energy.[27] These complex terms imply that the notion of *qi* cannot be easily fitted to English translations. *Qi* is not simply physical, psychological, or spiritual, but all of these; it is neither simply matter nor energy, but both; it is neither simply structural nor functional, but again both; it is also both vitalizing energy and what is vitalized. As Ames and Hall note, "*qi* is an image that defies categorizations into separate 'things,' 'actions,' 'attributions,' and 'modalities' (nouns, verbs, adjectives, and adverbs) of the sort that discipline our thought and language."[28]

Qi cosmology remains a persistent way of thinking by which Chinese describe the world as a continuity between the one and the many. It is "one" in the sense that all things and events are made of *qi*. It is, at the same time, "the many" because the myriad things, made of different portions and kinds of *qi*, have equal claim on reality. Thus, its qualities of "oneness" do not overwrite the claims of the particular. It is many and yet it does not preclude other particulars from sharing the field from which it emerges.

Qi cosmology provides two crucial implications as far as the current discussion is concerned. First of all, it offers a cosmological understanding that resonates with the sensibility of inclusive religiousness. Since everything is made of *qi* and animated by *qi*, it follows that spiritual beings are intrinsically correlated with humans and the myriad things and events of the shared ground. The difference, however, lies in degrees of refinement of *qi*.

The refinement of *qi* is a fundamental form of self-cultivation. It becomes one of the most important concepts as well as practices across various Chinese religio-philosophical traditions. Such a practice is called *yangqi* 養氣 by Mencius,[29] and is commonly termed as *qigong* 氣功. It emphasizes the day-to-day, moment-to-moment disciplines from breathing, gesturing, and posing to interacting with family and community members, to achieving the state of tranquility and acuity that implies harmony with one's social and natural environment. The practice of *yangqi* or *qigong*, therefore, can be seen as an expanding process of becoming more and more inclusive. Xu Bing reportedly enjoyed the "repetitive, meditative process of designing and carving the characters" in the process of making *Tianshu*,[30] and at times has associated this process with *qigong* and *zazen*.

Secondly, *qi* cosmology presupposes a version of perspectivism:

> If you look at them from the viewpoint of their differences, from liver to gall is as far as from Ch'u [Chu] to Yueh [Yue]; if you look at them from the viewpoint of their sameness, the myriad things are all one.[31]

Fundamentally, there is no viewpoint that is not limited and biased. A shared focus of self-cultivation among various Chinese religions involves expanding one's perspective so that it can be more inclusive.[32] However, the goal is never to achieve a God's-eye view and thus claim to be objective. The process of becoming inclusive is the same process of realizing that everything has equal claim on reality. In contrast to Foucault's "death of the author" idea, *Tianshu* anticipates multiple layers of unfolding meaning in the sense that the author is unable to make an authoritative or singular claim on reality.

Seriousness and Playfulness in Chinese Tradition

The sensibility of inclusive religiousness, together with the correlated *qi* cosmology, provides a very different perspective from which to consider seriousness and playfulness. Seriousness and playfulness are characterized not by static duality but by a dynamic and complementary correlativity in the Chinese religio-philosophical tradition. Seriousness is characterized by reverence (*jing* 敬). It is an overarching attitude towards things and events, from carrying out official duties and serving elders or higher authorities to observing ritual propriety and performing sacrifice. It is ultimately a sincere attitude toward other particulars and a focus of self-cultivation:

> Zilu asked about exemplary persons (*junzi* 君子). The Master replied, "They cultivate themselves by being reverent."[33]

Self-cultivation is not only, as commonly perceived, a moral project; it is also a religious project that extends human experience (*shen*) to the numinous (*shen*). It is not unusual for distinguished cultural heroes to become gods and to be conceived of as celestial bodies.[34] Again, the notion of reverence is not exclusively Confucian. It is shared by Daoism (especially institutional Daoism) and is included in the early discourse of Chinese Buddhism.

Seriousness alone, however, does not fully characterize the religious experience in Chinese tradition, which also has many playful aspects. A famous example in the *Analects* records an occasion on which Confucius asked several close disciples to speak out their aspirations when they were sitting in attendance on him. After three eloquent and ambitious responses, the last disciple, Zeng Xi, noted that his answer would be different from that of the others and played a few final notes on his zither before finally saying:

> At the end of spring, with the spring clothes having already been finished, I would like, in the company of five or six young men and six or seven children, to cleanse ourselves in the Yi river, to revel in the cool breeze at the Altar for Rain, and then return home singing.[35]

Confucius then says, "I am with Zeng Xi!"

The intention of Confucius here is not to depreciate the value of political involvement and achievement that he strives so hard to realize. However, at times it is playfulness that unifies every aspect of human experience. When this happens, it is a religious moment. The Altar for Rain is a religious site where rites of prayer for rain are performed; however, it is also a good place to enjoy a pleasant breeze that cheers people up and makes them feel like singing. Such playful moments do not suggest a lack of seriousness or religiousness. The serious and the playful do not necessarily contradict each other.

Being playful, therefore, serves as an important attitude and method for adding meaning other than merely being serious. The Altar for Rain becomes more meaningful when it can be experienced and associated with such elements. The *wu* 無-forms of Daoist terminology are playful and meaningful in this sense, negating readymade and serious ideas to open up a much broader range of possible meanings. For example, "acting/action (*wei* 為)" in a Confucian context is often associated with intentional behaviors, such as "acting governance (*weizheng* 為政)" and "performing ritual propriety (*weili* 為禮)." However, the seemingly negative term "*wuwei* 無為" signifies not "nonaction" as it literally conveys but, more accurately, "noncoercive action."[36] The negative term *wu* would initially shock listeners and readers, but then urge them to ponder and reinterpret the received meanings of *wei*. Through reflection one will realize that intentional action may be at times coercive. The whole point of *wuwei* is not to become static and do nothing, but to do things in a more reverent and less coercive manner.

The confusing answers given by Chan 禪 masters make use of similar effects to open the heart-mind of disciples to experience a broad inclusiveness. The void and emptiness in Chinese landscape painting and architecture also play a pivotal role in providing space for participation and interpretation, allowing multiple levels of meanings to be built. In playing with language, distance and space transform our ordinary ways of experiencing into something extraordinary.

Reexamined in this light, the profundity of *Tianshu* is arguably based on the dynamic dialogue between its seriousness and playfulness, which creatively invites its audience to participate in the meaning-generating process. In the following section, I shall further demonstrate how *Tianshu* triggers such processes by examining three concepts: noncoercive action (*wuwei*), readiness for awakening (*dunwu* 頓悟), and leaving off speaking (*buyan* 不言).

TEXT AND CONTEXT (II): A RELIGIO-PHILOSOPHICAL ARTICULATION OF *TIANSHU*

The Performative Nature of Tianshu: Wuwei

In Chinese traditions, writing is fundamentally an act (*wei*) and thus performative.[37] It presupposes enduring forms of meaningful patterns and knowledge, which are associated with *qi* and cosmic force. *Tianshu*, given its formal written format, is in this sense essentially performative.

Tianshu did not come into existence by chance. Enormous amounts of time and energy were invested in thorough study and implementation of traditional bookmaking methods; professional skills of writing and carving were thus cultivated. Concentration and sincerity permeate the laborious processes. As a testament to the serious efforts, this "book" is intentionally set up to act loudly.

Nevertheless, *Tianshu* acts in a different way from the conventional frameworks through which books perform their semantic meanings. *Tianshu* is a book devoid of any such meaning. Thus, the emptiness of meaning seems to negate the performative nature of the book. The question is: how do we conceive of this?

There are at least two readings. First, we can read the negation of the performative nature as "nonaction." Second, we can read the negation of the performative nature as "noncoercive action." The first approach assumes *Tianshu* to be a thoroughly serious work, while the second interpretation allows the existence of a playground upon which to negotiate possible meanings.

A Daoist reading prefers the second interpretation over the first. In Daoist texts, the seeming negations using *wu* are usually, if not always, associated with a broader context of function and utility:

> The thirty spokes converge at one hub,
> But the unity of the cart is a function of the nothingness (*wu*)
>   inside the hub.
> We throw clay to shape a pot,
> But the utility of the clay pot is a function of the nothingness
>   inside it.
> We bore out doors and windows to make a dwelling,
> But the utility of the dwelling is a function of the nothingness
>   inside it.
> Thus, it might be something that provides the value,
> But it is nothing that provides the utility.[38]

Wu, in the Daoist context, can be everything but a negation in the sense of formal logic. It follows that *Tianshu* is never simply nonacting; it aims at a broader range of action that will open up a space for inclusiveness and spontaneous negotiation.

The Mirroring Nature of Tianshu: Dunwu

Before being entitled *Tianshu*, this work was named *Xishijian* 析世鑑 (A Mirror that Analyzes the World).[39] There are two ways to understand a mirror: as representation, or as responsiveness. Chinese tradition, as already mentioned, favors the second reading. Probably one of the best-recognized examples concerning the metaphor of the mirror is that of Shenxiu 神秀 and Huineng 慧能. According to the *Platform Sutra*, Shenxiu, seeking to gain the title of the sixth patriarch, sneaks into a new meditation hall and writes an anonymous verse on one of the new walls:

> The body is the *bodhi* tree.
> The heart-mind is like a bright mirror.
> Moment by moment wipe and polish it,
> Not allowing dust to collect.[40]

In terms of the metaphor of the mirror, Shenxiu's idea is clear and to the point: a mirror should reflect the world perfectly. One's heart-mind is originally pure but becomes obscured because of the dusty world. Therefore, a person should wipe and polish it as a daily devotion so that our original heart-mind can shine and reflect accurately again.

However, a mirror is never free from bias in Chinese tradition. The reflections in a mirror change with the position of the mirror. From the religio-philosophical point of view, the value of mirroring is not perfect representation but readiness for responding. The story tells that the following day, the illiterate Huineng asked someone to write the following verse on the wall for him:

> *Bodhi* originally has no tree.
> The clear and bright mirror has also has no support.
> Buddha-nature is constantly purifying and clearing.
> Where could there be dust?[41]

Employing three negation words, Huineng rejected the dualistic perspective in Shenxiu's verse and opened up a space to rethink and reframe Buddha-nature. The difference between the teachings of Shenxiu and Huineng is traditionally characterized as a contrast between "gradual awakening" (*jianwu* 漸悟, of Shenxiu) and "sudden awakening" (*dunwu*, of Huineng). The contrast between "gradual" (*jian* 漸) and "sudden" (*dun* 頓) is most frequently framed as temporal difference; yet, as Hershock correctly notes:

> "*Dun*" can be translated as "sudden," but its root meanings are bowing the head, putting in order, preparing, or making ready. It refers to a dramatic turning point—the moment that a servant has bowed with forehead to the ground, received the master's directives, and is rising to go into action . . . The meaning of Huineng's use of "*dunwu*" is thus only partially and rather poorly captured by the term "sudden enlightenment." More accurately, "*dunwu*" might be rendered as "readiness to awaken" or "readiness for awakening."[42]

Read in this way, the value of *Tianshu* is not based on how it "reflects" people's assumptions but how it is "ready to respond" to these assumptions. It responds with its playfulness, saying nothing.

The Hermeneutic Nature of Tianshu: Buyan

Responding by saying nothing exists not solely in Chinese religio-philosophical tradition. The oracle of Delphi, as Heraclitus stated, "neither declares nor conceals but gives a sign (D. 93)." By saying nothing, the oracle urges interpretations. It is also interesting to note that the word "hermeneutics" is etymologically derived from "Hermes," a messenger god responsible for rendering the messages of gods into comprehensible forms for humans.[43] Hence, we may say that interpretation and translation are, in terms of etymology, religious tasks.

Tianshu is hermeneutic in nature, in the sense that it generates interpretations—the meaning and religiousness of it are concerned not with gods but with humans. A passage in the *Analects* reads:

> The Master said, "I think I will leave off speaking."
>
> "If you don't speak," Zigong replied, "how will we your followers find the proper way?"
>
> The Master respond, "Does *tian* speak? And yet the four seasons turn and the myriad things are born and grow within it. Does *tian* speak?"[44]

Tian, on which the term *tianshu* is built, is irreducibly a religious idea in Chinese religio-philosophical tradition. Confucius's description of *tian*, that it communicates well but does not speak, is meaningful because it serves as a reminder that there is a broader context of communication.

A sign or pattern devoid of semantic meaning does not imply that it is completely meaningless. On the contrary, a seemingly meaningless sign or pattern presupposes a plurality or complexity of meaning. What is needed is articulation and interpretation of the existing meanings. Articulation and interpretation, unlike the reflections of a mirror, are never neutral. They are forms of engaged knowledge, never external or apart from the interpreter. In this sense, *Tianshu* leads its audience to a broader context of communication and discourse, which is co-created not only by humans, but by other creatures in the world as well.

Meaning-making is a process of expanding productive relationships and becoming inclusive. From this point of view, meaning-making functions as a profoundly religious idea within a framework

of inclusive religiousness. The process of making something meaningful is the same process as making our lives significant. *Tianshu*
confronts its audience with their responsibility to make its contents
meaningful, which can be read as an act of "religiousness" in the
fullest sense of the word.

TEXT AND CONTEXT (III): *TIANSHU* IN THE POSTMODERN AND GLOBAL ARENA

Recontextualizing Tianshu

In our globalized and yet increasingly fragmented era, recontextualization and reinterpretation are of central importance. Therefore,
I would like to briefly examine the current religio-philosophical
context in order to articulate possible implications of *Tianshu* in the
international and transcultural arena.

In *After Christianity,* Gianni Vattimo remarks that the Nietzs-
chean announcement of "the death of (the moral-philosophical)
God" and the Heideggerian claim of "the end of metaphysics," two
of the most significant religio-philosophical events, share a continuum. The death of the moral-philosophical God depreciates "the
existence of a Supreme Being as a ground and ultimate *telos* of the
world"; while the end of metaphysics—a belief in the ideal world—
reflects the fact that "all the meta-narratives . . . that claimed to
mirror the objective structure of being have been discredited."[45]
When the presupposed metaphysical origins of reality yield influence, it is time to endow religious experience with a new meaning.
In resonance with Vattimo's observation, Aldo Gargain states:

> Contrary to the general trend, and to all those today for whom
> religion is an occasion to hand themselves over to a blind imme-
> diate feeling—like a leap into transcendence that they call faith,
> but which formally speaking can be anything that is not discur-
> sively and rationally mediated—the recovery and realization of
> religious experience occurs by way of a movement in exactly the
> opposite direction. To be precise, it consists *in the movement
> of reflection and experience that brings religion nearer again to
> immanence, picking out its symbols in the figures of our life.* Not,
> that is, in the inverse movement through which the human world
> is overturned by the antecedence of transcendent entities and
> events. Religious transcendence could not even be named were it

not a difference that emerged from the actual figures of our experience. Transcendence as the division of the ontological boundaries between classes of entities is therefore effaced; and yet it is not effaced as a critical point of interpretive activity at the heart of the flux of the phenomena of life and history. In the end, religion will not be the discourse that discovers and makes manifest an Other Object, an Other Entity, but rather a term of comparison according to which the situations, figures and processes of our life come to be interpreted.[46]

If, as Vattimo and Gargain have characterized it, the death of God and the end of metaphysics not only endow a renewed meaning to religious experience, but also "provide the general framework for characterizing late-modern experience,"[47] the paradigm of inclusive religiousness will be an appropriate framework to gradually replace the conventionally exclusive one for interpreting the late-modern religious experience. In other words, the religio-philosophical context nowadays will allow *Tianshu* to be appreciated in its full significance.

Amongst many possible religio-philosophical implications that can be derived from *Tianshu*, three of them are of significant importance and therefore deserve further exploration: reinstating playfulness, reframing seriousness and playfulness, and reconstructing meaningfulness and religiousness.

Reinstating Playfulness

Unlike psychologists and anthropologists, theologians and philosophers are usually much more dubious about the importance of playfulness.[48] For theologians, playfulness is at best spiritually innocent, while for moral philosophers, play and playfulness are at best morally indifferent. Usually they are construed much more negatively and are conceived to be, as Dewey accurately points out, "unnecessary, and worse, dangerous diversions from the path of useful action which is also the path of duty."[49] Therefore, there generally remains a feeling of distrust towards play and playfulness.

Such distrust is rooted in an exclusive framework of religiousness, in which there is a dichotomy between seriousness and playfulness. Playfulness presupposes an individual's intention to play and to actively have fun, and yet religious experience—when defined exclusively—is not supposed to be fun. Even though some people may experience a kind of overwhelming ecstasy, they experience it passively rather than intentionally. As a consequence, any active and playful intention will eventually be downgraded and end up being distrusted.

Playfulness also presupposes a sense of security. Otto asserts that Schleiermacher's softer version of the "feeling of absolute dependence"[50] is still problematic for accommodating playfulness because such a feeling is supposedly different from all other feelings of dependence. One will not think of playing when we are desperately dependent on someone or something. When people are close to dying of thirst, they are not likely to play with water. It follows that being fearful and being serious, rather than being playful, are much more appropriate emotions in response to the objects of religious experience. Thus, playfulness and fun are not associated with the realm of exclusive religious experience. Instead, they stand side by side with the secular, which will eventually and ultimately be devalued and depreciated in exclusive religious experience.

In addition, playfulness presupposes a kind of equality and mutual responsiveness. Even when a dog plays with a ball, the ball responds spontaneously to the dog's action and is considered as an equal in the play; yet within a framework of exclusive religiousness there is neither equality nor mutual response. In a religious experience, when characterized exclusively, the *numen* is everything and the experiencer is literally nothing. The experiencer has no choice but to respond to the *numen* while the *numen* does not necessarily respond to any person's calling.

If people choose to live inclusively and religiously, they need to address this inherited bias. Play—whether in its most fundamental form of having fun, or in its more sophisticated manifestations of playing games, drama, or various forms of art—is essential for human development and civilization. As children, we learned all kinds of "play." The basic body of knowledge involved in how to build and maintain interpersonal relationships—to share, to be polite, to respect others, and to play fairly—is established among children. With age, continuous engagement in play helps people learn various life skills while balancing stress and fatigue.

Play and playfulness are precisely incarnations of imagination, creativity, and novelty, as well as being the most essential form of adding meaning: we literally *play* things and meanings into being. We can observe that in many popular religious festivals where there are ritual performances of seriousness and purity there are also elements of play, amusement, and fun. These two aspects may be experienced respectively depending on time and place, but they are indeed co-constituents of what we mean by "religious festival."[51] In short, playfulness plays no less a role than seriousness in the making of religious experience. In Dewey's words, play—as well as art—is a "moral necessity."[52]

Reframing Seriousness and
Playfulness—A Complementary Model

In an inclusive framework seriousness and playfulness can coexist and correlate much more intimately than we might expect. A work of art is usually, if not always, an embodiment of the negotiation between seriousness and playfulness. *Tianshu* is just one example. While some audience members encountered its seriousness and felt overwhelmed, others discovered its playful aspects of inspiration, marvel, wonder, and pun.[53] If *Tianshu* is a joke, as Xu Bing has on occasion commented, then it is a sophisticated joke, containing a complex mix of playfulness, as well as sincerity and seriousness.

Seriousness lends *Tianshu* its form, which "mimics in every detail the characteristics of traditional Chinese printing and book-making."[54] The style of the carved characters on wooden blocks is of the Song period, developed for book-printing in the Ming Dynasty. There are nine rows on each page and each column usually contains seventeen characters. The paper (later folded and bound) is called *zangjing* 藏經 paper and is often used for printing Buddhist sutras. Each volume is stitch-bound in a six-hole pattern of the best quality, intended for the printing of important canonical or literary works. The format of the books' content seems to follow traditional arrangements: prefaces, tables of contents, main text, marginal notes, commentary, and finally postscripts. In order to do this, Xu Bing had to learn traditional techniques of bookmaking and printing. He also spent a year, cloistered in his dormitory, carving the characters to be printed in the book.

However, it is the playfulness that lends a transformational aspect to this work. While it seems to have a formal story to tell, it conveys nothing; while it appears to be full of sounds, it remains in silence; while it encourages the audience to read, it refuses to be read. These playful aspects not only transform this book from an ordinary book (*shu*) to an extraordinary, numinous book (*tianshu*); they also effectively transform the position of the audience from receivers of given meanings to interpreters and even co-creators of unfolding meanings.

The interplay between seriousness and playfulness thus generates a creative process of continually forming and transforming in which novel associations constantly emerge. Playful experiences at the Altar for Rain transform the formal rituals of praying for rain and lead to a re-forming of experience for the excursionists. Negative wording in a formal Daoist text transforms literal meanings of formal terms and opens up space for re-forming such meanings. Nonsensical answers given by Chan masters in formal conversations transform the ways that disciples think about Buddhahood, giving way to new realizations. Seriousness and playfulness, when working together, are like *yin* 陰 and *yang* 陽 in Chinese terms, and Apollo and Dionysus in Nietzsche's terms. On the one hand, they are as distinctively different as the North and South Poles. On the other hand, they form a continuum that can be regarded as one. In the case of *Tianshu*, it is obvious that playfulness does not have to entail disrespect, irreverence, insincerity, or chaos. It is more important to note that, in Gadamer's words, "play itself contains its own, even sacred, seriousness."[55] Such correlativity can only be found in an inclusive framework of religiousness.

Reconstructing Meaningfulness and Religiousness

In the framework of exclusive religiousness, finding the meaning of life is an issue that can never be overstressed. The logic is simple: if one believes that people are absolutely dependent on the transcendent, then one must find meaning in the transcendental realm instead of in this world among us. If people have to place ultimate value upon the *numen* while at the same time devaluing and depreciating themselves, it will make little sense to establish and develop their own meaningfulness, because doing so will eventually be in vain and therefore absurd.

Within the framework of inclusive religiousness there is no meaning that has been transcendentally given and *out there*. Meaning, as well as religiousness, is an end product rather than the starting point of living. It is not the root but the flower of human flourishing. Everyday living, through which one creates something novel and meaningful, is the process on which a religious person should focus. From such a perspective, the desire to access meaningfulness without paying any attention to this emergent process is a denial of life and simply misses the point of living.

The sense of time characterized by exclusive religiousness also has to be revised in an inclusive religiousness framework. As Dewey points out, time has long been seen as something negative, an unstable factor, and a threat, always signifying decay rather than perfection, or uncertainty rather than the assurance of fulfilling the given *telos*.[56] Therefore, the transcendental and spiritual realm is usually imagined as timeless. Everything seems to be kept in pre-established harmony and in static perfection. However, in an inclusive religiousness framework, one is much less likely to despise time because time is not an external factor but rather at the very heart of existence.[57]

A story told by Xu Bing, published as the artist's reflection on the work shortly after exhibiting the expanded version of *Tianshu* to the public in 1989, is an implicit statement of this kind of religious sensibility:

> For more than a year I ceaselessly invented, carved, and printed a set of twelve volumes of *Nonsense Writing* [*Tian Shu*] which no one in this world can understand. The unbelievable amount of work threw its audience into confusion . . . One of my printer friends once told me about a "crazy" guy in his home village, who always went out to collect waste paper at a certain hour, washing these papers in a river, carefully mounting them piece by piece, and then storing them under his bed after they had become dry and flat. I thought quite a long time about this person's behavior. Finally I realized that it was a kind of *qigong*—a kind of cultivation of the *Tao* [*dao*]. It was indeed a very powerful kind of *qigong*. [It exemplifies] an Eastern way of achieving true knowledge—obtaining sudden enlightenment and correspondence with Nature by endlessly experiencing a fixed point.[58]

The cultivation of *qi* (*qigong*) mentioned here is really "focusing the familiar," a term borrowed from Ames and Hall's translation of the title of the *Zhongyong*. By focusing on the familiar, that is, by concentrating on the context of co-experience, people can start to grow and extend their experience from the self to the community, and outward to society and the country, and finally to *tian*, which carries a religious quality that is the outcome of the co-creativity of humans and the natural world. This process, never-theless, always starts from the seemingly meaningless. The repetitive routine of the "crazy guy" in the village, the daily *zazen* of the monks, and the process of making *Tianshu* seem to be pointless and meaningless. However, because of such apparent meaningless-ness, one's choice—serious, playful, or both—to make something meaningful out of it can have its full significance. In other words, it is not that we have to find the meaning of life in order to be spiritual; on the contrary, it is through time that we cultivate our spirituality from meaninglessness.

CONCLUSION

The postmodern condition in which we are currently situated con-stantly urges us to find new words to tell old stories. As bodies of knowledge aggregate and different kinds of information enter a flow, it becomes increasingly challenging to tell a story well because articulating either a figure or a ground (but not both) may not make sense to all the members of an audience. Therefore, my cen-tral task in this chapter has been to interpret *Tianshu* in several different frameworks.

Starting with definitions of religiousness and two overall frameworks that people employ to understand religiousness, I have argued that the application of a framework of exclusive religiousness is limited in terms of cultural sensibility and compatibility, as well as explanatory efficacy. Even though the principle of hermeneutical generosity requires us to keep both options open, I have demon-strated that reading *Tianshu* within a framework of inclusive reli-giousness is more productive in terms of generating dialogue. I then articulated the Chinese context of *Tianshu* and attempted to make sense of it in its native contexts in order to excavate what is lost in translation. After pointing out that the interplay between serious-ness and playfulness is closely related to the process of becoming religious, I have also identified noncoercive action (*wuwei*), readi-ness for awakening (*dunwu*), and leaving off speaking (*buyan*) as key aspects of interpreting *Tianshu* based on my investigation of the Chinese religio-philosophical context.

Xu Bing describes his work and method of thinking as "searching for the living word." It entails unmediated transformation between experience, interpretation, and the reinterpretation of experience. In terms of searching for the living word, I have suggested that *Tianshu*, in the current international and transcultural context, implies appreciation for the value of playfulness. This entails a reconsideration of the interrelationship between playfulness and seriousness, as well as a reinterpretation of meaningfulness and religiousness as co-creative processes of discursive participants.

My interpretation, limited yet hopefully engaging, is only one response within the ongoing process of constituting the meaning of *Tianshu*. As a serious and playful writer, I hope this chapter will engender more discussions around the appreciation of this work. Now I would like to leave off speaking and be a listener of *Tianshu*.

NOTES

1. One possible explanation is that an articulation of the religiousness is in itself seemingly paradoxical: to speak about the unspeakable. The unspeakable nature of religious consciousness certainly does not imply that absolutely nothing can be asserted of it. Thus a responsible scholar of religious studies will endeavor to maximally approximate the unspeakable with languages and concepts. Another reason could be that religiousness, no matter whether it is regarded as the root or the flower of a flourishing community, is the most difficult topic to talk about. One simply has no way to access the most sophisticated expression or hidden assumptions of a culture without grasping more tangible and relatable facts. Unless a certain fundamental literature has been produced, it remains difficult, abstract, and even meaningless for most people to sketch any kind of religiousness.
2. Erickson, *The Art of Xu Bing*, 39.
3. The concept *tian* is difficult to translate. Taking a religious approach, the term *tianshu* can certainly be translated as "Heavenly Book" or "Book from Heaven." However, such rendering risks smuggling the connotation of the biblical Heaven. The usual title in English, *Book from the Sky*, may be free of such misdirection yet fails to convey the religious quality of *Tianshu* from its Chinese title.
4. Erickson, *The Art of Xu Bing*, 17–18. Quotation is from Xu Bing's own statement "Living Word," translated by Ann L. Huss.
5. John Dewey, "Religion versus the Religious," in *The Later Works*, vol. 9, ed. Jo Ann Boydston (Carbondale and Edwardsville: Southern Illinois University Press, 1986), 7.
6. Ibid.
7. Ibid., 8.
8. Ibid., 10.
9. Ibid., 11.
10. Ibid., 13.

11. Ibid., 11.
12. Rudolf Otto, *The Idea of the Holy: An Inquiry into the Non-Rational Factor in the Idea of the Divine and Its Relation to the Rational* (London: Oxford University Press, 1958), 5. My italics.
13. Ibid., 9–11, 25. Otto is making a strong claim here, consistent with his criticism of Schleiermacher's weaker notion of the "feeling of dependency."
14. Ibid., 70.
15. Ibid., 30.
16. Ibid., 69.
17. Ibid., 68.
18. Ibid.
19. K.C. Chang, *Art, Myth and Ritual: The Path to Political Authority in Ancient China* (Cambridge, MA: Harvard University Press, 1983), 65.
20. Tu Wei-ming, *Centrality and Commonality* (Albany: State University of New York Press, 1989), 78.
21. Chapter 2 of the *Zhuangzi*. Cited in A.C. Graham, *Chuang-tzu: The Inner Chapters* (Indianapolis: Hackett Publishing Company, 2001), 56.
22. Peter D. Hershock, *Chan Buddhism* (Honolulu: University of Hawai'i Press, 2005), 38.
23. Roger T. Ames, "*Li* and the A-theistic Religiousness of Classical Confucianism," in *Confucian Spirituality*, ed. Tu Wei-ming and Mary Evelyn Tucker, 174 (New York: The Crossroad Publishing Company, 2003).
24. *Qi* is the vapor or steam that arises from the heating of water and watery substances and subsequently appears as the actual air that we breathe. It appears in Shang and Zhou inscriptions as "three horizontal lines, similar to the modern Chinese character for 'three (*san*),' except the three parallel lines are usually shorter and somewhat more fluid," depicting "multiple layers of ascending and descending vapors." See Ames and Hall, *Focusing the Familiar*, 72.
25. Harold D. Roth, "The Inner Cultivation Tradition of Early Daoism," in *Religions of China in Practice*, ed. Donald S. Lopez, Jr., 125 (Princeton, NJ: Princeton University Press, 1996).
26. Notably, scholars such as Wang Aihe, Li Ling, Robin Yates, and Mark Lewis have been arguing that both intellectuals and ordinary people shared the correlated *qi* cosmology as a symbolic discourse. See Ames and Hall, *Focusing the Familiar*, 19.
27. Stephen F. Teiser, "The Spirits of Chinese Religion," in *Religions of China in Practice*, ed. Donald S. Lopez, Jr., 33 (Princeton, NJ: Princeton University Press, 1996).
28. Ames and Hall, *Focusing the Familiar*, 22.
29. See *Mencius 2A.2*.
30. Erickson, *The Art of Xu Bing*, 37.

31. Chapter 5 of the *Zhuangzi*. Cited in Graham, *Chuang-tzu*, 76–77.

32. It also has an impact on Chinese debate: an argument stops not with the demonstration that one party is wrong, but rather not inclusive enough. The Mohist school is probably a distinctive exception.

33. The *Analects* 14.42.

34. See the *Analects* 19.24.

35. See the *Analects* 11.26. Cited in Roger T. Ames and Henry Rosemont, Jr., *The Analects of Confucius: A Philosophical Translation* (New York: Ballantine Books, 1998), 150.

36. See Roger T. Ames and David L. Hall, *Dao De Jing "Making This Life Significant": A Philosophical Translation* (New York: Ballantine Books, 2003), 39, 44–45, for relevant discussion.

37. Angela Zito, *Of Body and Brush: Grand Sacrifice as Text/Performance in Eighteen-Century China* (Chicago: University of Chicago Press, 1997), 42. Zito's examination is focused on calligraphic writings of the Qianlong Emperor in Qing Dynasty. However, it is well suited to characterize the long history of writing in Chinese culture.

38. See *Dao De Jing*, chap. 11. Cited in Ames and Hall, *Dao De Jing*, 91.

39. It is interesting to see how varied people's responses and interpretation can be when they face a seemingly meaning-void work like *Tianshu*. If a person was shocked by what happened in the Tiananmen Square incident, *Tianshu* would appear to this person as an unspeakable criticism and accusation of the harsh control with which Chinese communists run the country. *Tianshu* would seem to be just another exhibition of Chinese calligraphy to people who do not recognize Chinese characters unless they are intentionally reminded. It could also be an exotic work for people who know a little about Chinese culture yet do not have a chance to fully understand and embrace it. For people who are habituated to read Chinese characters, *Tianshu* requires that they spend a long time to find a word to read, which reminds them of the frustrating experience of learning to read Chinese characters.

40. See *Platform Sutra*, section 6. Cited in Hershock, *Chan Buddhism*, 98.

41. See *Platform Sutra*, section 8. Cited in Hershock, *Chan Buddhism*, 99.

42. Ibid., 102–103.

43. Richard E. Palmer, *Hermeneutics* (Evanston, IL: Northwestern University Press, 1969), 13.

44. See the *Analects* 17.19. Cited in Ames and Rosemont, *The Analects of Confucius*, 208.

45. Vattimo, *After Christianity* (New York: Columbia University Press, 2002), 13, 15.

46. Aldo Gargain, "Religious Experience as Event and Interpretation," in *Religion*, ed. Jacques Derrida and Gianni Vattimo (Stanford, CA: Stanford University Press, 1998), 114–115.

47. Vattimo, *After Christianity*, 12.

48. John Finn lists "play" as one of the seven basic forms of good (among life, knowledge, aesthetic experience, friendship, practical reasonableness, religion) and is among a few philosophers who appreciate the value of play in their philosophy. Dewey, as we will see, is another. See John Finn, *Natural Law and Natural Rights* (Oxford: Oxford University Press, 1980), 90.

49. Dewey, *Human Nature and Conduct* (Mineola, NY: Dover Publications, Inc., 2002), 159.

50. Otto, *The Idea of the Holy*, 9.

51. Li Feng-mao, "Seriousness and Playfulness: Daoist San-yuan Festival and Customs of Tang Dynasty," in *Anthology of the Tenth Annual Conference of Institute of Chinese Literature and Philosophy* (Taipei: Academia Sinica Press, 2001), 90.

52. Dewey, *Human Nature and Conduct*, 160.

53. Erickson, *The Art of Xu Bing*, 39.

54. Alice Yang, *Why Asia?: Contemporary Asian and Asian American Art* (New York: New York University Press, 1998), 25.

55. Hans-Georg Gadamer, *Truth and Method* (New York: Crossroad Publishing Company, 1985), 91.

56. Dewey, "Time and Individuality," in *The Later Works*, vol. 14, ed. Jo Ann Boydston (Carbondale and Edwardsville: Southern Illinois University Press, 1988), 99.

57. Ibid., 102.

58. Xu Bing, "Looking for Something Different in a Quiet Place," *Beijing Qingnian Bao* [Beijing Youth Newspaper], February 10, 1989.

CHAPTER FOUR

Making Natural Languages in Contemporary Chinese Art

RICHARD VINOGRAD

Since the mid-1980s Xu Bing and other contemporary Chinese artists have explored problems and contradictions of textual language, the interplay between textual and visual meanings, or between meaning and nonsense, and the status of cultural versus natural languages in a series of ongoing projects. Several of these projects involve aspects of what can be termed *natural languages*, although this term can comprise various topics that may not be immediately or transparently interrelated. For the present discussion, I use natural language to refer to four major categories that operate in contemporary art practice:

1. everyday, native language, as opposed to artificial or machine language
2. signs and talismans such as the trigrams and hexagrams of the *Book of Changes* (*Yijing* 易经) or talismans of the Five Sacred Mountains that are conventionally said to be of divine or heavenly, nonhuman origin
3. legible signs in the natural world or landscape
4. embodied texts in or on animal or human bodies, from surface tattoos to genetic codes

Broadly speaking, then, natural language references appear in the linguistic realm—primarily textual rather than spoken language, given the visual arts context of most projects—in the geophysical realm of landscape, and in the biological realm of animal and human

95

bodies. The notion of the natural is of course not self-evident or unproblematic, any more than is a simple distinction between the cultural and the natural. Some version of that distinction seems often to function in contemporary art practice, however, even while being problematized and complicated, and thus it seems a useful starting point for discussion. Similarly, the identification of these artists as "Chinese" acknowledges the locus of their early training and fields of activity, as well as culturally based references to Chinese language practices and texts, without overlooking the international or trans-national contexts in which many of these projects appeared, or the conditions of intercultural encounter that precipitated many of them.

Xu Bing has engaged all of these types of natural language in his work, where in one or another form it is an intensive and ongoing preoccupation, but a concern with language, writing, and the problematics of meaning is very widespread in post-1985 Chinese art. There may be particular historical reasons for this, having to do with the coming of age of artists whose formative years were passed under the hypertrophied semiotic regime of the Cultural Revolution. Ideological slogans, big character posters, the ubiquitous Little Red Book, and other visual-textual machinery of political discourse and propaganda were so pervasive that both language and its material embodiments were an inescapable part of public consciousness. In a manner similar to the torrent of Mao imagery (often parodistic or critical) that was unleashed in the same post-1985 era as a kind of return of the impressed, involving a working out of the overload of Mao image exposure during the Cultural Revolution, we might see the wave of language-based art—often nonsensical and deliberately obscure—as a long-duration response to collective linguistic trauma.[1]

The deployment of natural language concerns in contemporary Chinese art practice is, however, so diverse, and so full of ambiguities and self-reflexive positions that any univocal explanatory context—even one so potent as the political horizon of Maoist China—is bound to seem inadequate. Indeed, the same post-1985 era was also marked by the introduction of waves of literary, semiotic, and cultural theory into Chinese academic and intellectual circles.[2] It is not difficult to see a widespread concern with language, text, and meaning issues in the visual arts as either a deployment of such critical and semiotic theory, or as a reactive manifestation of weariness toward a theoretical oversaturation that might have seemed as pervasive and as inescapable as Maoist rhetoric.

There are still other, historically more deeply situated horizons to the language-centered arts of recent decades. China has always been marked in the European worldview as the site of ultimate linguistic and communicative difference—difficult or impenetrable language combined with inscrutable embodied facial expression. Paradoxically, for Leibniz and others in the late seventeenth century, China held out hope as the source of universal language: in the *Book of Changes* (*Yijing* 易经) hexagrams conveyed to him by the Jesuit Father Bouvet, and whose invention he attributed to the ancient Fohy (Fuxi 伏羲), Leibniz saw the origins and counterparts of his own binary arithmetic.[3] The idea of a universal language, especially one of purportedly deep antiquity, was in turn linked in some ways with the quest for humankind's original, more or less pictographic, natural language by Kircher and others.[4] Such deeply situated cultural forms as the hexagrams are referenced in contemporary Chinese art practice, but the broader residue of this deep history of cultural encounters may have been the felt need on the part of contemporary Chinese artists to negotiate the horizon of linguistic difference as part of their reengagement with the international art world.

It is a long way round from Mao to Leibniz to Fuxi to Xu Bing, but the centrality of paradox at least survives the journey. Natural language is to begin with a vexed term. The most common usage nowadays is to distinguish natural spoken or written languages from artificial languages, that is to say, computer languages or codes, or machine languages. Native language ability is indeed, according to Steven Pinker and Noam Chomsky, natural or instinctive—humans seem to be prewired for language use and understanding and for the employment of a universal grammar.[5] At the same time, it is a commonplace of semiotic theory that language systems are constructed sign systems, arbitrary in the sense that they have no natural relationship to their referents, with such exceptions, important in the present context, of such phenomena as onomatopoetic sounds or pictographic scripts.

The notion of "making" natural language also seems intrinsically paradoxical, and similarly, many of the uses of natural language in contemporary art contexts involve paradox or internal contradictions: natural languages are made or performed, rather than discovered; natural languages are made unnatural, unfamiliar, and difficult; and natural languages are often deployed to unmake meaning.

LIMINAL LEXICONS

While most of the projects we are concerned with do not involve ordinary or natural language in the current usage, some of Xu Bing's projects deal with natural language in the most common sense. The *Square Word Calligraphy* (Figure 4.1) project, for example, involves natural English-language words that are deformed and defamiliarized in their graphic representations. Thus the tension between the natural and the artificial/constructed that is intrinsic to the natural language concept is echoed in the tension between familiar and defamiliarized native language in the square word calligraphy mode. The English or other Roman alphabetic language-using reader enters into a liminal or interlinguistic space, in which the 'natural,' relatively automatic, or unconscious process of reading and decoding is made laborious and strange. This is a space of a certain discomfort, puzzlement, and, ultimately, of wonderment, in which the visitor/reader may feel that she has become all at once literate in a new language. The *Square Word Calligraphy* "classroom" installations are ultimately congenial and rewarding spaces. The lightened semantic load of the texts involved—often nursery rhymes or personal names—has something of the accommodating character of Chinese primer texts such as the *Three-Character Classic* (*Sanzi jing* 三字经). In that way, the classroom spaces of *Square Word Calligraphy* take on some of the retrospective, nostalgic aura of preschool or primary school classrooms or other early reading spaces.

One might say that *A Book from the Sky* (*Tianshu*, Figure I.1) also plays on the same tension between familiar natural language forms and the estrangement from, or defamiliarization of, the invented graphs. Compared to *Square Word Calligraphy*, the emotional tone of *A Book from the Sky* is much less accommodating, and more fraught with frustration and anxiety, which may account in part for the vitriolic critical reaction it stimulated in China, within its primary and "natural" audience. Native natural language is made illegible and difficult for readers of Chinese, who are cast into a psycholinguistic limbo of elusive meaning, always in sight but not quite within reach. It is a psychic space of deliberate illiteracy and dis-ease, with some of the symptoms of illness in its discomforts and self-alienation. It can be at the same time a liberating and exhilarating space of neologism, populated by fragmentary sememes awaiting reformulation into a poetics of nonsense.

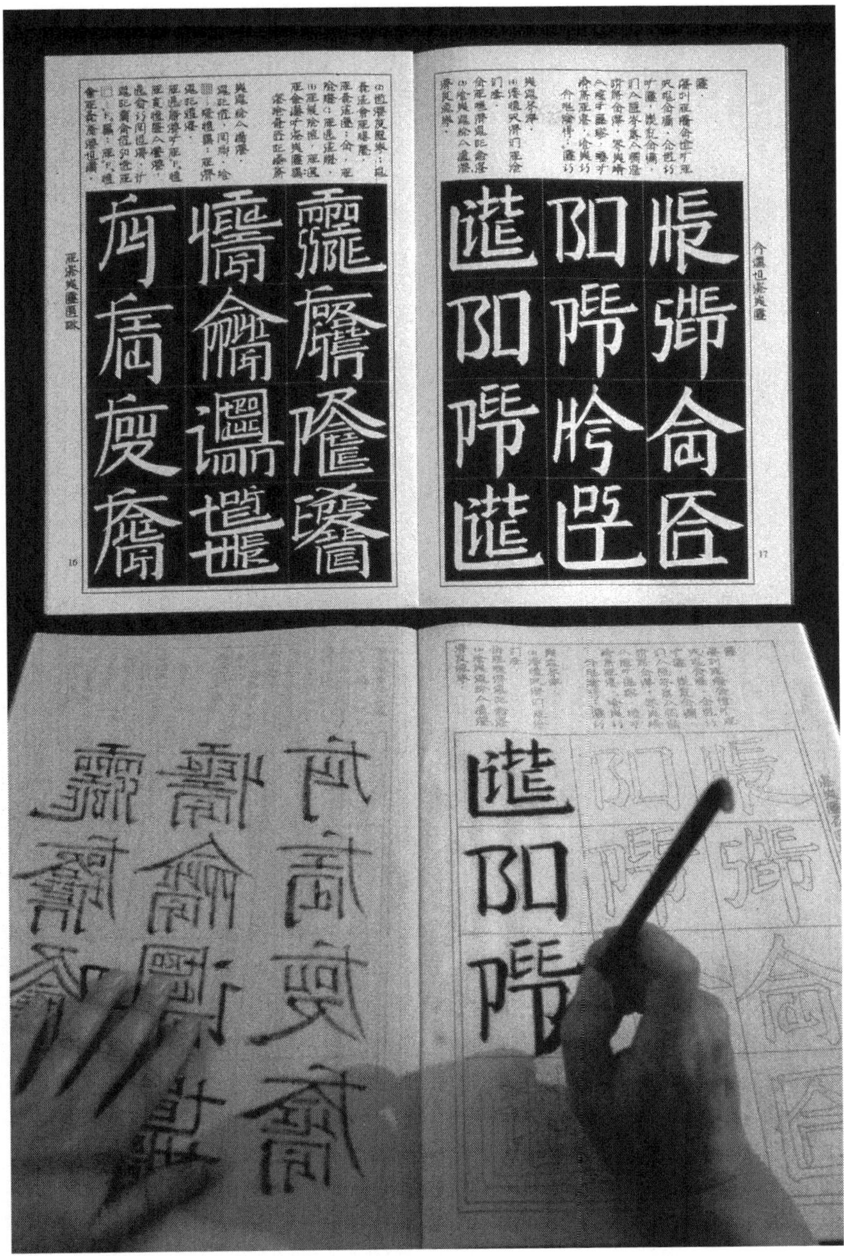

FIGURE 4.1. *Square Word Calligraphy*, Xu Bing, mixed-media installation, 1994–1996. (Courtesy of the artist.)

In both *Square Word Calligraphy* and *A Book from the Sky*, exhilaration and disquiet alike arise from the blurring between the cultural and the natural. In their loss, the cultural codes of reading and language are felt to have the status of natural abilities, whose absence occasions the same kind of disorientation as the failure of space-time coordinates. This loss is all the more poignant for being surrounded by dense material environments of reading, a lectic landscape that reminds us that reading is not purely a mental or psychological act, but one situated in reading places and supported by the physical and tactile presence of books, paper, and even computer screens. The sensorium of reading and printed matter is offered in abundance, from the relief of carved woodblocks to the drape of thread-bound volumes, even as the reader is cast into an alexic state.

SIGNS OF DISPLACEMENT

The concept of natural languages had a deep historical basis in China and elsewhere in the world. The idea of a legible world, or of the phenomenal world as a panoply of signs, had a central position in the European medieval worldview, and in Chinese metaphysics as well.[6] In China the idea of revealed heavenly images or signs as the origins of writing was very powerful, and often located the idea of natural language in the visible, written, or graphic primarily, rather than in spoken language. The trigrams were viewed as a form of natural language, related variously to the state of primordial chaos, to phenomenal reality, and to the revealed cosmic diagrams known as the River Diagram and Luo Writing that were supposed to have emerged out of the Yellow and Luo Rivers on the backs of tortoises.[7] Another form of putatively natural language script involved the Daoist talismans (*fu* 符) or esoteric magic scripts used as amulets or sometimes representing the Five Sacred Mountains, in diagrammatic forms that map the infrastructure or inscape of those sites.[8]

Such forms of natural language were often referenced in Chinese avant-garde art of the mid-1980s and afterwards. Huang Yongping's *Roulette Wheel: Paintings Created According to Random Instructions* of 1985 used trigram signs as part of artistic divination techniques related to the *Book of Changes* to guide his painting production.[9] These deployments of versions of "natural" signs were in every case deeply cultural, and even intercultural, in their contexts. Huang Yongping's divination paintings reference aleatory production methods of the early twentieth-century Dada and

Surrealist artists, Breton and Duchamp chief among them, a connection elsewhere indicated by Huang's leading role in the Xiamen Dada anti-art performances.[10] The *Book of Changes* signified not only primordial Chinese culture but also its reception in the West, as perhaps the best known (if not necessarily the best understood) of the Chinese classics through Wilhelm's interpretive translation accompanied by Carl Jung's forward.[11]

Huang Yongping also produced large-scale land art projects in France that reference *Book of Changes* trigram patterns and Daoist talismanic signs.[12] These evoke a context of geomantic practice, with geomancy involving a kind of nature code that renders the landscape readable. At the same time, the location of Huang's talismanic and *Book of Changes* signs in the French landscape recalls the context of his participation in the multicultural program for *Magiciens de la Terre*, in which Chinese geomantic traditions were both respected and re-exoticized in the company of African, South American, and Oceanic cultural practices.[13] Gu Wenda's projects also reference the gamesmanship of Chinese artists positioning themselves in an international art world arena, in which the currency of a familiar exoticism played a helpful role. Gu's serial *United Nations* projects suggest a globalizing agenda through a copresence of multiple invented scripts—with the pseudo-Chinese script possessing some of the unreadable familiarity of Daoist talismanic signs—that are "naturally" interrelated by their realization in ethnically differentiated human hair samples, another "natural" biological language of ethnic typology.[14]

Many of these early examples of cross-cultural natural language are magnified, hypertrophied, and one might say outspoken in size and scale—visual shouts across the geographical and cultural divides that separated China from the rest of the world. Xu Bing's *A Book from the Sky* installations were amplified in another way, in the sheer quantity of their invented graphs (Figure I.1). There is an enveloping sea of text on the floor, surrounding walls of text, and ceiling/tent/sky of text in these installations that materializes the omnipresence of language and semiosis—a very real prison house of encompassing language for the visitor, and a psychological space of detention/attention for the Sinoliterate viewer, who cannot easily get the alluring promise of signification out of his or her head.

Despite the enormous and obvious labor of making that went into projects like *A Book from the Sky* and *United Nations Series*, the viewer/visitor's role is paramount. Whatever significance, or nonsignificance, there is in such projects is not a message communicated from the artist to viewer but rather is produced in the space of encounter between graphs or environments and the viewer's response, even if it is only one of bewilderment. The visitor's active and participatory role in making natural languages is explicit in the *Square Word Calligraphy* (Figure 4.1) writing stations, but it was no less central to *A Book from the Sky*. Indeed, that now commonly employed title for the installation seems to have been adopted by Xu Bing as a replacement for the earlier *Mirror to Analyze the World* because of the response of certain visitors, in the same fashion that the critical response to his Great Wall rubbing project contributed the now standard title *Ghosts Pounding the Wall*.[15]

The Chinese language equivalent of *A Book from the Sky* (*Tianshu* 天書) might be rendered in a fuller and more historically based translation as "Heavenly Scriptures." This version acknowledges the long-duration importance of "Heaven" (*tian*) in Chinese political cosmology, and the specific locution of *Tianshu* as a label for Daoist talismanic writings, one of the kinds of purportedly natural languages discussed earlier, which may be considered "scriptures" because of their religious aura and contexts. The Daoist *Tianshu* may be considered a form of natural language because they are ostensibly not human productions and are not translatable into the codes of conventional language.

Because *Tianshu* are religious and untranslatable graphs, the labeling of Xu Bing's installation with that term seems pejorative in terms of socialist aesthetics. The term suggests incomprehensibility, and thus inutility and social isolation, as well as Daoist mysteries or mystifications, and hence at least a tinge of religious superstition. The title *Ghosts Pounding the Wall* similarly had critical and pejorative implications, including futile activity and the taint of counterrevolutionary orientation.[16] Xu Bing's openness to adopting pejorative characterizations of his works suggests that for him, meaning is not just unstable in the poststructuralist sense, but is literally what the viewer makes of it. "Making" natural languages thus refers to an at least tripartite process: the invention of new symbols by the artists; the facture of material embodiments of such symbols, in print or woven hair or other media as the case might be, and with all the consequent significance attached to those choices of materials and media; and the meaning-making produced by the reader/viewer/visitor in his or her perceptual, bodily, and psychological/intellectual engagement with the texts.

This insistence on making and production, and the accompanying magnification of scale and quantity of pseudo-semantic forms seems compensatory for the evacuation of discursive meaning in projects like *A Book from the Sky*. One might say that the making is the meaning. Or, in another and equally valid sense, the meaning lies in the unmaking of meaning, especially if we emphasize the interpretation of such projects as critiques of the vacuousness of political discourse. In a curiously complementary way, the later *Square Word Calligraphy*, which seems to offer restitution of meaning and communication, and even a mildly utopian international translatability, diminishes in significance by focusing on personal names and nursery rhymes for its demonstration texts—texts whose discursive significance is less important than their phonetic structure. It seems entirely characteristic of Xu Bing's artistic strategy to offer something and then take it away, presenting a perpetual horizon of things just out of reach.

GROUNDING NATURAL LANGUAGES

While most of the natural language projects discussed in the preceding were pure text or reading environments, however densely materialized, Huang Yongping's talismanic graphs in the French landscape are reminiscent of land art, large-scale shapings, borrowings, or employments of the geophysical landscape for art projects. Since some Daoist talismanic graphs were semi-iconic signs of sacred mountains, this grounding of graphs in the landscape seems appropriate. There is a cultural grounding at work here as well; a reference to deep cultural practices that lends the contemporary projects a certain historical weight and resonance. This strategy is also at work in *A Book from the Sky*, with its referencing of Song dynasty printing and bookbinding practices, and in many other contemporary Chinese art projects. Typically, in both Huang's and Xu's projects the displacements and distortions of deep cultural practices—into the French countryside or into nonsensical graphs—makes it clear that the contemporary artists are leveraging the cultural capital invested in those practices for their own purposes, rather than simply invoking tradition.

Any kind of large-scale inscription of or on the landscape evokes both casual graffiti on rocks and cliffs at famous scenic sites or pilgrimage spots, and programmatic monumental cliff carvings like those of Sutra Stone Valley in Shandong.[17] Some of Xu Bing's

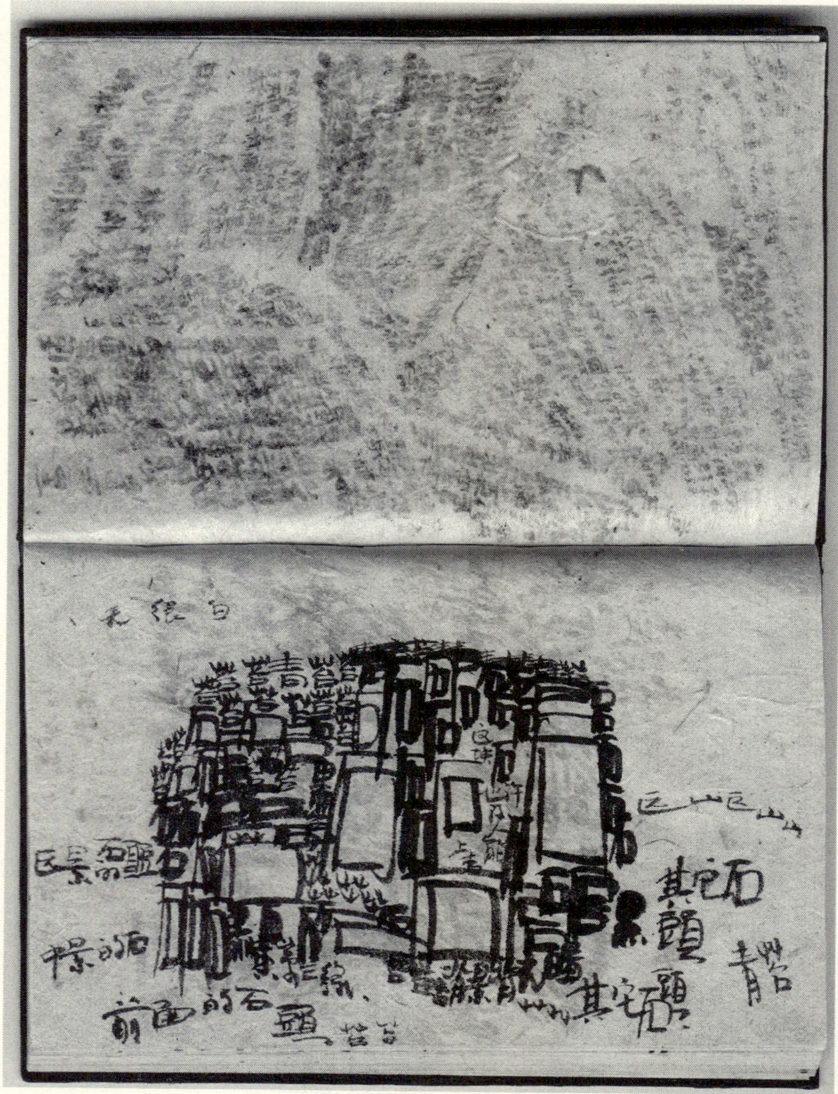

FIGURE 4.2. *Helsinki-Himalaya Exchange*, Xu Bing, ink on paper, 1999–2000. (Courtesy of the artist.)

recent projects such as *Helsinki-Himalaya Exchange* of 2000 (Figure 4.2) involve not inscriptions on the landscape but landscape as inscription, in which the visually constitutive elements of landscape painting designs are composed of legible graphs—forests composed of *mu* 木 or *shu* 樹 'tree' or *lin* 林 'grove' graphic clusters; ridges and cliffs composed of *shi* 石 'stone' graphs, *qiu* 丘 'hill' graphs and the like.[18]

Xu Bing's strategy has a somewhat removed, deep historical antecedent in the Japanese Heian period *ashide*, or reed writing, in which pictorialized *kana* syllabary graphs, originally derived from Chinese characters, were woven into pictures in semi-disguised forms to convey religious or poetic sentiments through a hybrid picture-text.[19] Whatever Xu's awareness of this Japanese genre, which has some congruencies with his interest in visual games, interactivity, and acts of recognition, he shifts the parameters from text embedded within, or underneath, a dominant pictorial design, to a more thoroughly textualized form in which the landscape design is entirely composed from graphs. The effect is to visualize and foreground the process of linguistic categorization and conceptualization that lurks behind perception and recognition, pictorial or otherwise. Do we "see" visual forms of rocks and trees? Or rather linguistic-conceptual categories of "rocks," and "trees"? Characteristically, by fashioning his graphs into a landscape painting rather than a landscape, Xu Bing simultaneously interrogates the status of pictorial representations, as alternatively iconic or symbolic, in C.S. Peirce's terminology.[20]

Equally characteristically, Xu pushes the interrogation further and in several directions in this and other work. In *Helsinki-Himalaya Exchange* (Figure 4.2), graphic forms become iconic in two ways. Some like, *mu* 木, 'tree' or *tian* 田 'farm field,' or *cao* 艸 'grass' look like schematic versions of their referents, and are thus loosely pictographic. Others are grouped in ways that visually resemble, through their density, tonality, rhythm, or arrangement, trees on a hillside or a ridge of stones above fields. Symbolic forms can suggest diagrammatic maps or mental notations, as when graphs are strung together in phrases, such as 'a strip of red emerges from the ground.' Thus the total ensemble of *Helsinki-Himalaya Exchange* has elements of sketch, map, and diary notation all at once.

In the related *Landscript* installation for the Biennale of Sydney (2000), Xu shifted his arena from representational to perceptual space with a mixture of Chinese and *Square Word Calligraphy* graphs painted on the glass windowpanes of the Art Gallery of New South Wales that echoed the forms of urban landscape visible through the same glass. Since almost everything in the field of vision except for a few trees is humanly produced, there is little tension here between even a represented or illusionistic nature and cultural forms of writing as in *Helsinki-Himalaya Exchange*, an aspect emphasized by the outspokenly geometric arrangement of the graphs in *Landscript 2000*. What does seem at issue again is the interplay or inextricability of perception and conception or categorization, or, to put it another way, the filtering or screening effect that mental categorizations have on perceptual experience.

Helsinki-Himalaya Exchange takes place entirely within representational space, while the Sydney version of *Landscript* involves "real" perceptual space of the cityscape that is framed by the picture-plane-like glass of the gallery windows, so that it too has the quality of a pictorial or mediated experience. *Reading Landscape: After Yuan Jiang* (Figure 4.3) for the Sackler exhibition engages both the representational space of the Yuan Jiang landscape painting and the physical space of the gallery and the viewer's perceptual field. By extending the now three-dimensional, materialized carved graphs for landscape elements like 'grass,' 'water,' and 'cloud' into the intermediate space between viewer and flat scroll painting, Xu Bing suggests that linguistic forms are in some sense more "real" than the illusionistically representational forms of the landscape painting. At the same time, the extension of the operative space of the painting beyond its mounting into three-dimensional space tends to emphasize the physical status of the painting as an object, comprised as much by its framing silk mounting as by its pictorial representational content. This double transposition—from pictorial representation to textual graph, and from flat picture to interspatial sign—further suggests that language is always present in nature as a kind of interference pattern. By juxtaposing graphs for landscape elements with the pictorial representation of landscape by Yuan Jiang, Xu presents a world thoroughly inhabited by linguistic signs. He further conveys a materialization of cognitive perception, as the pictorial images are transposed into linguistic categories in the process of perception/reception, literally "before our eyes."

Song Dong's 1996 performance work *Printing on Water* provides an instructive precedent and comparison for Xu Bing's engagements of language with the natural world.[21] Song's performance, though earlier than Xu Bing's projects discussed here, took the further conceptual step of trying to physically imprint textual language on the natural world, without the mediation of representation, paintings, or gallery spaces. In place of the traditional practice of accomplishing that through carving enduring text on stone cliffs, Song Dong sat in the Lhasa River and repeatedly plunged a carved seal into the flowing water. Song Dong's event is saturated with

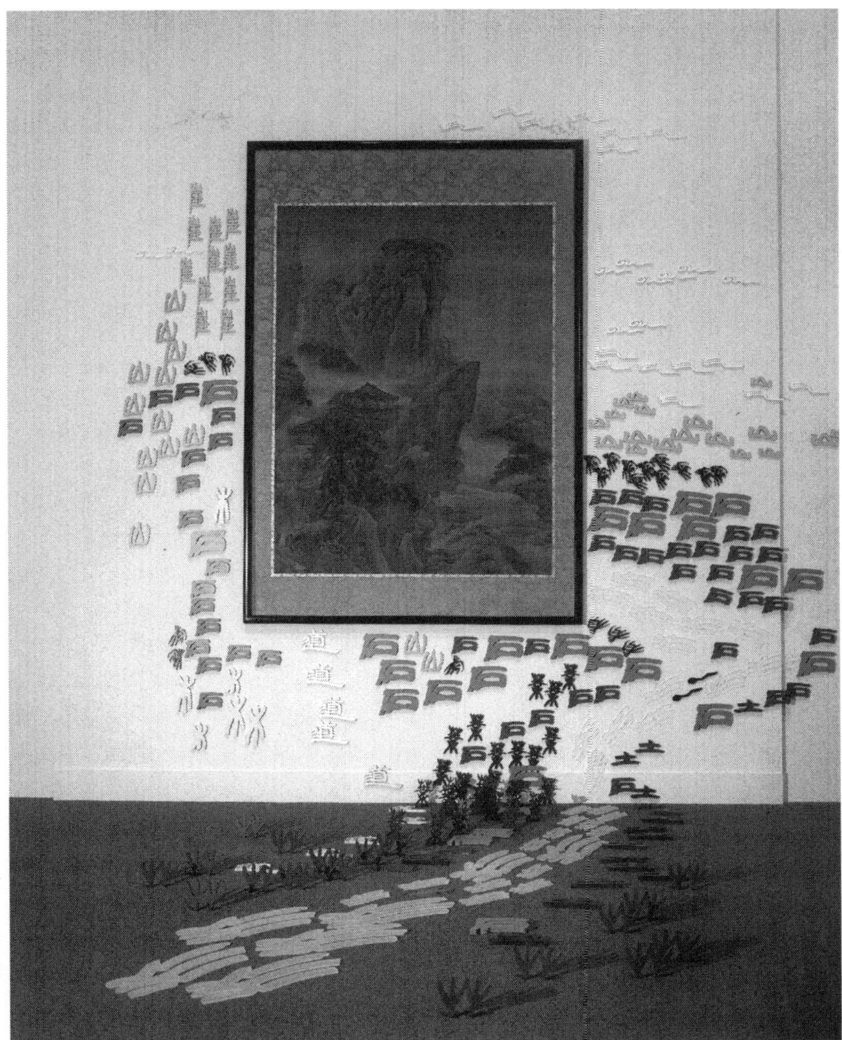

FIGURE 4.3. *Reading Landscape: After Yuan Jian.* Xu Bing, 2001. Wood, PVC, acrylic paint, and Chinese landscape painting, installation view. (Courtesy of the artist, photo: Tsao Hsingyuan.)

futility, made all the more poignant through a near-ritualistic reiteration. The flowing river refuses the imprint of Song's carved seal, in the way that the natural refuses the imprint of the cultural, and just as the phenomenal world refuses containment by linguistic categories. Song's performance is an exercise in negation of meaning, other than that invested in the performativity of the event.

SOMATIC TEXTS

Printing on Water dissolves textual significance, but produces a kind of performative meaning through the rhythmic, embodied gesture of stamping the water surface. Gu Wenda's *United Nations Series* involves another kind of embodied language, or pseudo-language, in its use of braided human hair as the medium for invented graphs and scripts, conveying specific physical and ethnic messages that transcend the ambiguities of the scripts. In a number of recent projects Xu Bing and other contemporary Chinese artists have explored biological languages separate from ordinary speech and written language. These could potentially include facial expressions, gestural and body language, identifying markings, and color display, all the way down to forms and behaviors as expressions of genetic traits, which are in turn embodied in genetic codes, conventionally represented by an alphabetic language of DNA sequences. As with many other forms of natural languages explored by Xu and his contemporaries, biological and genetic languages prove often to be competitive with, or destructive of, standard language and its understanding. Such bio-art projects move the problematics of natural languages from the relatively uneventful realm of landscape into the proximate and unsettling arena of animal and human bodies.

Xu's 1995 *American Silkworm Series Part I and II*, for example, involved in its second phase, silkworm larvae scattered upon the pages of books, other printed matter, and even computer monitors to spin their cocoons (Figure 4.4).[22] In the process, the silkworms covered the texts with an increasingly dense filigree of silk, ultimately obscuring and disfiguring the texts beneath. The Chinese word for silkworm, *can* 蠶, is also a homonym for disfigurement and destruction 殘, an apt description for the effects of the silkworms' biological expression on the texts. Silk threads have something of the quality of a text in their linearity and their suitability for spinning and weaving into a textile, just as yarns are spun and stories are woven into texts. The silkworms' texts are thus in some ways an overwriting of the printed texts, and suggest the obliteration of culture by the relentlessly natural expression of languages of the biological world, as well as by the destructive processes of time and history.

Xu Bing's *Guangdong Wild Zebra Herd* (Figure 4.5) borrows the natural language of species-specific markings to transform

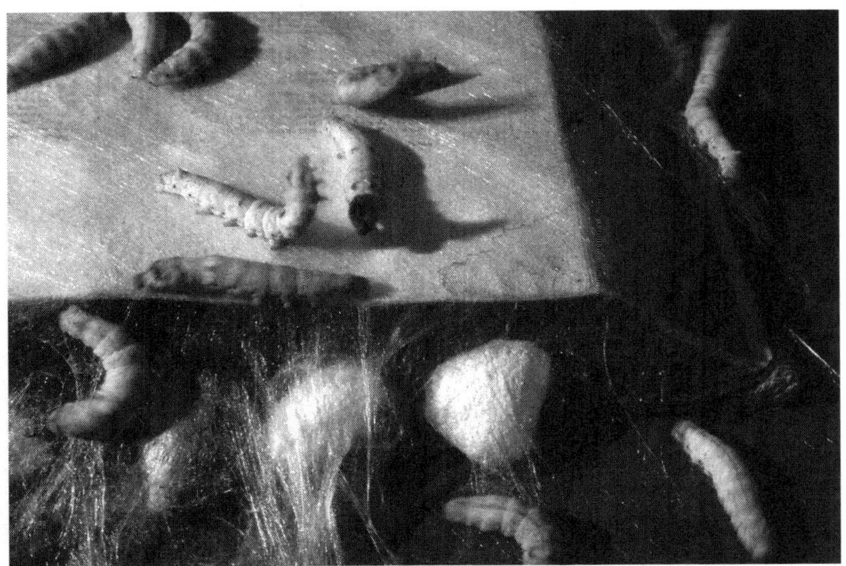

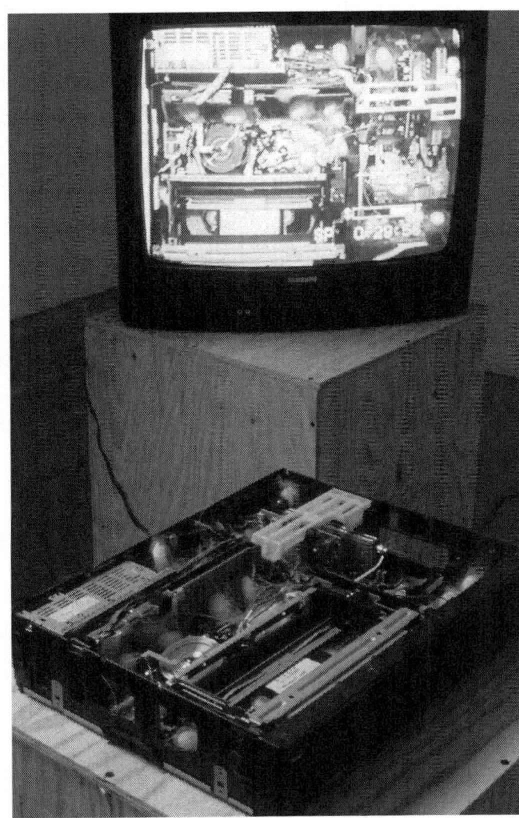

FIGURE 4.4. *American Silkworm Series Part I and II,* formerly known as *Can Series,* Xu Bing, installation with live silkworms, books, and objects, 1994–1995. (Courtesy of the artist.)

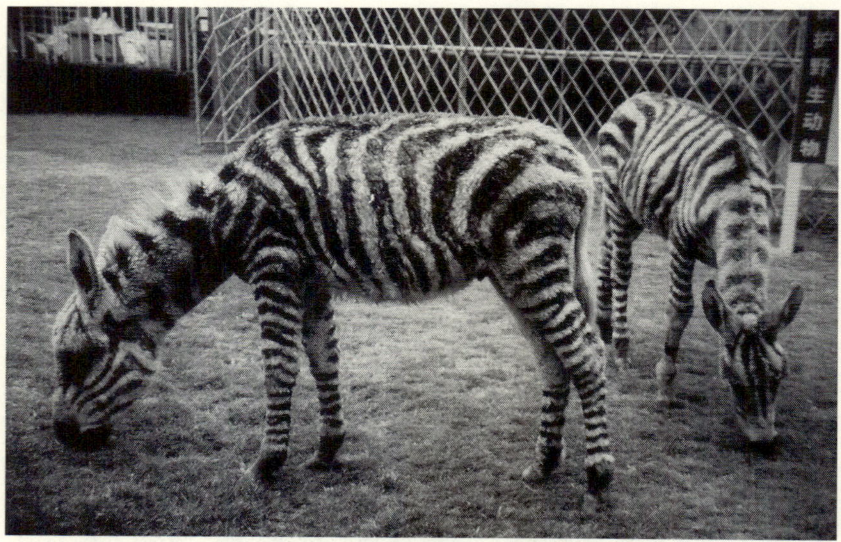

FIGURE 4.5. *Guangdong Wild Zebra Herd*, Xu Bing, installation with live donkeys, Guangzhou Biennale, 2002. (Courtesy of the artist.)

ordinary donkeys into something exotic through painted zebra stripes.[23] This both imitates and denies natural signs in a way that evokes camouflage, makeup, visual mimicry, and deception as fundamental counterfoils to the legibility of nature. Camouflage and visual mimicry are, of course, part of "natural" strategies of deception practiced by plants, invertebrates, and mammals alike, even if unselfconsciously. *Guangdong Wild Zebra Herd* (2002) and the related *Panda Zoo* (1998) installation of masked pigs with real bamboo and a painted mountainscape backdrop, all within a gallery space's "nature preserve," involve a deliberate human deception that differs from the human intervention and arrangement of the silkworm larvae in *American Silkworm Series*.[24] At the same time, these projects can yield a reflexive interrogation of the conditions of painting as well as of human visual deception: is painting in some ways a natural activity as much as a cultural one, a human counterpart to natural deception strategies?

Similarly, we might ask if language use is ultimately natural, even with, or perhaps especially because of, all its artifice, ornament, rhetoric, and lying. Xu Bing's work constantly probes and critiques language culture as an instrument of political manipulation and deception, as a mental prison, as a pretext for controlling and abusing animals, and as an interference pattern in our visual perception of the natural world. At the same time, this critique is not protected from a reflexive realization that language and textuality are pervasive human activities, perhaps distinctively natural ones.

Xu Bing's *Net and Leash* installation of 1998 involved a human constraint of animals, not through species counterfeiting but through language.[25] Sheep were leashed with a chain of poetic text, and caged within a materialized and enclosing exhibition statement, as if to show that language conceptions are as much a source of human dominion over animals as are physical constraints, and that both humans and animals are perpetually caged by conceptual structures that are invisible without a special effort of attention. Like the natural world landscapes of *Helsinki-Himalaya Exchange*, other animal bodies are, it would seem, only perceivable through a scrim of linguistic consciousness.

Xu Bing's *A Case Study in Transference* performance involved copulating pigs whose skins were imprinted with invented pseudo-Chinese graphs from the *A Book from the Sky* lexicon and nonsense English words, all the while trampling on books underfoot (Figure 4.6).[26] The project seems to celebrate the triumph of animal instinct over linguistic culture, and simultaneously to satirize utopian hopes for intercultural communication, since what is being transmitted here, however primally, is in any case nonsense text. Some subtexts of the project involved questions of cultural and gender dominance and subordination, since the male pig was imprinted with pseudo-English text and the sow with pseudo-Chinese graphs. Further, since the pigs were culturally marked, their mating could be considered a kind of mock miscegenation. Whether intended or not, the genetic implications of the performance do in fact provide a frame for the event, against which matters such as the uncontrollable dissemination of the semiotic process take on further resonance. The ultimate controlling language for animal sexual behavior is not the imprinted nonsense text on the pigs' skins, but the sequences of the genetic code that they exchange, a reminder that "the genetic code must be regarded as the most fundamental of all semiotic networks and therefore as the prototype for all other signaling systems used by animals, including man."[27]

Questions of genetic dissemination and miscegenation do not seem so far-fetched in the context of the extended version of *A Case Study of Transference*, the follow-up *Cultural Animal* performance where the pseudo-English pig attempted to mate with a male

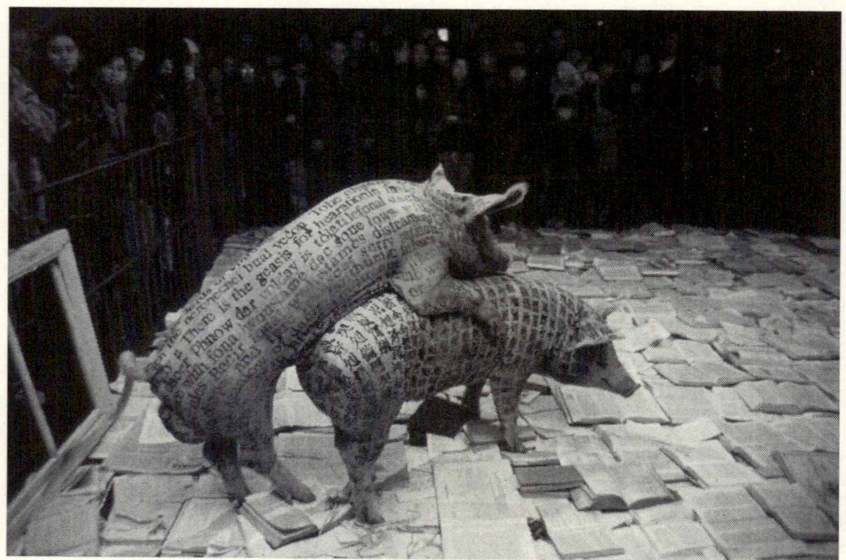

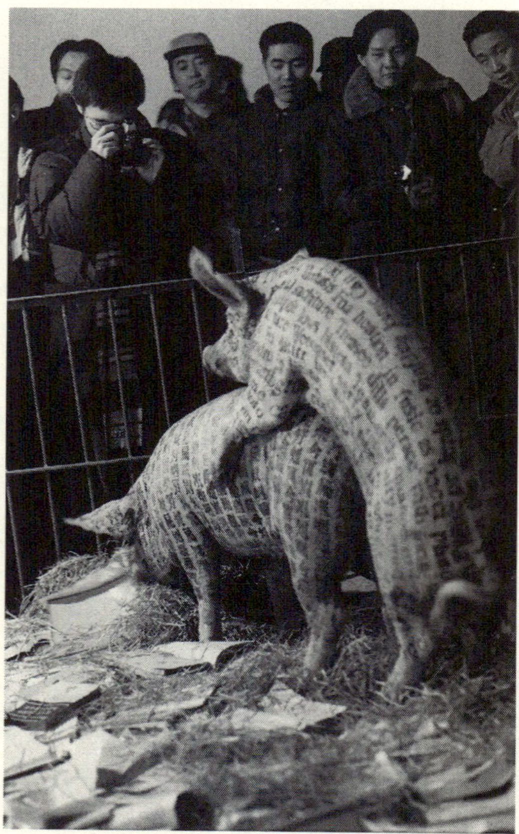

FIGURE 4.6. *Case Study for Transference #1*, Xu Bing, performance at the Han Mo Art Center in Beijing, 1994. (Courtesy of the artist.)

mannequin imprinted with pseudo-Chinese graphs.[28] This mock reverse bestiality sets the terms of language, gender, culture, reality, and artifice into a whirling spiral toward the abyss from which it is hard to pull out into any stable plane of interpretation. At least the animal–human interaction in this, and in less flagrant and disturbing forms in Xu Bing's animal art, reminds us that related aspects of the genetic, the natural world, and the linguistic horizon of identity all operate in the human sphere as well.

This has most often been visualized through the imprinting medium of the tattoo, including Huang Yan's 1999 *Chinese Landscape—Tattoo*, in which the figure is no longer in the landscape as in traditional Chinese landscape painting, but the landscape is on the human figure. This is an act of self-exoticization but is also a reminder that the natural world is perceived through a cultural lens, even at the stage of embodied, physical perception. Zhang Huan's *Family Tree* photographic series visualizes genealogy not as an internal genetic process nor wholly as a physical manifestation of appearance, but rather as a simultaneously cultural-linguistic-physical category in which the nominal genealogical sequence is tattooed on the face in gradual overlay to the point of a complete erasure and self-negation of personal identity.[29] Textual language repeated and overlaid is transformed into bodily marking. Qiu Zhijie's *Tattoo 1* photograph of 1997 utilizes the body and face as a natural surface for a graph that is similarly self-negating and marks a full and reciprocal incorporation of language into the human subject, and of the human subject into language.[30]

Each of the modes of natural language we have encountered represents an alternative to conventional language. Even *Square Word Calligraphy*, which comes closest to ordinary natural language in the most widespread usage of the term, involves a radical deformation and defamiliarization of scripts so that a conscious effort of recognition is required for decipherment, unlike the more or less automatic recognition of natural languages. This search for alternatives suggests a pervasive horizon of dissatisfaction with or mistrust of conventional language, whether from its liability to political or commercial manipulation, its openness to ambiguity, or from an exhaustion of impact through overuse and abuse. The kinds of natural language alternatives that are employed—linked variously to elemental sign systems, to the geophysical world, or to biological bodies—do not, however, provide the security of authenticity, simplicity, and directness of meaning that might be expected.

The overarching outlook of the various projects ranges from the extreme distrust and pessimism about the possibility of meaningful communication in *A Book from the Sky* (Figure I.1) and *Printing on Water* to the hopeful transculturalism of *Square Word Calligraphy* (Figure 4.1) and *United Nations Series*, but in each case the starting point is at least a condition of frustration of expectations, defamiliarization, and categorical disorientation.

To counterbalance these insecurities, these projects offer primarily the materiality of natural language-making contexts, as process of facture (*A Book from the Sky* and *United Nations Series*), as embodied text (*American Silkworm Series*, Figure 4.4), or as perceptual horizon (*Landscript*). Natural languages are thus sometimes deployed in ways that are compensatory for language loss and corruption, or restorative of deep cultural identities. More often than not, however, natural languages are referenced in ways that deny, suspend, complicate, and interfere with legibility and meaning. In contrast to the intrinsic promise of natural language as a universal code of intelligibility, contemporary art practice often denatures language.

NOTES

1. For a sampling of Mao imagery in this period see Wu Hung, *Transience: Chinese Experimental Art at the End of the Twentieth Century* (Chicago: Smart Museum of Art, 1999), 43–53.

2. See, for example, Fredric Jameson, *Postmodernism and Cultural Theories: Lectures in China (Houxiandaizhuyi he Wenhualilun.* (Xi'an: Shaanxi Teacher's University, 1987). See also Jing Wang, *High Culture Fever: Politics, Aesthetics, and Ideology in Deng's China* (Berkeley and Los Angeles: University of California Press, 1996); also Erickson, *The Art of Xu Bing*, 14.

3. See Frank J. Swetz, "Leibniz, the Yijing, and the Religious Conversion of the Chinese," *Mathematics Magazine* (October 2003).

4. See Haun Saussy, "*China Illustrata:* The Universe in a Cup of Tea," in *The Great Art of Knowing: The Baroque Encyclopedia of Athanasius Kircher*, ed. Daniel Stolzenberg, 111–112 (Stanford, CA: Stanford University Libraries, 2001), for the "supposed natural stage common to Egyptian and Chinese writing."

5. See Steven Pinker, *The Language Instinct: The New Science of Language and Mind* (New York: Morrow, 1994).

6. For medieval theories of natural signs, though the primarily linguistic rather than the theological, see Andrea Tabarroni, "Mental Signs and the Theory of Representation in Ockham," in *On the Medieval Theory of*

Signs, ed. Umberto Eco and Costantino Marmo, 195–224 (Amsterdam and Philadelphia: John Benjamins Publishing Company, 1989).

7. See Stephen Little, ed., *Taoism and the Arts of China* (Chicago: The Art Institute, 2000), cat. no. 14, p. 139.

8. See ibid., cat. nos. 53–55, pp. 201–205, for early, Tang dynasty examples of Daoist talismanic manuscripts from Dunhuang.

9. See Gao Minglu, ed., *Inside Out: New Chinese Art* (San Francisco: Museum of Modern Art, 1998), 15.

10. Ibid., 198–199.

11. Wilhelm and Baynes, *The I Ching or Book of Changes*.

12. *Sacrifice au feu*, at Saint-Victoire, France, in 1990.

13. See Jean-Hubert Martin, et al., eds., *Magiciens de la terre* (Paris: Editions du Centre Pompidou, 1989), 152–153.

14. See Gao Minglu, *Inside Out*, 4.

15. For the background of the titles of both projects, see Erickson, *The Art of Xu Bing*, 41–52.

16. Ibid., 41.

17. See Wen Fong, et al., eds., *Images of the Mind: Selections from the Edward L. Elliott Family and John B. Elliott Collections of Chinese Calligraphy and Painting at The Art Museum, Princeton, University* (Princeton, NJ: The Art Museum, 1984), 82.

18. See Erickson, *The Art of Xu Bing*, 72–73.

19. See Julia Meech-Pekarik, "Disguised Scripts and Hidden Poems in an Illustrated Heian Sutra: Ashide and Uta-e in the Heike Nogyo," *Archives of Asian Art* 31 (1977–1978): 53–78.

20. See Robin Allott, "Language and the Origin of Semiosis," in *Origins of Semiosis: Sign Evolution in Nature and Culture*, ed. Winfried Noth, 255–268 (Berlin and New York: Mouton de Gruyter, 1994).

21. See Gao Minglu, *Inside Out*, 9.

22. See Erickson, *The Art of Xu Bing*, 63.

23. See Wu Hung, Wang Huansheng, and Feng Boyi, eds., *The First Guangzhou Triennial: A Decade of Experimental Chinese Art (1990–2000)* (Guangzhou: Guangdong Museum of Art, 2002), 480–481.

24. For *Panda Zoo*, see ibid., 2.

25. Ibid., 41.

26. Cf. the discussion in ibid., 60–62.

27. See Thomas A. Sebeok, "Goals and Limitations of the Study of Animal Communication," in *Perspectives in Zoosemiotics* (The Hague: Mouton and Co., 1972), 117.

28. See Erickson, *The Art of Xu Bing*, fig. 44, p. 62.

29. For both Huang Yan and Zhang Huan works, see Wu Hung and Christopher Phillips, eds., *Between Past and Future: New Photography and Video from China* (Chicago: Smart Museum of Art, 2004), cat. 101, p. 140, and cat. 107.

30. See Wu Hung, *Transience*, 173–174, 22.

CHAPTER FIVE

The Living Word

Xu Bing and the Art of Chan Wordplay

APRIL LIU

Since emigrating from China to the United States in 1990, Xu Bing has developed a unique format of art connected to his position as an artist of the Chinese diaspora. Featured in prestigious exhibitions around the world, his work has received critical acclaim across Asia, Australia, Europe, and North America. As for many Chinese artists who moved abroad after the 1989 Tiananmen Square demonstrations, Xu Bing's use of "traditional" Chinese cultural elements has become a particularly problematic topic of discussion. In a highly competitive contemporary art market, artists of the diaspora are often criticized for self-exoticizing their works by using "traditional" themes and media. At the same time, they are accused of borrowing too much from the "West," to the extent of having lost touch with their native cultures.[1] Perpetually framed by such debates around cultural identity and authenticity, diasporic artists face significant challenges in creating works that transcend these predetermined categories.

Xu Bing is particularly skilled in dealing with this double bind. Keeping his foreign audience in mind, his strategies for introducing "traditional" Chinese elements are cleverly combined with a deconstruction of basic cultural categories. Inspired by Chan Buddhist philosophy, Xu Bing's influential works have dealt with the liminology of language and an evocation of what Chan masters call "living words" (*shengyu* 生语), including nonsensical, paradoxical, or tautological wordplay. These themes allow the artist to access and perform "tradition" while simultaneously denying its fixed identity and meaning. Starting with his earliest works as a studio art student in China (*Five Series of Repetition*, 1987) and continuing through to his recent installations in Europe and North America (*Where Does the Dust Itself Collect?*, 2004), Xu Bing's interest in Chan is enacted at the level of process and experimentation. However, the majority of critical texts concerning his work only give brief mention to this salient theme. Existing critiques have addressed his interest in language from the perspective of cultural identity, ideology, and postmodern discourses of Euro-American academia.[2] By drawing connections between Chan texts and Xu Bing's art, I intend to map out an alternative reading of his interest in language and wordplay. A close examination of several key works will illustrate the rich diversity of Chan linguistic strategies that have inspired Xu Bing's art.

Before setting out on this project, it is important to keep in mind Xu Bing's intention behind accessing a Chinese cultural discourse, which is to speak to a larger audience. Xu Bing has stated, "I have no choice but to draw from my own cultural tradition, which has been filtered by Mao's Cultural Revolution. I feel that to use Chinese cultural elements to address global issues, to participate in global cultural debates, is a positive development . . . the real problem is not what materials or cultural elements one uses, but the level of one's reflection."[3] By citing the Cultural Revolution, Xu Bing reminds audiences of the disorienting ideological campaigns that have challenged the very foundations of traditional culture in his generation. For Xu Bing, the nebulous concept of "traditional culture" is thus less important than an artwork's potential for engaging in global dialogue. These statements reflect his desire to transcend his local context to speak to a larger, global community. This is a challenging task since non-Western artists participating in such "global dialogue" are often denied the global perspective, whereas "Western artists must always transcend their particular context and be representative of a universal perspective. The same status of universality is not extended globally."[4]

In a statement that encapsulates a unique dilemma of Chinese diaspora artists, Gu Wenda has pointed out the cultural misreadings of their works:

Artists like Xu Bing and I use Chinese elements, but not in a traditional way. This is difficult for non-Chinese audiences unfamiliar with Chinese culture to understand. They think we are using traditional Chinese elements when we are not. At the same time, conservative Chinese intellectuals criticize us for revisionism. This is a dilemma we face because of the isolation and the ensuing level of incomprehension between different cultures.[5]

The problematic positioning of diasporic artists, displaced from conventional categories, yet caught between the presumed access/denial of their own cultural "traditions," is further exacerbated by the tradition versus modernity divide. Nikos Papastergiadis emphasizes the lack of discussion on the "diasporization" of culture, where "tradition and modernity appear to be caught in a duel to the death over the identity of culture." By setting up a contestatory model between tradition and modernity, one overlooks the "resilience of the old in the form of the new, the unconscious repetition of previous habits within current practices, the subtle transpiration of traditional values in contemporary norms."[6]

In the midst of many competing claims to authentic "tradition," it becomes impossible to identify any singular and unified "Chinese cultural tradition." For instance, generalized terms such as "Chan Buddhism" and "Daoism" evolve from Euro-American scholarly constructions that bundle together the immense diversity of Buddhist and Daoist practice. Xu Bing's references to Chan Buddhist ideas are also broadly construed rather than having close connections to any specific Buddhist school. His invocation of Chan takes place primarily within the contexts of his personal art practice and the international art world. By keeping this discussion grounded in the specific contexts of his art production, one can avoid generalizations of "Chinese tradition" while locating Xu Bing's subtle acts of enacting and translating Chan ideas.

TRANSLATIONS OF THE LIVING WORD

In particular, I shall focus on the Chan notion of the "living word" (*shengyu* 生语), which has inspired Xu Bing's works on multiple occasions. The term, which can be traced to the Tang dynasty (618–907 CE) or earlier, signals a long and varied history of skillful linguistic strategies used by Chan masters to evoke experiences of "sudden awakening." To unpack this notion of the "living word," one must turn to the corpus of historical Chan texts, including master–disciple dialogues, instructional sayings, poetic verses, and anecdotal narratives. Many early Chan records were collected and assembled during the Song period (960–1279 CE), providing the foundation for classic anthologies such as the *Blue Cliff Record* (*Biyanlu* 碧岩录, 1125 CE) and *Transmission of the Lamp* (*Jingde Chuandenglu* 景德传灯录, 1011 CE).[7] Primarily based on oral transmissions rather than doctrinal treatises, these records embody the soteriological functions of "living words" as they are used in specific situations. In comparing Xu Bing's use of the "living word" with that of Tang and Song Chan masters, I shall focus on the Chan interest in paradox, tautology, and poetic or indirect language. In *Linguistic Strategies in Daoist Zhuangzi and Chan Buddhism: The Other Way of Speaking* (2003), Wang Youru takes a "liminology of language" approach to study these Chan linguistic strategies and examines how spaces of meaning are opened up beyond the confines of conventional language.[8] I will draw from his approach to explore a similar function in Xu Bing's use of creative wordplay.

In an artist statement titled "The Living Word," Xu Bing's opening paragraph explains his interest in Chan:

> Many strange dialogues are recorded in the annals of Chan (禅, Zen) Buddhism. In the *Collected Works of Buddhism* is the question, "What is Buddha?" the master responds: "The neigh of a wooden horse." How could the Buddha be the neigh of a wooden horse? A student might ponder this all day without coming to a conclusion, yet perhaps the day will come when he "suddenly bumps upon the proper road and realizes what has been clouding his vision." Such "sudden realization" in Chan Buddhism is called Enlightenment. This Chan method of revelation can lead you to understand the errors in your thinking and everyday logic. The real origins of truth cannot be found in a literal, logical answer but instead must be searched for in the living word.—Xu Bing[9]

According to Xu, the absurdist answer given by the master provokes thought and exploration on the part of the student. Since a wooden horse cannot neigh, the student is asked to ponder an obvious paradox until a moment of spontaneous clarity occurs. It is not quite clear exactly *what* is being realized in the "sudden realization." Is it an awakening to the mind's attachment to logic, which can never solve a paradox? Or is it simply the awareness that one is trying to read too much into the master's response, which has performed the important function of prompting a moment of reflection and introspection? Instead of providing a literal, logical answer that would bring about an end to the questioning, the master used a nonsensical response to catalyze the student's probing search.

I would like to highlight two key features of the Chan "*gongan* 公案" dialogue as quoted by Xu Bing. First, the answer points to itself as a nonsensical answer, prompting an increased awareness of expectations in ritualized speech. In other words, this state of awareness becomes the "answer" to the question; or, one could say, the master's answer prompted the student to "see" the answer rather than "know" the answer. The process of "seeing" can be understood as an unmediated and embodied experience of self-awareness. In contrast, the process of "knowing" entails a mediated understanding of an answer that only makes sense within a preexisting set of assumptions or expectations. A nonsensical answer is one that evades any such framework. It therefore halts the mediated process of "knowing" while provoking a direct experience of "seeing." In *Daodejing: "Making This Life Significant": A Philosophical Translation* (2003), Roger Ames and David Hall draw this distinction to explain some key aspects of Chinese cosmology and its expression in language:

> A comparison with the analytical epistemic language of "getting," "grasping," "comprehending" is important here. Rather than a language of mediation in which the essences of things are abstracted through concepts, the Chinese language tends to be dispositional in that it promotes the "having" of the unmediated experience through a correlating and focusing of the affairs of the day.

Taking the aesthetic experience as an example, Ames and Hall illustrate the differences between a cognitive knowledge that abstracts from experience and "felt experience as the concrete content of knowledge."[10]

A second key feature of this Chan dialogue is the use of language to question the adequacy of language itself. The distrust of language as a medium for transmitting wisdom is commonly found in Chan texts and can be traced to Acharya Nagarjuna's (ca. 150–250 CE) *Fundamental Wisdom of the Middle Way (Mūlamadhyamakakārikā)*, a philosophical treatise that significantly influenced Mahayana Buddhism in China. Nagarjuna's nondualist perspective speaks of the human mind's tendency to be trapped in language and dual concepts, a problem that must be dealt with repeatedly in a fully conscious manner. Any dichotomizing of mind into subject and object, being and nonbeing, enlightenment and delusion, is an illusory grid work that prevents one from experiencing and understanding situations as they really are. Thus Nagarjuna's formula of "neither *x* nor not *x*" was intended to halt a habitual process of linguistic reification in which one side is favored over the other. Binary language perpetuates the false belief that opposites can exist as two independent entities, separate from contextual circumstances. Thus phenomena are described as "empty" in Buddhist literature; it generally signifies this lack of independent existence and closed, fixed identity. Nagarjuna, who insisted that the Buddha himself held no views, developed the critique of dualistic thinking to include all philosophical positions and concepts, which can only exist in opposition to an antithesis.

Wang Youru explains how Chan Buddhists of the Tang period adapted Nagarjuna's thinking by replacing its modes of rigid logical analysis with the simplified use of paradox (juxtaposition or negation of opposites). This practice coincided with the Chan attitude of nonreliance on theoretical teachings and of seeking realization in mundane activities.[11] As a distinct characteristic of Chan discourse, paradoxical language was used to disengage from rational philosophizing and to awaken a practitioner from dualistic thought. Wang cites Tang dynasty Chan master Baizhang Huaihai's (百丈怀海, 720–814) account of living words (*shengyu* 生语) as differentiated from dead words (*siyu* 死语): "Those sayings that there is cultivation and there is realization, that this mind is Buddha . . . are *dead words*. Those sayings that there is neither cultivation nor realization, that it is neither mind nor Buddha . . . are *living words*" and "Neither identity nor difference, neither impermanence nor permanence, neither coming nor going- these are *living words* . . . [the binary distinctions of] coming, going, impermanence, permanence, Buddha and sentient beings, are *dead words*."[12] This account negates a series of opposites to illustrate a pattern of dualism within conventional language. The use of living words is thus a strategy to resist any kind of predication. In doing so, one stumps the logical, either/or mentality of mind to open up new spaces of experience.

These two features of living words—the unmediated experience of knowledge and wordplay's soteriological function of catalyzing nondual states of mind—are both found in Xu Bing's works, including his acclaimed *A Book from the Sky* (1987–1991, Figures I.1). In this piece, Xu spent nearly four years hand carving four thousand nonsensical characters made of reconfigured Chinese radicals. The paradox of creating a noncommunicative language is facilitated by the illusion of being a "real" language. Thus a heightened tension is achieved between the familiar and the unfamiliar. *A Book from the Sky* lures viewers in via familiar cultural signifiers, then proceeds to disrupt all expectations for meaning. By visually "halting" the access to meaning, there is no mediation of meaning through language. As "empty" symbols, the nonsensical characters reflect back on the expectations of the viewer and thus create a heightened awareness of the viewing experience. This can be compared to the poetic phrasing of "the neigh of a wooden horse" response, which uses visual and auditory associations to "hook" one's imagination before stumping all expectations for a logical "answer."

Existing interpretations of *A Book from the Sky* have addressed it as an act of "anti-writing" or "anti-ideology," first in the context of Chinese politics in the late 1980s and later, in the context of the international art world.[13] The earlier interpretations positioned the work as an antiauthoritarian piece, in reaction to a totalitarian Chinese regime. The nonsensical texts were compared to the ideological texts that flooded the Cultural Revolution landscape and Xu Bing's experience as a propaganda painter was often cited.[14] Since Xu Bing's move abroad, interpretations have focused on the work's position in the global art circuit and its potential for casting "traditional" Chinese features in a "modern" (i.e., Western) idiom. Patricia Karetzky, for example, wrote an article entitled "A Modern Literati: The Art of Xu Bing" (2001).[15]

These various interpretations elucidate important aspects of *A Book from the Sky* and form part of its historical trajectory in contemporary art; however, they reflect a common fixation on issues around political and cultural identity. This reflects the curatorial concerns of Euro-American art institutions in the 1990s, which tended to focus on the "cultural memory/identity/art equation" when introducing contemporary Chinese art to international audiences.[16] However, if we take Xu Bing's interest in Chan as an important factor of his work, there are other possible readings for *A Book from the Sky*. The Chan approach to deconstructing structures of knowledge is not merely focused on evading meaning or challenging authority, nor is it interested in forming theoretical frameworks around identity or tradition. Instead, the Chan texts are geared towards the pragmatic goal of catalyzing an unmediated, embodied experience of nonduality. By revealing the inseparable nature of content and form, of message and mode of delivery, Xu Bing's nonsensical language draws attention to the experiential realm.

How can a contemporary art piece translate a Chan idea? Is it possible to engage translation as a creative, transformative act rather than an objective transfer of meaning? How can Chan concepts translate into Anglo-European discourses that have evolved from a fundamentally logocentric perspective? A possible response to these questions is to convey meaning through direct experience rather than linguistic means. Xu Bing's works suggest that Chan concepts are best translated when they are not mentioned at all. While *A Book from the Sky* employs paradox and indirect communication without making direct reference to Chan, Xu Bing's artist statements inform us that he draws from Chan ideas. Xu Bing's "silent" enactment of a Chan strategy points to the Chan idea that meaning is more effectively communicated through "showing" and not "telling."

Wang Youru quotes the view of mid-Tang dynasty records of the Hongzhou Chan School, where the enlightened person "always speaks in terms of function, having no fixation whatsoever on either affirmation or negation." There are thus no contradictions in the Chan teachings as long as they prompt a "sudden awakening."[17] Living words are thus pragmatic tools, playing a *therapeutic* or *prescriptive* role within specific teacher and student interactions. A literal translation of these words into the theoretical or descriptive norms of Euro-American philosophical discourse would necessarily entail a loss of the dialogues' original function and intended effects. The act of translation thus entails an entire paradigm shift in the linguistic structuring of human interaction. Put simply, an English translation becomes descriptive of Chan practice, a fixed representation of Chan thought, rather than conveying the lived experience that is considered inseparable from its functional usage.

Given the spatiotemporal dimensions of installation art, this is where an artist can step in to enact creative translations beyond language. As an artist who has traversed the world to engage multiple cultural contexts, Xu Bing's sensitivity to translation is an integral factor of his international success. Drawing from Chan linguistic strategy to engage audiences experientially, he has explored the liminology of language through visual art. To borrow Wang Youru's definition of liminology in Chan wordplay, there are three major features[18]:

1. the radical problematization of the limit of language
2. insight into the mutual connection and transition between two sides of the boundary of language, between speaking and nonspeaking, etc.
3. play at the limit or boundary of language

These three aspects are identifiable in *A Book from the Sky*, which illustrates the limit of language by altering its visual form just enough to deny access to meaning. It also plays on the tension between speaking and nonspeaking by feigning the appearance of language. In doing so, it erases the hierarchical relationship between speaker and listener, between transmitter and receiver. As in the Chan dialogue quoted by Xu Bing, the student/listener must take a creative and engaged role in seeking transformation; one cannot simply duplicate the master's experience. Although one may harmonize or resonate with the master's experience, enlightenment must be experienced in the context of the present moment. To illustrate this point, Wang cites the following Chan story from *Transmission of the Lamp*:

> When Mazu Daoyi heard Master Damei Fachang lived in the mountain, he sent a monk there to ask, "What have you learned from Master Mazu so that you live in this mountain?" Damei answered, "Master Mazu taught me that mind is Buddha; accordingly I have settled here to live," The monk said, "Nowadays Master Mazu teaches a different Buddha-dharma." Damei asked, "What is the difference?" The monk said, "In these days he also teaches that there is neither mind nor Buddha." Damei said, "This old man confuses people without an end. No matter how you insist on saying 'There is neither mind nor Buddha,' I will pay attention only to 'Mind is Buddha.'" When Master Mazu heard the story after the monk's return, he remarked, "Oh brothers, the plum is now ripe." (For the Chinese word *damei* means big plum.)[19]

The creative relationship between master and student is emphasized, as is the student's freedom to choose a suitable path for his particular situation. The responses given by the master, "Mind is Buddha" or "Neither mind nor Buddha," are not more than empty phrases used to catalyze a student's realization in a temporary situation. This is an important teaching within itself, thus Damei is admired for having grasped the message. His nonattachment to the master's words is a sign of maturity and freedom.

Likewise, Xu Bing's translation of Chan wordplay invites a co-creative approach to meaning-making that levels the hierarchical playing ground of conventional dialogue. A logocentric view of culture privileges language as the site of knowledge, yet Xu Bing's work suggests just the opposite. By disconnecting the signified from the signifier, Xu Bing's invented "pseudo-language" opens up the field of communication across language barriers. For Xu Bing, the accessibility of a piece is what leads audiences to a deeper contemplation of meaning:

> I became troubled by the hierarchical relationship between contemporary art and its public audience. When people enter an art museum it is as if they have entered a place of worship. The audience often feels bewildered by the art they see. They then react with a feeling of guilt, as if their confusion was a reflection of their lack of education in art or culture. In fact, many works of contemporary art are lacking in thought and creativity although they present a shocking appearance to the audience. I hope that my works are clear and accessible to its audiences. I hope they are works that the audience can easily engage with. Once they are engaged, I hope that the audience can discover the deeper meanings in the work and become inspired in their own ways of thinking.[20]

In seeking to create accessible works, Xu Bing has also borrowed the spare and restrained aesthetics of Chan wordplay. For example, in his performance/installation piece *Parrot* (1994, Figure 5.1), Xu Bing bought a pair of parrots in Beijing and had them trained to recite phrases such as, "Why are you holding me prisoner? You bastards!" and "Humans are so boring! Modern art is crap!"[21] The simple repetition of stock phrases is humorous because it sets up an experience of paradox and absurdity. Knowing that the parrots' "words" are only mimicked sounds achieved through repetitive training, the listener becomes suddenly aware of his/her own conditioned responses to linguistic comprehension. When one laughs at this piece, is one prompted by the parrot's oblivious speech or one's own sense of awkwardness? The parrot's speech can be likened to the Chan master's tautological use of living words, where the master simply repeats the student's words:

Question: What is one drop of water from the source of Caoxi?
Answer: [It is] one drop of water from the source of Caoxi.
Question: What is the Buddha dharma?
Answer: The Buddha dharma
Question: What is the dharma of all dharmas?
Answer: The dharma of all dharmas . . . [22]

These "tautological answers" are meaningless but not useless. Within Chan soteriological practice, Wang explains tautology as a tool for "therapeutic shock," which violates normal rituals of predication by refusing to formulate a definition.[23] Any predicated answer to these questions would only reify the oppositional thinking of a dualistic frame of mind. Therefore, the unconventional and tautological response is intended to reverse the direction of predication.

The repetitive announcements of Xu Bing's parrots bring this strategy to life with a tongue-in-cheek playfulness, poking fun at the audience's expectation for meaning when none exists. According to Wang, the linguistic structure of Chinese is particularly suited to such practice: "The lack of strict subject-predicate structure in Chinese grammar facilitates the Chan master's deliberate

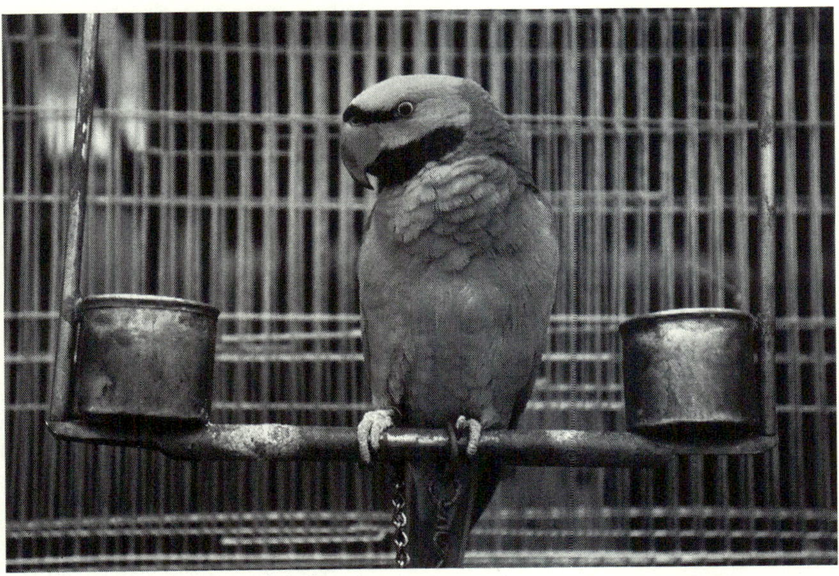

FIGURE 5.1. *Parrot*, Xu Bing, mixed-media installation and performance of live parrots, 1994. (Courtesy of the artist.)

rejection of definition."[24] Xu Bing's ingenious use of animals and trained mimicry allows a translation of Chan tautology in an English context. This is yet another form of the "living word" because it reveals the limits of language in a way that stumps the either-or pattern of thinking. Is the parrot speaking or not speaking? Is speech to be found in the speaker or the listener? It appears that the act of "speaking" is in of itself a relative concept, culturally constructed and contingent on the definitions we attach to it. The multivalent, contingent, and indeterminate nature of language is thus brought to the fore in a highly experiential manner.

This act of relativizing the limits of language is closely tied to the nonduality of speech and silence: "Once the absolute, impassable demarcation between silence and speech is obscured, the path for playing on the borders of language is opened."[25] Furthermore, it is this very freedom from fixating on silence or speech that "enables the Chan Buddhists, first of all, to relocate (or redefine) the positive role of language within the framework of the liminology of language."[26] In other words, Chan wordplay is not a rejection of logical language or an attempt to escape the inevitable use of language. Instead it attempts to draw out the full potential of language and its ability to be self-referential or "self-erasing." Wang therefore argues that Chan expressions are not "illogical" or "irrational" but "translogical" or "paralogical."[27]

This transformative, self-erasing effect of liminal language is conveyed in Xu Bing's installation, *The Living Word* (2001, Figure 5.2). The work illustrates the historical development of the Chinese character for "bird" (*niao* 鸟) from its ancient pictographic version to its contemporary simplified form. Displaying over four hundred variants, the bird characters "de-evolve" into their earliest forms as they fly away through the gallery stairwell. Visually, the characters appear to break free from the very limits of "language" and gradually enter the realm of the "image." This simple yet engaging work communicates the false boundaries between word, image, and meaning. These categories are revealed as culturally constructed concepts, inadequate for describing the multivalent nature of semiotic signs. The many versions of the bird character portray a state of spontaneous flux, as well as a return to the early origins of language. From the Chan perspective, the "living word" disrupts fixed meanings to bring about this dynamic state of being. Consider this passage by Tang dynasty Chan master Linji Yixuan (临济义玄, ?–886):

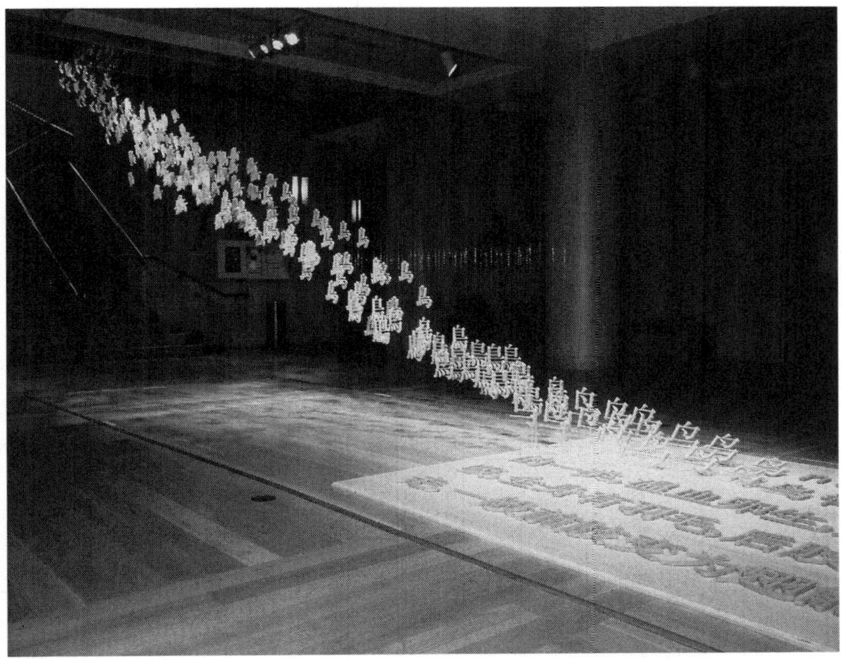

FIGURE 5.2. *The Living Word*, Xu Bing, installation of acrylic "bird" characters at the Arthur M. Sackler Gallery, Smithsonian Institution, 2001. (Courtesy of the artist; photo: Tsao Hsingyuan.)

> The mind changes in accordance with the myriad circumstances;
> The way it changes is truly profound.
> If you can realize its nature through this flow,
> You will have neither joy nor sorrow.[28]

In commenting on this passage and other similar examples, Wang emphasizes how "Chan thinkers never regard liberation or enlightenment as isolation or escape from the flowing reality of the everyday world. They rather consider it as a return from our isolated or fixed state of mind to this world of perpetual change and flux."[29] In Xu Bing's work, this state of flux is found in language itself, the "living word" that mirrors the natural, spontaneous state of the enlightened mind.

Let me now return to a central question of this chapter: What are the implications of reading these works from the Chan perspective? Xu Bing is not a Chan practitioner and his audiences may not be familiar with Chan discourse. Furthermore, his enactment of Chan strategies are generalized interpretations, taken out of the historical and practical Chan contexts, then applied in the removed formats of contemporary installation art. It may be a stretch of the imagination to see his art as a form of "Chan" art. Nonetheless, Xu Bing's interest in testing the limits of language produces successful translations of Chan strategies because they function at the experiential level. This allows his work to open up spaces for inter/cross/transcultural communication.

While the appropriation/circulation of cultural identities in the international art market sets the conditions for an artist's professional survival, Xu Bing's invocation of *living* words speaks to a desire to evade the *death* of imposed and fixed representations. Living words are those that point to a realm of experience beyond words and identity; they conjure up a realm of freedom unfettered by external constraints and dogmatic schemas. They also evoke a sense of transient and fleeting speech, alive only in the moment-to-moment acts of embodied enunciation. Likewise, this notion resonates deeply with Xu Bing's international touring, a mode of cultural exchange that constantly shifts as it enters into momentary dialogues with disparate cultures and locales.

Xu's work draws attention to the undertheorized notion of cultural translation, the possibility of mobilizing knowledge across multiple cultural contexts. However, this urgent topic is complicated by the difficulty of locating cultural boundaries, if only as shifting gray areas within performative contexts. Although one can identify broad distinctions between cultures, there is no simple way to identify how such differences come into play in contemporary contexts. There is no identifiable space from which to make objective, culturally neutral comparisons between different cultural traditions. Xu Bing's art embodies this dilemma by reorganizing disparate cultural signs so that their origins become undistinguishable. In the following section, I will address this strategy of "cultural camouflaging" and how it entails erasures of the artist's identity.

CULTURAL CAMOUFLAGE AND ERASURES OF IDENTITY

Starting with his earliest works, Xu Bing's interest in Chan philosophy has been connected to erasures of personal identity. In *Five Series of Repetitions* (1986–1987, Figure 5.3), a set of prints records the stages of a solid woodblock becoming gradually carved into scenes of fields and ponds until the entire surface is carved away, leaving only a blank hole in the center of the last image. Patricia Berger recognizes the work as an allusion to the famous *Ten Ox-Herding Pictures* theme, which usually portrays a symbolic Chan narrative of a herdboy (symbolic of "self") tracking and taming a wild ox (symbolic of "mind").[30] The herdboy's taming of the ox-mind succeeds in the end when they both disappear in the final image, an empty circle that suggests a transcendence of the subject–object duality. Xu Bing's carving of the block concludes in the same image, suggesting this unity of opposites. While referencing a traditional Chan narrative, Xu Bing's destruction of the image and the woodblock itself speaks to a circular process of being and nonbeing; the act of carving is seen as creating and erasing at the *same* time. This circular process is also found in his later works such as *American Silkworm Series Part I and II* (1994, 1995, Figure 4.4) and *The Case Study of Transference* (1994, Figure 4.6).

In *American Silkworm Series Part I and II*, Xu arranges silkworm eggs in linear strips onto a blank book so they appear as lines of "text." Once the eggs begin to hatch, the "text" literally comes alive and the neatly organized rows begin to wriggle off the page. As the worms grow, they continue to transform the book into

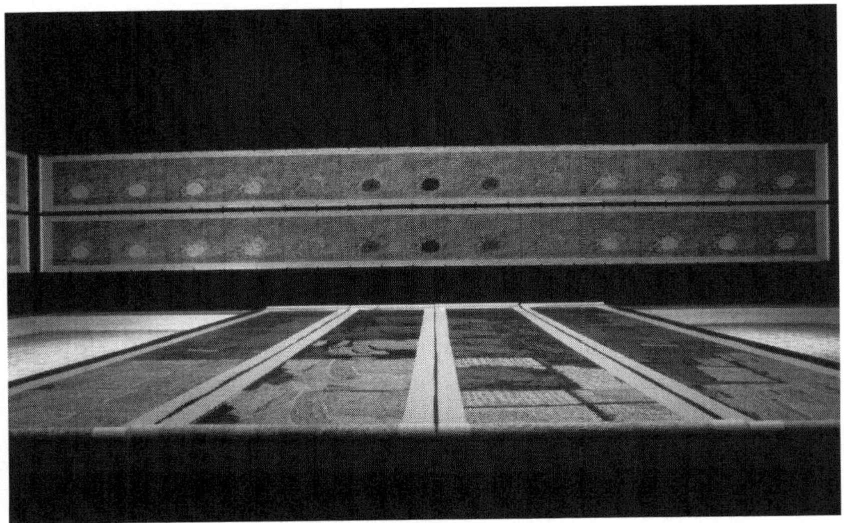

FIGURE 5.3. *Five Series of Repetition*, Xu Bing, series of woodblock prints on paper, 1986–1987. (Courtesy of the artist.)

illegibility by spinning silk over it. In the second part of the series, the worms spin their threads onto various objects, such as Cultural Revolution artifacts, newspapers, and a computer system. Although the worms appear fragile and small, their collective labor renders the modern objects illegible. By creating, they are also erasing or obscuring. Being and nonbeing evolve simultaneously, naturally, and without any regard for "meaning." This work can be read as a vivid metaphor for "living words" that surpass "dead words," where the spontaneous "writing" of the silkworms is contrasted by the lifeless artifacts of communication. The silkworms' uncontrolled labor takes over the objects and the artist's agency/identity is thus significantly downplayed and subjected to chance.

Xu Bing has likened the repetitive acts of carving characters, practicing calligraphy, or harvesting silkworms to a form of Buddhist meditation in daily activity. By merging with the present moment of each act, the mind loosens its fixation on identity, its habitual distinction between subject and object, or doer and act. Xu recalls his dedication to traditional calligraphy as being an aspiration towards this liberating effect rather than an interest in content: "I have written so much, and now as I think back, it seems as if I was then like the Buddhist copiers of old. They did not need to understand the meaning of each sutra that they copied. They only had to copy and recopy a lifetime's worth of sutras to gain entrance into the next world."[31] Xu Bing has often commented on his interest in craft as an introspective act. He describes calligraphy as combining "artistic expression and spiritual energy. From the first stroke of a word to its completion, our entire bodies are involved. It is a process of communing with nature, of experiencing consummate beauty, and of discovering our inner selves."[32]

Although some critics suggest that Xu Bing's works are successful because they put elements of exotica or "traditional" culture on display for foreign audiences, I would like to entertain another possibility—that Xu Bing's works are successful because they make use of elements that are rather culturally familiar to Euro-American audiences. For example, Xu Bing's overarching interest in language coincides with the "linguistic turn" in postmodern discourse as led by French intellectuals such as Roland Barthes, Michel Foucault, and Jacques Derrida. On a more popular level, Xu Bing's monumental works engage the general public with commonly seen media, including books, computers, modern appliances, and animals. Using the well-established idiom of installation art, Xu overwhelms the senses with these objects, from piles of books and scrolls to live animals squirming and mating before one's very eyes. There is also a great deal invested in getting the audience actively involved in the work, as seen in *Square Word Calligraphy* (1994–2000, Figure 4.1), where audiences are taught to write different languages in a manner that looks like Chinese calligraphy.[33]

This dual function of engaging scholarly tastes as well as that of the general populace reflects a skillful manipulation of familiar elements. Whether making the foreign familiar or making the familiar foreign, Xu Bing's works often confuse an audience's expectation for locating the multiple "cultural origins" at play. Xu Bing has described this strategy as a form of "cultural camouflage."[34] By masking or disguising one's ideas in a conflation of cultural references, the artist can take subterfuge from various forms of imposed meaning. Many contemporary Chinese artists have experimented with this strategy; a notable example is the Paris-based installation artist, Huang Yongping. Huang began his career as the leader of Xiamen Dada, a subversive collective of experimental Chinese artists in the 1980s. Known for his famous statement, "Chan is Dada, Dada is Chan," Huang employed the rhetoric of European Dada and Fluxus movements to challenge the theoretical foundations of Socialist Realism and expressive trends in art. By invoking Chan, Huang simultaneously sought access to a traditional Chinese discourse that provided the philosophical bases for deconstructing the foundations of culture and ideology. By locating the same set of ideas in multiple philosophical discourses, it becomes impossible to pin down the origin of his ideas.

By equating Chan and Dada, Huang strategically elides any conflicting tensions between Chinese and European traditions. Instead, he celebrates their commonalities: "Postmodernism thus is the modern renaissance of Chan Buddhism. Both are known by their openness and depth, and have no aesthetic significance. They are concerned with the fact that the real cannot be real, they doubt and do not believe."[35] Martina Koppel-Yang has interpreted this as an effort to "catapult contemporary Chinese art and culture directly from the phase of post-impressionism and expressionism into that of postmodernism."[36]

Huang's works from this period, including the *Roulette Series* (1986–1988), *Four Paintings Created According to Random Instructions* (1985), and *"A History of Chinese Painting" and "A Concise History of Modern Painting" Washed in a Washing Machine for Two Minutes* (1987/1993) are experiments in combining Eastern and Western philosophical traditions. In *Roulette Series,* he altered roulette wheels to include markers ranging from *Yijing (Book of Changes* 易经) diagrams to everyday gestures. Inspired by John Cage, who used the *Yijing* as a composition tool for his "chance-controlled music" in the 1950s, Huang also used it to generate "random" instructions directing the actions of the artist.[37] Huang thus eliminated the artist as an operative subject and used chance as the determining agent for creating art. Similar to Xu Bing's works, this cross-referencing of different artistic and philosophical sources can also be read as a form of "cultural camouflage."

Both Xu Bing and Huang Yongping moved overseas and began referencing Chinese "tradition" in new contexts. While in China, their references to tradition came under the scrutiny of totalitarian authorities; in the move overseas, these same references have become muted and depoliticized. In response to their new audiences, both artists have diversified their approaches to reference many different cultural sources. This reflects a period of adjustment and uncertainty as they redefine themselves amidst their skyrocketing popularity. Comprised mostly of young males who left China in the late 1980s, artists such as Xu Bing, Huang Yongping, Cai Guoqiang, and Gu Wenda are pioneers in defining what it means to be a diasporic Chinese artist. Without any precedent to follow, these artists were suddenly thrust into the role of representing "China" at the same moment of being displaced from their homelands. As newly minted celebrities of the international art world, these artists remain hardly known within China. The rapidly changing dynamics of China's unprecedented economic growth further magnifies the artists' displacement from China while raising the stakes of their interaction with Euro-American institutions.

PERFORMING DIFFERENCE: THE CASE STUDY OF TRANSFERENCE (1994)

In this situation, Chinese diasporic artists face a particularly heightened sense of being put on display to perform a Chinese cultural identity. The strength of Xu Bing's works lies in his continued attempts to enact Chan-inspired intellectual strategies at the level of process rather than physical representation. For example, in the mid-1990s, Xu began using nonsensical language and cultural camouflage to perform public spectacles. In *The Case Study of Transference*

(1994, Figure 4.6) and *Cultural Animal* (1994), Xu Bing creates a nonsensical language with Roman letters to be contrasted with the one made of Chinese radicals in *A Book from the Sky* (Figure I.1). In *The Case Study of Transference*, a male pig is "linguistically tattooed" with the nonsensical English while a female one is marked with the nonsensical Chinese. The live pigs are then placed inside a pen to mate in front of an audience that is being videotaped for spontaneous reactions. The pigs, oblivious to their markings, proceed to the task of mating while prompting viewers to examine their own "cultural baggage."

Xu Bing explains how the piece "juxtaposes culture and something primordial, something prehistoric, to clarify a certain aspect of culture. . . . When the people watch the pigs, they think of themselves more than the pigs. This is the point of the piece. I want people to think of their human selves, not to know more about pigs. Their embarrassment demonstrates how far we are from nature."[38] The work's blatant use of shock value implies an underlying sarcasm towards the sensationalist modes of representation in contemporary art. The procreating pigs are put on display as the artist-creators, exposing their vulnerability as well as their blissful ignorance of the cultural games they've become pawns for. I am tempted to read *The Case Study of Transference* as a metaphor for Xu Bing's ongoing struggle to define his work within a diasporic context, caught in a chaotic battlefield of cultural identities and imposed media representations. Xu Bing's creation of "Chinese" and "English" nonsensical languages diminishes their cultural differences to the visual, a "cultural camouflaging" of fixed identity.

Critics of contemporary "non-Western" art have observed how the identity/difference dialectic ultimately serves to fix and subdue the "Other" into a represented object. Commenting on the Third Asia-Pacific Triennial of Contemporary Art (1999), Charles Green observes, "Difference is not now treated, in exhibitions and art magazines, as ceaseless flow and change, but as a new look—as a set of fixed cultural distinctions and a grid of emblematic contrasts and significations."[39] Similarly, in relation to Latin American art, Nelly Richard speaks of how the reorganization of cultural signs is an old tactic for cultural and economic colonization. The Latin American "difference" is called upon "to illustrate how the mentality of the center today finds itself ready to break out of its Eurocentric closure." Thus Richard critiques the use of the word "difference" and suggests using "situational specificity" in its place, reminding authors to ground their discussions in concrete and reflective locations so that socioeconomic and cultural imbalances are not easily overlooked.[40]

As marginal groups gain acceptance in mainstream institutions, slogans such as the 'crisis of the subject' or 'death of the author' are deployed as misleading mottos suggesting a significant collapse of power and authority. Take, for instance, the 'death of the author' notion, which originates from Roland Barthes's efforts to liberate the text from authority by shifting the production of knowledge away from the author and into the hands of the readers. Using linguistics as an analytical and deconstructive tool, Barthes's 'death of the author' radically challenged the master narratives of the Euro-ethnic modernist tradition.[41] The death of the modernist author thus played a key role in the subsequent dismantling of the modernist canon's foundations, and by extension, its oppressive exclusion of marginal culture. However, by the 1990s, the institutional acceptance of the 'death of the author' topic depoliticized its usage as it was endorsed by the very cultural authorities it had initially sought to challenge.

In response to this situation, Nelly Richard has articulated the "reterritorialization of the center," which would signify not a collapse of power but a reinscription of "symbolic institutional credit."[42] According to Richard, these terms locate an international network of symbolic capital that grants authority and legitimacy (credit) through the use of language and the signaled endorsement of recognized institutions. The management of 'symbolic institutional credit' is enacted by a Eurocentric network of social and economic structures that reinforce the international imbalances of cultural power, including (but not limited to) museums, universities, publishing houses, cultural centers, and mass media corporations. This network of symbolic capital transcends geographic boundaries, controlling cultural exchange throughout the global market. The 'death of the author' or the 'crisis of the center/subject' become likened to marketable catchphrases that signify nothing more than an institution's readiness to embrace a fashionably postmodern image for itself.

Read within this context, Xu Bing's explorations of authorial erasure, wordplay, and cultural difference are well streamlined to lend 'symbolic institutional credit' to the major institutions that circulate his works. This is particularly evident in the major biennales that exhibit Xu Bing's art, such as the 45th Venice Biennial

(1993), the Gwangju Biennale (1997), the Sydney Biennale (2000, 2002), and the 26th Sao Paulo Biennial (2004), just to name a few. As cities catch on to the "biennale fever," various groups have jumped on the wagon to pump out art prizes, publications, and commercial promotions. Implicated in the metropolitan agendas for raising a city's international profile and cultural status, Xu Bing's widely circulated works have become hallmark pieces in the growing canon of "global art." In describing the commercialization of Chinese artists in the 1980s, Geremie Barme pointed to how artists were providing foreign collectors with "dissent on tap."[43] As Chinese diasporic artists move into the limelight, "liberated" from the constraints of Chinese nationality, one can observe a similar art market demand for "difference on tap." In the following section, I will explore the driving forces behind this desire for difference, especially when it references China.

CHAN AS CULTURAL CAPITAL: WHERE DOES THE DUST ITSELF COLLECT? (2004)

The increasingly sought after 'symbolic institutional credit' of high-profile contemporary Chinese art is a direct reflection of China's increasing influence in the geopolitical power plays of global affairs. Starting in the early 1990s, business periodicals and mainstream news sources began announcing China's economic boom and rise to global power. In 1993, *Time* magazine published a special report on China titled "The Next Superpower." By the late 1990s, leading industrialized nations (including the United States, Canada, France, Germany, and Great Britain) had sent their heads of state to China to intensify trade relations, coming home with billion-dollar deals. In 2001, China's fifteen-year bid to enter the World Trade Organization was finally granted, securing China's role as a serious global player.[44]

Embedded in the euphoric reports of China's rise to power is a sense of threat and awe. Images of Xu Bing's works have been repeatedly implicated in these discourses. A recent example is the inside cover of *The Atlantic* (July/August 2007), which featured a two-page reproduction of *A Book from the Sky* as a background image for its table of contents; the headlines read: "Special China Issue: China Makes, the World Takes," "Why China's Rise Is Good for Us," and "Superiority Complex: Why America's Growing Nuclear Supremacy May Make War with China More Likely."[45] Juxtaposed with these ambivalent headlines, the imposing color photograph of nonsensical Chinese text conveys the monumentality of China's power, size, and foreignness. However, the neutral visual aesthetics of the modern art gallery serves to tame and contain the menacing content of the headlines. The headline "Why China's Rise Is Good for Us" effectively positions the image as that of the Chinese "Other," in opposition to the American "us."

The political and cultural currency of Xu Bing's art is nowhere more clearly demonstrated than in his winning the first Artes Mundi Prize in 2004. Supported by a number of Welsh organizations and the Welsh Assembly Government, the award is part of a high-stakes bid to win the status of European Capital of Culture for the Wales capital of Cardiff. Valued at roughly US$72,000, Artes Mundi is the largest visual art prize to ever be awarded an individual artist. Open to artists from around the world, the Welsh Culture Minister Jenny Randerson said the prize would help put Wales on the "cultural map of the world."[46]

Xu Bing's winning submission, an installation titled *Where Does the Dust Itself Collect?* (2004, Figure 5.4), was commissioned for exhibit at the National Museum and Gallery in Cardiff. Using a leaf blower, Xu Bing covered the gallery floor with the 9/11 dust he collected near Ground Zero on September 11, 2001. Using large letter stencils that were removed once the dust settled, Xu inscribed onto the floor two lines of poetry: "As there is nothing from the first, where does the dust itself collect?" The English quote is a translation of two lines from a famous poem attributed to the Sixth Patriarch of Chinese Chan Buddhism, Huineng (惠能, 638–713), the leader of the Southern or "Sudden Awakening" School of Chan practice. Viewers enter the space on an elevated catwalk above the dust. On an adjacent wall, five photographs document how Xu Bing collected the dust and cast it into a toy doll for transport through international customs. The doll was then ground back into powder upon arrival in Cardiff.

By couching the controversial topic of 9/11 in the mysterious rhetoric of a Chinese Buddhist patriarch, Xu Bing's installation evades direct political or social commentary. At the same time, the physical presence of the 9/11 dust lends shock value to the simple installation. This combination of depoliticized content and visual sensationalism works well for the strategic interests of the Artes Mundi project. By choosing this installation to represent the debut of their award and biennial, the Welsh cultural authorities are well

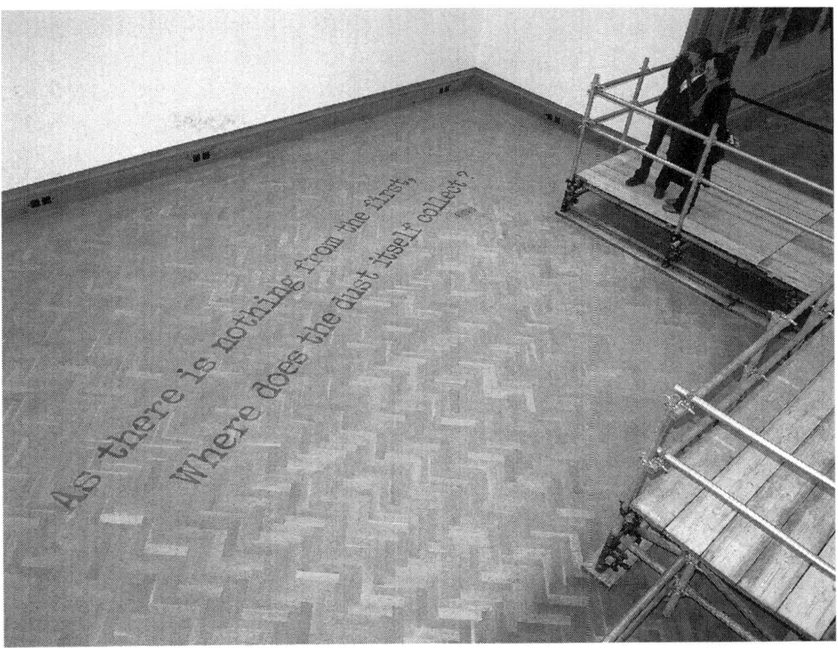

FIGURE 5.4. *Where Does the Dust Itself Collect?*, Xu Bing, installation with Chan quote and collected 9/11 dust from Ground Zero, 2004. (Courtesy of the artist.)

positioned to catch media headlines without taking a clear political stance. The Artes Mundi award can capitalize on its calculated "risk" of addressing the 9/11 events, a sign of contemporaneity and its engagement with the so-called "New World Order." Furthermore, by awarding a Chinese artist of the diaspora, the Artes Mundi team projects a progressive image of multicultural diversity and cultural exchange. The commission of this installation is thus closely aligned with institutional, national, and political agendas, clearly illustrating how a multitude of cultural signs are reorganized to dissolve the possibility of conflict or threat.

What can we make of Xu Bing's quotation of a Chan poem in this context? Although the quote provides an entry point to the Chan philosophy of Huineng, its translation into English removes the subtle connotations and culturally embedded meanings of the Chinese version. The phrase "As there is nothing" is a misleading English translation of *wu yi wu* 無一物, which literally means "not (empty of)-one-thing(ness)," an ontological concept based on a worldview of nonduality. Huineng's quote is taken from a longer poem, which is recognized as his response to a poem by his contemporary Shenxiu (神秀, 606?–706). The famous legend has it that Huineng and Shenxiu were both disciples of the Fifth Patriarch, Hongren (弘忍, ca. 601–675). Shenxiu, the elder disciple, is said to have sneaked into the quarters of the aging Fifth Patriarch under cover of night to affix the following poem to the wall:

Body is the Bodhi (wisdom) tree,	*shen shi pu ti shu*	身是菩提樹
Mind is like a bright mirror-stand.	*xin ru ming jing tai*	心如明鏡台
Take care to wipe it continually,	*shi shi qin fu shi*	時時勤拂拭
And allow no dust to cling.	*mo shi yo chen ai*	莫使有塵埃

The next night, Huineng, who was said to be illiterate, asked the servant boy to write down his response and tack it to the Fifth Patriarch's wall:

There is no Bodhi-tree,	*pu ti ben wu shu*	菩提本無樹
Nor stand of mirror bright.	*ming jing yi fei tai*	明鏡亦非台
As there is nothing from the first,	*ben lai wu yi wu*	本來無一物
Where does the dust collect itself?	*he chu you chen ai*	何處有塵埃

(*The Sutra of Huineng*, chap. 1[47])

From Shenxiu's standpoint, the mind is like an untainted mirror that reflects all the contents of the dusty world. To reveal the pure brightness of mind one must diligently engage in the meditation practices taught by Hongren, which is likened to a continual process of "wiping" or dusting. Shenxiu's dust refers to the impure attachments to thoughts, perceptions, and sensory distractions that would disturb or cloud the true state of inner tranquility.

Huineng's poem, however, holds that there is no such dust and no such purity of mind apart from the world, nor any concept or phenomena that can be said to exist as a singular, independently existing "thing." This nondual view shatters dichotomous notions of being/nonbeing or enlightenment/delusion. At first it appears that this is a refutation of Shenxiu's view through absolute negation. Yet this would only hold true if Huineng intended to affirm an opposing view in its place, a position that would bind him to the same dualism of his critique. Instead, by pointing to the empty nature of *all* phenomena, including any concepts of mind or wisdom, the statement must also admit to its own emptiness of meaning and is thus a "self-erasing" statement.[48] A dialectical rather than contradictory relationship is then established; Shenxiu's poem speaks at the level of *practice* where there is still a subject-practitioner and object of practice while Huineng's poem speaks at the level of *attainment* where notions of subject and object have dropped away spontaneously.[49]

Xu Bing's use of the last two lines from Huineng's poem highlights the crucial point of his response, and the underlying principle of the Southern School's perspective on sudden awakening. As mentioned earlier, the correspondence of *wu-yi-wu* 無一物 to the English phrase "there is nothing" is what alters the translation significantly. The character *wu* 無 is a philosophical concept that comes into regular usage through being combined with other characters. This body of terms has been referred to as the "*wu*-forms," to borrow Ames and Hall's explanation of their usage in the *Daodejing*.[50] The *wu*-forms embody a wide range of applications that describe the cultivation of a balanced, skillful, and nonwillful disposition, one that takes into account the lack of independent selfhood. In contrast, the English phrase "there is nothing" implies a static state of nihilistic void, a pervasive state of absolute nothingness. In seeking to be accessible, Xu Bing's use of an English translation fails at recognizing the cultural transformations that occur at the level of language.

Unlike *A Book from the Sky* and other works involving nonsensical languages, there is no creation of an ambiguous, disruptive space to reflect back onto the viewer's role. In these earlier works, there is no explicit use of a Chan dialogue, yet one can locate the elusive and paradoxical spirit of "living words," words that defy definition by playing at the very limits of language. Conversely, in *Where Does the Dust Itself Collect?*, there is an explicit translation of a famous Chan saying, yet the ontological connotations that are meant to disrupt dualistic thinking are lost in its English phrasing. Although Xu Bing privileges English to reach a specific audience, the reference to Chan is ironically more successful when there is no direct mention of Chan.

When asked about the symbolic meaning of this installation, Xu Bing calls attention to the elemental qualities of the dust itself: "In the West, it is possible that dust is not considered a material object of significance. However, within a Chinese cultural context, dust is in itself an important material object imbued with great substance. Of all materials, dust is an elemental entity that is both consistent and stable. The sudden collapse of the Twin Towers can be understood as an accumulation of too much material tension. Yet if you look at it from the perspective of Christians or Buddhists, both would agree that 'everything comes from dust and goes back to dust.'"[51] The dust thus achieves an equalizing effect in which all things are shown in their emptiness of identity. In observing the neutral gray dust, viewers cannot distinguish the fragments of building, concrete, and human debris, much less the remains of those who were "innocent" or "guilty." Like the self-erasing poem of Huineng, the dust is but a fleeting trail of the actual event that has long disappeared into the unapproachable past. This emphasis on the dust's neutrality allows Xu Bing to take a broader, more removed perspective on the events of 9/11. By reframing the event in apolitical terms, the controversial topic is presented in a way that is nonthreatening for its institutional sponsors and the general public.

CONCLUSION

While addressing Xu Bing's diverse application of Chan ideas, I have taken a twofold approach in this chapter. The first half focused on the philosophical implications of reading Xu Bing's work in a Chan context. In particular, his experiments with the liminological features of language have opened up spaces for moving Chan ideas across linguistic barriers. Works such as *A Book from the Sky*, *Parrot*, and *Living Word* are creative enactments of Chan wordplay without making direct reference to Chan. By functioning at the experiential rather than the representational level, these works expose the limits of language in both visual and aural terms. By playing at the limits of language, Xu Bing points to the transformative and therapeutic potential of language to catalyze nondual states of experience. This interpretation is a departure from earlier critiques that position his deconstruction of language as a subversive form of "anti-writing" or "anti-meaning." Most importantly, Xu Bing's art speaks to the profound richness of intellectual strategies available in Chan discourse as well as contemporary arts potential for greater inter-cultural contact and exchange. Despite the international media's tendency to flatten this richness into simplistic representations of cultural identity, Xu Bing's works invite a deeper contemplation of Chinese cultural resources.

As a way of situating these ideas in the specific contexts of their display, the latter part of this chapter highlights the institutional agendas that problematize his works' reception. This includes Xu Bing's complex position as a diasporic artist as well as the alignment of creative concerns with institutional, political, and commercial interests. Although my observations may suggest the artist's complicity in aligning his art with institutional agendas, I would emphasize the contrary. Xu Bing's works, especially his experiments with nonsensical languages and "cultural camouflage," provide interesting possibilities for challenging dominant discourses from within. Instead of going blindly for the bait, Xu Bing resists playing the facile role of the cultural "Other." His strategies of erasing identity and confusing cultural origins are at the very heart of this ongoing struggle. As seen in his creative wordplay, his invocation of Chan explores an experiential and imagined space outside of conventional paradigms of thought.

Without being compelled to locate an authentic Chan tradition in Xu's art, one can explore the constructive aspects of appropriation and translation. In 1983, Eric Hobsbawm and Terence Ranger published their influential anthology, *Invented Traditions*, which redefined the notion of "tradition" to highlight its socially constructed nature as well as its contemporaneity.[52] By using the term "invented," the authors problematize tradition's explicit link with a specific past and its formations of continuity. At the same time, they emphasize the significant ritual or symbolic functions of "tradition" in differentiation from similar concepts such as 'custom,' 'convention,' or 'routine.'

An appreciation of "tradition" as an invented cultural practice can shed light on the contributions of diasporic Chinese artists, who often draw upon Chinese cultural discourses to define the terms of representation and communication. In addressing this problem of who is speaking for whom, Nelly Richard has called for a realignment of institutional practices so the 'subject of difference' is given the resources to discuss/articulate their differences, modify the rules of enunciation, and "negotiate the conditions of the critical functioning of that difference in cultural systems."[53] Yet her tone remains skeptical towards the ability of prominent cultural institutions to actualize such a goal.

The institutional framing of Chinese identity is encapsulated by Bernhard Fibicher's "four topoi" for the curatorial representation of contemporary Chinese artists: "the topos of the Chinese artist as dissident, the topos of the exotic Chinese artist, the topos of the formerly Chinese, global artist; the topos of the Chinese artist as threat."[54] As rhetorical themes, these frameworks have all been used to describe Xu Bing's role in contemporary art at one time or another. All four paradigms are narrowly focused on the cultural identity of the artist, forming a unified set of shared characteristics for all contemporary Chinese artists despite the diversity in subject matter and media. Ironically, Chinese artists have come to represent "global diversity" through a categorical designation that downplays their own diverse backgrounds. This effect is compounded by stereotypes of a unified "Chinese cultural tradition or past" that all Chinese artists are expected to relate to. With great labor and dedication, Xu Bing has enacted Chan strategies to open up new spaces of communication and to coax audiences towards a more probing critique of culture itself.

NOTES

1. For a discussion on the critique of self-exoticizing in Xu Bing's art, see Simon Leung et al., "Pseudo-Languages: A Conversation with Wenda Gu, Xu Bing, and Jonathan Hay," *Art Journal* 58, no. 3 (Autumn 1999): 91–92. For a broader discussion on this topic in global art, see Ria Lavrijsen, ed., *Global Encounters in the World of Art: Collisions of Tradition and Modernity* (Amsterdam: Royal Tropical Institute, 1998).

2. See the annotated bibliography by Erickson, *The Art of Xu Bing: Words without Meaning, Meaning without Words* (Seattle and London: University of Washington Press, 2001): 78.

3. Leung et al., "Pseudo-Languages," 91.

4. Nikos Papastergiadis, "The Limits of Cultural Translation," in *Over Here: International Perspectives on Art and Culture*, ed. Gerardo Mosquera, 332 (London: MIT Press, 2005).

5. Leung et al., "Pseudo-Languages," 91–92.

6. Papastergiadis, "The Limits of Cultural Translation," 331.

7. See Heinrich Dumoulin, *Zen Buddhism: A History, India and China, Volume I* (Bloomington, IN: World Wisdom Inc., 1988, 2005), 245–256.

8. For a discussion of the "living word" concept in Chan discourse, see Wang Youru, *Linguistic Strategies in Daoist Zhuangzi and Chan Buddhism: The Other Way of Speaking* (London and New York: Routledge Curzon, 2003), 175–186.

9. Xu Bing, "The Living Word," trans. Ann L. Huss, in *The Art of Xu Bing: Words without Meaning, Meaning without Words*, 13.

10. See Ames and Hall, *Dao De Jing: "Making This Life Significant": A Philosophical Translation* (New York: Ballantine Books, 2003): 52.

11. Wang Youru, *Linguistic Strategies*, 114.

12. Ibid., 177.

13. See Wu Hung, *Transience: Chinese experimental art at the end of the Twentieth Century* (Chicago: University of Chicago Press, 1998).

14. For a discussion of the English-language interpretations of *Book from the Sky* through 1994, see Stanley K. Abe, "No Questions, No Answers: China and *A Book from the Sky*," *boundary 2* 25, no. 3 (Autumn 1998): 169–192.

15. Patricia Karetzky, "A Modern Literati: The Art of Xu Bing," *Oriental Art* xlvii, no. 4 (2001): 41–52.

16. For a discussion of curatorial paradigms around cultural identity, see Bernhard Fibicher, "Cultural Partnerships, Maybe More: On the Reception of Contemporary Chinese Art in the West," in *Mahjong: Contemporary Chinese Art from the Sigg Collection*, ed. Bernhard Fibicher and Matthias Frehner, 41–48 (Ostfildern-Ruit: Hatje Cantz Verlag, 2005). See also Charles Green, "Beyond the Future: The Third Asia-Pacific Triennial," *Art Journal* 58, no. 4 (Winter 1999): 85.

17. Wang Youru, *Linguistic Strategies*, 119–120.

18. Ibid., 6.

19. Ibid., 173.

20. For the entire interview transcription, see April Liu, "An Interview with Xu Bing: Nonsensical Spaces and Cultural Tatoos," *Yishu Journal of Contemporary Chinese Art* (December 2005): 88–95.

21. Erickson, *The Art of Xu Bing*, 63.

22. Wang Youru, *Linguistic Strategies*, 181.

23. Ibid., 180–186.

24. Ibid., 181.

25. Ibid., 118.

26. Ibid.

27. Ibid., 179.

28. Ibid., 178.

29. Ibid.

30. Patricia Berger, "Pun Intended: A Response to Stanley Abe, 'Reading the Sky,'" in *Cross-Cultural Readings of Chineseness: Narratives, Images, and Interpretations of the 1990's*, ed. Yeh Wenhsin, 88–89 (Berkeley: Institute of East Asian Studies, UC Berkeley, 2000).

31. Xu Bing quoted by Erickson, *The Art of Xu Bing*, 16.

32. Xu Bing quoted by Erickson, *The Art of Xu Bing*, 69.

33. For background information on this work, see Erickson, *The Art of Xu Bing*, 69–70.

34. Xu Bing discussed the issue of "cultural camouflage" in his public lecture "Meaning, Image, and Word" at the University of British Columbia, March 3, 2005. Video archive available at the UBC Visual Resources Library.

35. Huang Yongping, "Xiamen Dada—Postmodern?," in *Chinese Art Weekly* (*Zhongguo Meishu Bao* 中国美术报) 46 (1986): 1.

36. Martina Koppel-Yang, *Semiotic Warfare: The Chinese Avant-Garde, 1979–1989. A Semiotic Analysis* (Shenzhen: Timezone 8, 2004) 145.

37. For a discussion of this work, see Koppel-Yang, *Semiotic Warfare*, 132–149.

38. Quoted by Linda Weintraub, "Allegorical Personal," in *Animal. Anima. Animus*, 43–49 (Pori, Finland: Pori Art Museum, 1998).

39. Green, "Beyond the Future," 86.

40. Nelly Richard, "Postmodern Decentrednesses and Cultural Periphery: The Disalignments and Realignments of Cultural Power," in *Over Here: International Perspectives on Art and Culture*, ed. Gerardo Mosquera and Jean Fisher, 267 (London and Cambridge: MIT Press, 2004).

41. Roland Barthes, "The Death of the Author," in *The Death and Resurrection of the Author?* ed. W. Irwin, 3–9 (London: Greenwood Press, 2002).

42. Richard, "Postmodern Decentrednesses," 264.

43. See Geremie Barme, "Exploit, Export, Expropriate: Artful Marketing from China, 1989–93,"in *New Art from China, 1989–93*, ed. Johnson Chang, 47–51 (Hong Kong: Hanart, 1993).

44. Fibicher, "Cultural Partnerships," 41.

45. See inside cover and table of contents in the *Atlantic* 300, no. 1 (July–August 1997).

46. See BBC website: http://news.bbc.co.uk/1/hi/wales/3577285.stm and Artes Mundi website: http://www.artesmundi.org/.

47. Thomas Cleary, trans., *The Sutra of Hui-Neng Grand Master of Zen with Hui-neng's Commentary on the Diamond Sutra* (Boston: Shambala, 1998).

48. Wang Youru, *Linguistic Strategies*, 119.

49. For a discussion of this view, see D.T. Suzuki, *The Zen Doctrine of No Mind* (London: Rider and Company, 1969).

50. Ames and Hall, *Dao De Jing*, 36–48.

51. April Liu, "An Interview with Xu Bing: Nonsensical Space and Cultural Tattoos," in *Yishu Journal of Contemporary Chinese Art* 4.4 (2005): 88–95.

52. E. Hobsbawm and T. Ranger, eds., *Invented Traditions* (Cambridge: Cambridge University Press, 1983).

53. Richard, "Postmodern Decentrednesses," 264.

54. Fibicher, "Cultural Partnerships," 41.

CHAPTER SIX

Transmission of Meanings

A Study of Shen Wai Shen 身外身
(Body Outside Body) by Xu Bing 徐冰

KAZUKO KAMEDA-MADAR

INTRODUCTION: CULTURAL ALLIANCES

This chapter aims to explore Xu Bing's *Shen Wai Shen* (身外身, *Body Outside of Body*, Figure 6.1, hereafter, *Shen Wai Shen*), literally "body outside body," an installation that focuses on issues around the transformability of languages in the computer and digital age.[1] This installation recontextualizes how the Chinese written language, in the form of calligraphy, transcribed spoken Japanese and Korean languages of the past. It also explores how East Asian languages have been affected by the emergence of recent technologies. East Asia may be defined in either cultural or geographic terms, yet these definitions are not always taken into account in discussions concerning the art of the region. Considering the cultural instability and linguistic ambiguity of this region, I would like to propose that *Shen Wai Shen* is crucial for a study of the political, sociological, and ideological functions of Chinese-based writing systems, often considered a source of the congenial cultural alliances in East Asia.[2]

The work of Xu Bing, which addresses issues around the meaninglessness of words, has generally been viewed from poststructuralist perspectives such as the deconstructionism of Jacques Derrida.[3] Often perceived as "universal," Western academic approaches may invite exciting interpretations of Xu Bing's works and allow them to communicate in larger contexts. At the same time, however, these

147

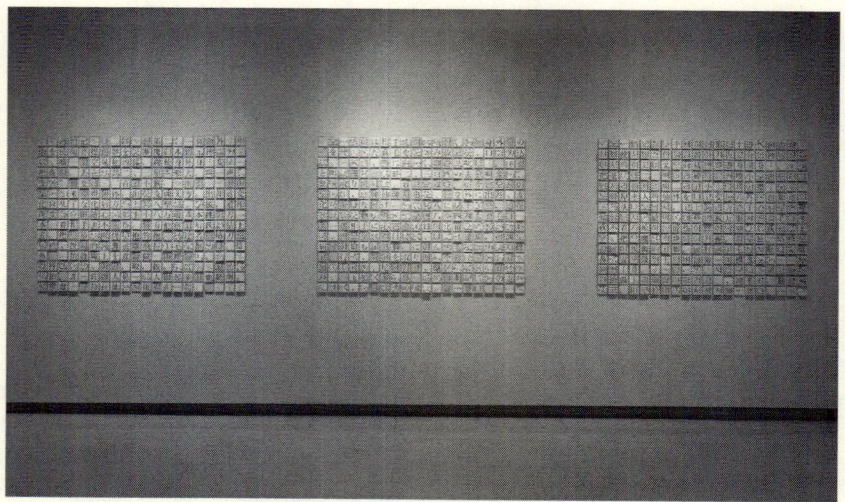

FIGURE 6.I. *Shen Wai Shen*, Xu Bing, installation of printed Post-it notes, Ginza Graphic Gallery, Japan, 2000. (Courtesy of the artist.)

ideas may violently silence the localized sensibilities of East Asian art and culture. As long as the "non-Western" subject continues to be discussed within "Western" narratives, the unbalanced political situation will never improve. Needless to say, neither the term "East" nor "West" has any innate stability; as a hangover of colonialism, each is merely a social construction used to promote the notion of the "Other" for political purposes.[4] Are there, then, any possibilities of interpreting Xu Bing's works using the long tradition of Eastern philosophies? Can contemporary East Asian art be independent from Western interpretations and still share mutual respect in the global art community? In order to investigate these issues from East Asian perspectives, I will consider *Shen Wai Shen* through the lens of Confucian and Buddhist cosmologies as well as eighteenth-century Tokugawa-era philosophies.

Shen Wai Shen was presented in an exhibition at Ginza Graphic Gallery (GGG) in December 2000. It was organized by The Book and Computer, a nonprofit experimental Japanese publishing association with international branches.[5] The GGG focuses exclusively on exhibits of art that involve graphic design and written characters. Subtitled "The Transformation of Books in Asian Times and Spaces 書物変容・アジアの時空," the goal of The Book and Computer Exhibition 本とコンピューター展 was to explore, on the eve of the twenty-first century, the possibilities of electronic publishing for the book industry among regions that share a common heritage of Chinese-based scripts.

Due to Japan's aggressive actions toward other Asian countries since the Meiji 明治 period (1868–1912, especially the "crimes" committed during the Second World War, ending in 1945) and its current submissive ties with the United States, East Asia struggled to achieve political unification while European countries overcame their differences and established the European Union. Facing the hegemony of the Euro-American world, the organizers of the exhibition felt an urgency to seek a solution by exploring a shared linguistic, artistic, and cultural expression.[6] In doing so, they hoped to create a friendly artistic coalition among three countries: China, Korea, and Japan. Three artists, Xu Bing 徐冰 of China, Ahn Sang-Soo 安尚秀 of South Korea, and Hirano Kōga 平野甲賀 of Japan, were invited to Tokyo to produce artworks dealing with a specific passage from the Chinese classical story *Journey to the West* (*Xiyouji* 西遊記 *Saiyūki* in Japanese).[7]

Based on oral and written folklore, *Journey to the West* is a popular mythological novel completed by Wu Cheng'en 呉承恩 (1500–1582), a scholar-official of the Yangtze region, and published in 1592 in Ming 明 China (1368–1644).[8] This novel echoes how the writing system, in the form of Buddhist sutras, was transported from one place to another, an allegorical vehicle for many cultural and linguistic transformations. The story is set in the Tang 唐 dynasty period (618–907), when Sun Wukong 孫悟空, the Supernatural Monkey (often called the Monkey King), and his fellow animal spirit guardians, Zhu Bajie 猪八戒 the Pig Monster and Sha Wujing 沙悟浄 the River Monster, acted as bodyguards to Sanzang 三蔵, the Buddhist priest. Sanzang traveled the Silk Road westwards to India (Tianzhu 天竺), the birthplace of Buddha, to bring Buddhist sutras (written in Sanskrit) back to China.

Among the main characters in this story, Sanzang is based on the historical figure of Xuanzang 玄奘 (602–664), a Tang Buddhist priest who is credited with transporting and translating seventy-four fascicles (1,335 volumes) of sutras, including six hundred volumes of *The Great Heart of Wisdom Sutra* (*Dabanreboluomiduoxingjing*, 大般若波羅蜜多心経 *Daihannyaharamitashin-gyō* in Japanese).[9] While translating, Xuanzang radically condensed and essentialized these volumes into a version that consists of 260 Chinese characters, titled *The Heart of Perfection Wisdom Sutra* (*Mahebanreboluomiduoxinjing*,

摩訶般若波羅蜜多心経 Makahannyaharamitashin-*gyō* in Japanese).
The Heart Sutra (*Reboxinjing*; 若波心経 *Hannyashin-gyō* in Japanese), the shortened form of the name, has been one of the most
widely used texts by Mahayana Buddhists of the various sects and
schools in East Asia. Although chanted in the different pronunciations of Mandarin, Cantonese, Korean, Japanese, and so forth, the
identically scripted sutra has transmitted its teachings without altera-
tion in form and meaning, and hence formed a Pan-Asiatic tradition.

Similar to how Xuanzang unified the religious views of neighboring regions through his translation of sutras, Xu Bing narrowed
the gap between China, Japan, and South Korea by highlighting
the intercommunicability of their written languages in the production of *Shen Wai Shen*. The title, *Shen Wai Shen*, refers to one of the
magical powers performed by Sun Wukong in the selected passage:

> Seeing how ugly the demon king had turned, Sun Wukong used
> his hairs, popped it in his mouth, chewed it up, and blew it out
> into the air, shouting, "Change!" It turned into two or three hun-
> dred little monkeys, who all crowded round him. Sun Wukong
> now had an immortal body, and there was no magic transforma-
> tion of which he was not capable. Since he had followed the Way
> he could change each of the eighty-four thousand hairs on his
> body into anything he wanted. The little monkeys were too quick
> and nimble for sword or spear. Look at them, leaping forwards
> and jumping backwards, rushing up and surrounding the demon
> king, grabbing him, seizing him, poking him in the backside,
> pulling at his feet, punching him, kicking him, tearing his hair
> out, scratching at his eyes, twisting his nose, each picking him up
> together and throwing him to the ground.[10]

In order to defeat *Mowang* 魔王 the Demon King, who attempted to
block their journey, Sun Wukong pulled out the hairs on his body,
blew them into the air, and transformed them into an army of two or
three hundred little monkeys, all identical "clones" of himself.

Unlike the two other artists—Ahn Sang-Soo and Hirano
Kōga—who dealt with each of their own languages in reproducing
this passage, Xu Bing incorporated all three languages (Chinese,
Korean, and Japanese) into his *Shen Wai Shen*. The work consists of
over ten thousand small, square sheets of paper in pads, stacked in
nine hundred piles. One word or illustration from a passage of *Journey to the West* is printed on each single removable sheet of paper. At

the beginning of the exhibition, these nine hundred piles are neatly separated into three blocks of text that are identical in content but written in three different languages: pink colored paper for Chinese, blue for Korean, and yellow for Japanese. Each pad consists of twelve sheets of paper divided into the three layers of linguistically coded colors, with each language conveying identical content. The viewers are then invited to remove sheets of paper from these pads, which are then mounted on the wall of the gallery.

In this installation, Xu Bing compares the "body" of Sun Wukong to the Chinese writing system and employs the action of pulling hairs out of his body and blowing them into the air to metaphorically suggest the process of transporting the Chinese writing system from China to peripheral regions. The multiple bodies of little monkeys resemble duplicates of the original body, but each one is distinct in strength and intelligence for battling the demon. Thus, these bodies are understood as the new writing systems that developed in the region to which their prototype was transported. Each of the new languages are related but have developed distinctively to satisfy regionalized cultural agendas and needs.

COSMOLOGY AND THE POWER OF WRITING

The power of *Shen Wai Shen* lies within its demonstration of the translatability and transplantability of a written language from one culture to another. Xu Bing's work often involves the passage of time, which transforms the appearances of his installations.[11] As the exhibition proceeds, the three blocks of neatly divided languages and colors become mixed because the audience removes the sheets of paper at different rates. Some parts reveal the words in different languages just three days after the opening, but other parts are not removed until the last day of the exhibition. The work is designed to eventually resemble a chaotic computer screen affected by a virus. This transformative process is an essential element through which Xu Bing expresses the interrelation of languages in East Asia, which constantly change through mutual influence over many centuries.

When explaining his works that involve books/writing (*shu* 書), Xu Bing often refers to the Chinese legend of Cang Jie 蒼頡, a legendary four-eyed sage who invented the writing system after being inspired by bird claw prints.[12] The Japanese and Koreans have had similar legends describing their first encounters with their own writing systems. According to an episode of *The Masters of*

Huainan (*Huainanzi* 淮南子), the cosmological text complied by King of Huainan Liu An 劉安 (180–122 BCE), the invention of a writing system by Cang Jie frightened heaven and earth and made the spirits cry.[13] As interpreted by K.C. Chang, "the written record held the secret of the governance of the world; the inscriptions were identified with the information they contained because when writing began they themselves were part of the instruments of the all important heaven-earth communication."[14]

In the Chinese cultural context, the written word (*yan* 言) has been considered a valid agent of moral and political authority. The earliest examples of writing date to the Shang 商 dynasty period (ca.1523–1028 BCE), when questions posed by kings to their ancestors were engraved on oracle bones (*jiaguwen* 甲骨文). The hexagrams (*bagua* 八卦) of the *Book of Changes* (*Yijing* 易経), have been traditionally regarded as the prototypes of written characters.[15] These line patterns of yielding *yin* 陰 and unyielding *yang* 陽 were said to have derived from the celestial images and patterns discerned by the legendary sage-king Fu Xi 伏義. Accordingly, human nature and moral code were established when the harmonious processes of change were inscribed in the linear patterns of the hexagrams, a system of balance from which Chinese characters are derived. Further, Nishi Kōjirō 西孝二郎 has pointed out that each of the one hundred chapters in *Journey to the West* is connected to one of the sixty-four cycles of hexagrams in the *Book of Changes*.[16] The hexagrams indicate the intertwined relationship between ancient cosmology and language, illuminating hidden meanings that are often implied in classical literature.

Xu Bing has attempted to show viewers how the writing system, since its very inception, manifested itself as a tool for rulers to legitimate their sovereignty. Numerous examples of such rulers can be found throughout the course of history. Qin Shihuangdi 秦始皇帝 (Qin 秦 dynasty 221–206 BCE), the first emperor of China, standardized the Chinese writing program in order to centralize power and unify the Warring States. Likewise, once the People's Republic of China was established, the communist government issued a few hundred simplified characters to align them with Mao Zedong's 毛沢東 (1893–1976) political vision and to spread literacy among less educated people in rural areas.[17] Xu Bing's works implicitly reflect his experience of Maoist campaigns. Not only did Xu print over ten thousand sheets of paper for *Shen Wai Shen* in a manner similar to the way Mao's *Red Book* was reproduced, he also chose the simplified characters 簡体字, a signature of the Maoist China, to produce the Chinese text in the installation. The simplified characters are used despite the fact that the original text of *Journey to the West* was written in traditional characters 繁体字, the form actively used in Taiwan today.

Nearly all East Asian citizens in the Chinese cultural sphere began his or her education by memorizing thousands of characters that consist of form (*xing* 形), sound (*yin* 音), and meaning (*yi* 意). This learning process can be read as a type of initiation ritual into the culture, creating a strong sense of respect for the written word (*yan* 言). Nevertheless, the generation represented by Xu Bing grew up during the Cultural Revolution in Mainland China and experienced the promulgation of new characters, as well as the abandonment of old characters that had already been mastered. This remodeling of characters confused Xu over the fundamental conception of culture, and, in turn, made him realize the arbitrary nature of one's cultural identity.[18]

By using simplified Chinese characters in *Shen Wai Shen*, Xu Bing reduces the hierarchical relationship between the three languages. Since Korean and Japanese characters were derived from simplified versions of traditional Chinese, the relationship between Chinese and Korean/Japanese languages parallels that between parent and children, or master and disciples, implying a tangible hierarchy in accordance to Confucian tradition. If one considers the simplified Chinese script to be just one of the many transformed versions deriving from an original script, then it may be compared to just one of the bodies that Sun Wukong created from his hairs. From this perspective, the relationship among the three languages becomes less clearly hierarchical. It is a strategy of the artist to mitigate existing hostilities and to encourage an amiable relationship among the countries involved.

Another strategy employed by Xu Bing involves the incorporation of calligraphy in his works. The digitally printed letters on the sheets of paper in *Shen Wai Shen* were written in regular script, which is one of three standard calligraphic scripts.[19] The art of calligraphy developed out of diverse writing practices and was considered brought to perfection by Wang Xizhi 王羲之 (303–361) in the Eastern Jin 東晋 dynasty (317–419).

His *Preface to the Orchid Pavilion Gathering* (*Lantingxu* 蘭亭序, Figure 6.2) is considered one of the finest examples of early Chinese calligraphy.[20] Similar to the art of *Shen Wai Shen* performed by

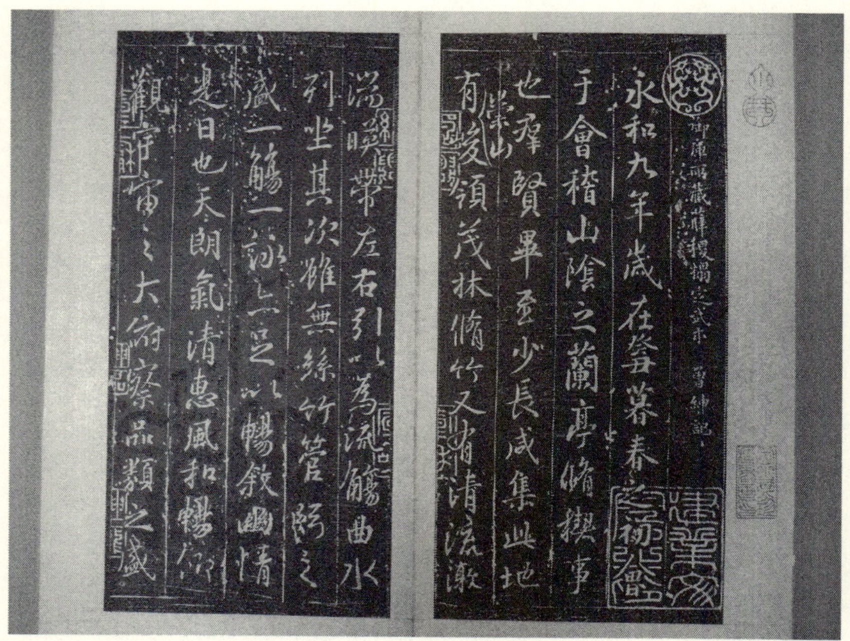

FIGURE 6.2. *Preface to the Orchid Pavilion Gathering (Lantingxu* 蘭亭序*)*, attributed to Wang Xizhi, ink rubbing on paper, originally scripted in Eastern Jin period, Ming period copy, Dingwu version, Kyoto National Museum. Photograph by Kazuko Kameda-Madar.

Sun Wukong, Wang Xizhi's calligraphic style was seen as a sign of power and spread to many peripheral regions. Through the copying of sutras, Buddhism in particular played a significant role in spreading the art of calligraphy. For instance, numerous copies of *The Lotus Sutra* (*Miaofa lianhua jing* 妙法蓮華経) are inscribed in Wang's style and were reproduced in Korea during the Koryo 高句麗 dynasty period. The teachings of Buddhism were received with enthusiasm in Korea, especially in the southern kingdom of Paekche 百済. According to tradition, in 538, the king of Paekche sent learned monks with the gift of a statue of Buddha as well as Buddhist scriptures to the Japanese ruler, Emperor Kimmei 欽明天皇 (509–571), thus officially introducing Buddhism and a writing system to Japan.[21]

The *Bucchō Sonshō Darani-kyō Sutra* 仏頂尊勝陀羅尼経 was copied in Japan during the Nara 奈良 period (710–794).[22] The original version of this sutra was directly imported from Tang dynasty

China to Japan through the official imperial mission. According to the inscription appearing at the end of scroll, in 739, Emperor Shōmu 聖武天皇 (701–756) ordered the production of one thousand copies of the sutra in order to cure the sickness of Priest Genbō 玄昉. In 717 Genbō left the shore of Japan and traveled to the Tang dynasty as an imperial diplomat, studied in the Hossō sect 法相宗 of Buddhism, and in 735 brought back five thousand Buddhist sutras for Emperor Shōmu.[23] The consort of Emperor Shōmu, Empress Kōmyō 光明皇后 (701–760), was a famous practitioner of calligraphy and a pious proponent of the Wang Xizhi style. She established the imperial calligraphic standard, which was largely based on the manner of Wang Xizhi, an imperial inclination reflected in the sutra. Because this sutra includes the white and red marks indicating the four tones of spoken Chinese, we can assume that it was chanted with the Chinese phonetic tones.[24] The historical evidence proves how Wang Xizhi–style calligraphy was glorified as it crossed cultural boundaries. In contemporary times, a similar trend is reimagined in the tale of Sun Wukong, the digital monkey of *Shen Wai Shen*.

TRANSFORMATION FROM *XIYOUJI* TO *SAIYŪKI*

As represented in *Shen Wai Shen* by Xu Bing, Japan began to develop its own written characters just like one of Sun Wukong's many bodies. Having a written language allowed Japanese culture and history to blossom in writing, whereas the oral tradition was constantly at risk of being forgotten. During the transmission from China, important modifications occurred in Japanese calligraphy. The Japanese developed *kana* 仮名, characters that indicate sound in contrast to ideographic characters. *Manyōgana* 万葉仮名, named after the eighth-century poetry anthology, *Collection of Ten Thousand Leaves* (*Manyōshū* 万葉集), are certain kinds of *kanji* 漢字, Chinese characters used phonetically to represent the syllables of Japanese.[25]

The transformation from *kanji* to *kana* was largely accomplished by female calligraphers at the Heian 平安 court (794–1185), and thus, *kana* are called 'woman's hands' (*onna-de* 女手) as opposed to 'man's hands' (*otoko-de* 男手), which refers to *kanji*.[26] The Japanese calligraphic expression reached its peak when the twelfth-century Heian court developed *sōgana* 草仮名, a set of "aestheticized" cursive scripts, as exemplified in *Thirty-Six Immortal Poets* 三十六人家集, a collaborative project of the *Nishihonganji* 西本願寺 Buddhist temple in Kyoto. This phonetic usage and drastic simplification of cursive script gave birth to the two syllabaries of *hiragana* 平仮名 and *katakana* 片仮名. At first, *katakana* was used in combination with *kanji* to denote verb endings while *hiragana* was used independently. Later, *hiragana* also came to be used in combination with *kanji*, and this practice continues to the present day. Xu Bing purportedly used a reader-friendly, contemporary combination of *kanji* and *hiragana* in order to write the Japanese text of *Shen Wai Shen*.

During the Tokugawa 徳川 period (1603–1868), approximately two centuries after the publication by Wu Cheng'en, Japanese authors began to write *Journey to the West* in their own characters; they retold the same content but used different scripts. The story was initially imported as a didactic tale to disseminate the True Pure Land (Jōdo Shinshū 浄土真宗) sect's Buddhist teachings. Soon after the story was imported to Japan, it was quickly secularized and popularized as entertainment for the urban masses. *Popular Journey to the West* (*Tsūzokusaiyūki* 通俗西遊記, 1758) and *Illustrated Journey to the West* (*Ehonsaiyūki* 画本西遊記, 1806) were two major early translations of the Chinese *Xiyouji* 西遊記 into Japanese, pronounced *Saiyūki*.[27] Along with the *kanji Tsūzokusaiyūki*, the earlier version was transcribed and woodblock printed in *katakana* for easy reading for the increasingly literate Japanese consumers. Compared to this, *Ehonsaiyūki*, the later version, was published in an even more reader-friendly format that combined *kanji* and *hiragana*. This was accompanied by illustrations produced by the *ukiyo-e* (picture of floating world) studios of Ōhara Tōno 大原東野, Utagawa Toyohiro 歌川豊広, and Katsushika Hokusai 葛飾北斎. This version was not only woodblock printed, but also produced by offset printing systems to satisfy the higher demands of the Meiji era. The manner is which Xu Bing uses print and digital mass media in *Shen Wai Shen* to engage a wide audience could be related to this stage of *Saiyūki*. The adventures of the supernatural monkey, familiarly known as Son Gokū 孫悟空 in Japanese, have become deeply integrated into Japanese culture since its arrival.

TRANSFORMATION OF SUN WUKONG

Sun Wukong is able to transform himself into seventy-two different forms, including a tree, a bird, a beast, or an insect small enough to sneak into an enemy's belly. Sun Wukong's shape-shifting ability is a metaphor for the constantly changing faces of languages and cultures, as emphasized by Xu Bing in his *Shen Wai Shen*. Different cultures have modified the images of Sun Wukong in order to meet the needs of their own audiences. In Japan, for example, *Journey to the West* has been adapted to many forms of cultural expression, such as *bunraku* 文楽 (puppet theater), *manga* 漫画 (narrative comics), *anime* アニメ (Japanese animation), and TV games. Today, virtually every Japanese adult has grown up with a Son Gokū of one variation or another that reflects the social background of its producers and audiences.

An *anime* film adaptation of the *manga* by Tezuka Osamu 手塚治虫, entitled *My Son Gokū* (*Boku no Son Gokū* 僕の孫悟空, 2003), is done in the tradition of Tezuka Gokū.[28] This film spotlights the beginning episodes of the first chapter of *Journey to the West*, when Son Gokū, born from a rock fertilized by the grace of Heaven, masters all the magic tricks of Daoist master Xupudizushi 須菩提祖師 (*Shubodaisoshi* in Japanese). However, due to his mischief, Son Gokū was imprisoned under a rocky mountain. Five hundred years later, Buddha sent Sanzang to dig him out and take him on his journey to the West. Tezuka Production shot another animated film of the same subject, released by Tōei 東映 Animation in 1966 along with the TV series, which became an animation classic in Japan. With the goal of entertaining young children, the Tezuka versions of *Journey to the West* are constructed around hopeful and didactic messages. These messages were informed by the social conditions of the 1960s, when the Japanese experienced a growing economy and a hopeful desire to build the nation.

Authored by Toriyama Akira 鳥山明, the story line of *Dragon Ball* ドラゴン・ボール is a simplified version of *Journey to the West*. A *manga* version of this work first appeared in 1985 in *Shōnen Jump* 少年ジャンプ, a monthly boy's comic magazine, or *shōnen manga zasshi* 少年漫画雑誌. *Shōnen Jump* appeared in the midst of the "bubble economy," when economically mature Japanese corporations were still heavily dependent on the American investments they had received since the post-Second World War. The political and economic situation of the US–Japan Security Treaty was manifested in the characteristics of Japanese popular culture, which conveyed a combination of pretentious immaturity, exaggerated sweetness, and twisted eroticism. As a part of this cultural phenomenon, Son Gokū from *Dragon Ball* is represented as a cute and innocent child.[29] In the story, he dwells in the isolated mountains until the girl Bulma ブルマ arrives to inform him that if he collects all seven

Dragon Balls, a wish would be granted. Their journey in search of Dragon Balls begins, and Son Gokū trains himself to fight against monsters and ghosts along his way.[30] Although the representation of Heavens and Hells is inspired by the classical tradition, the narrative seems to evade religious and ideological issues.[31] In contrast, this version of *Journey to the West* penetrates virtually every possible area of marketing. It was first adapted as a TV series, followed by a film, videos, collectable cards, and games promoted by Sony's PlayStation 2.[32] Filled with violent actions and slapstick jokes, the TV episodes are primarily organized into a three-part series: *Dragon Ball* and *Dragon Ball Z*, later followed by *Dragon Ball GT*. The long-running series finally ended in 1997, but *Dragon Ball*'s popularity and commercial success continues to flourish in the North American market today.

Saiyūki 最遊記 (Figure 6.3) is the most ambiguous and intriguing remake of *Journey to the West* in Japan in recent times. Authored by Minekura Kazuya 峰倉かずや, this *manga* was serialized in the monthly comic magazine *G-Fantasy*, which has since been followed by *ZERO-SUM*.[33] For Japanese readers, this title is a wordplay that conveys the identical pronunciation of *Saiyūki* 西遊記; however, Chinese readers would pronounce it *Zuiyouji* 最遊記. By replacing *xi* 西 with *zui* 最, the meaning of the title is altered from *Journey to the West* to *Ultimate Playfulness*. As suggested in this title, all the characters are depicted as playful hooligans who are also strong fighters, despite an appearance of radical femininity; they are exquisite, frail, and elegant. All of the characters, male and female alike, have slim bodies, long hair, and large shining eyes with curly eyelashes. In addition to his regular helpers (Sun Gokū, Cho Hakkai, and Sa Gojō), Sanzō is assigned to work with the hermaphroditic figure, Kanzeonbosatsu 観世音菩薩, the Goddess of Mercy. The series obviously emphasizes confusion in the gendered features of its characters. Why is a tough fighter like Son Gokū depicted as a girl-like figure in this version of *Journey to the West*?

The social construction of gender modes in Japan is rooted in the Japanese language and cultural practices that extend back at least to the tenth-century Heian 平安 era (794–1185). During this time, the Japanese vernacular was transcribed in feminized Chinese scripts, the so-called *onna-de* calligraphy discussed earlier. It was a time when the Japanese saw Japan as having only marginal (feminine) status in the vast cultural sphere of which China was the center (masculine). It is therefore evident that the study of Japanese art

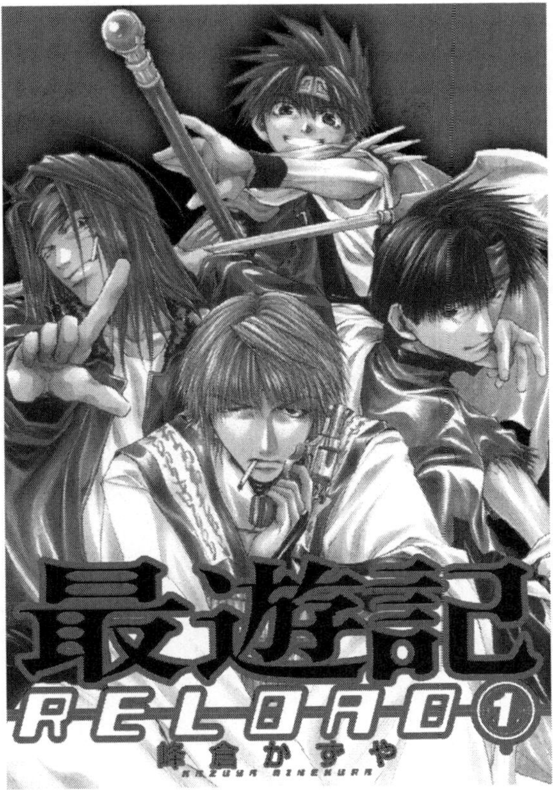

FIGURE 6.3. *Saiyuki*, image from the *manga* by
Minekura Kazuya.

and culture cannot be comprehended by simple binaries between
Occidental/superior/masculine versus Oriental/inferior/feminine
as suggested by Edward Said's *Orientalism* of 1978 or Linda Nochlin's feminist discourse of 1989.[34] According to Japanese aesthetic
sensibility, "femininity" reigns over "masculinity" in the sense
that it is traditionally linked with "courtliness, refinement and ele-
gance," the value system of the "ruling" class. Hence, Chino Kaori
千野香織, who introduced contemporary gender studies to the art
historical discipline in Japan, advocated a second binary structure
that consists of public/Sinophile/masculine and private/native/
feminine modes. Today, this "double-layered binary structure" theory is one of the most effective theoretical tools available to understanding political identity as represented in Japanese art.[35]

With Chino's theory in mind, one may assess the peculiar tendency of medieval Japanese men to define their cultural identity in the "feminine" mode. For example, this is reflected in the *onna-de* calligraphy of *Thirty-Six Immortal Poets*.[36] It is as though Japanese men concealed themselves behind a comfortable "feminine" mask to displace the fear of a real and masculine China coming to obliterate them. Such paranoia in men seems to continue to exist in the heavily Westernized society of contemporary Japan. While battling to get to the west, the characters of *Saiyūki* 最遊記 learn of each other's vulnerability and painful backgrounds.[37] In this version of *Journey to the West*, the term "West" could doubly refer to India (Tenziku 天竺) and Euro-America *Seiyō* 西洋. Unlike the earlier variations, this version of *Journey to the West* contains darker, more pessimistic feelings that reflect the increasingly insecure socioeconomic condition of the post-bubble-economy era. The characters of *Saiyūki* are all threatened by various insecurities, and thus bear the feminine qualities that fortify them.

ART AND LANGUAGE IN THE COMPUTER AGE

Using golden clouds (*jindouyun* 金斗雲) as a vehicle, Sun Wukong can travel 108 thousand miles (this number refers to a phrase in Chinese, 十万八千里, which means a very long distance) in a single somersault. His cloud vehicle may be read as a metaphor for the accessibility of written communications using electronic publishing through the Internet. Viewers of *Shen Wai Shen* are invited to remove any of the printed sheets of paper on display, a process that allows successive layers to appear with the same words in different languages. The audience's participation transforms the monumentality of fine art into the ephemerality of pieces of paper. As a result, the two seemingly antagonistic qualities of the monumental and the ephemeral coexist harmoniously in this work. Xu Bing's official website address is written on the back of every single sheet of paper. As site-specific installations, most of his works disappear when the exhibition ends. This work, however, existed as a concept on his website both before and after the gallery exhibition. In conjunction with the exhibition, a special website was also set up by The Book and Computer.

By visiting Xu Bing's official website, audiences continue to interact with *Shen Wai Shen* beyond the constriction of time and space. The in-progress construction of this work (Figure 6.4) was designed to appear on the website prior to the exhibition. Selecting the section of "My Projects" allows the website visitor to view the process of making *Shen Wai Shen* and its proposal sketches. From these sketches, we can see the meanings implied in the name Sun Wukong, such as Xu Bing's special consideration for the word *wu* 悟, which is a character in Sun Wukong's name, 孫悟空. The word *wu* references the Chan (or Japanese, Zen) 禅 concept of enlightenment. The word *kong* 空 references a well-known passage from Xuanzang Sanzang's *Hannyashinkyo* sutra 般若心経, where the two concepts of *se* 色 (form, body) and *kong* 空 (space, emptiness) are equated 色即是空、空即是色. Although the Confucian *Analects* relates *se* 色 to amorousness, Buddhist teachings define it as anything that has physical substance, or "body." Thus, the name *Wukong* literally suggests "one who understands the materiality of things."

Sun Wukong is a Buddhist name, which was given by the master Daoist, Xupudizushi 須菩提祖師.[38] At the completion of discipleship, all twelve disciples of Xupudizushi received new names that included one of the twelve characters in his system of core principles: 広大

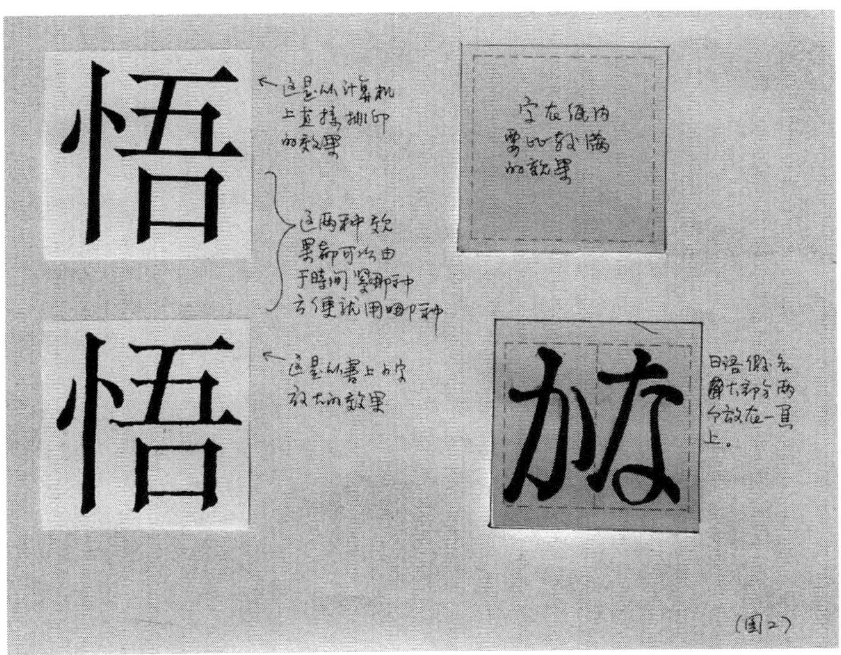

FIGURE 6.4. Character for *wu* 悟, from a detail of a sketched project proposal for *Shen Wai Shen*, Xu Bing, 2000. (Courtesy of the artist.)

智慧 (wide, large, wisdom, merciful); 真如性海 (trueness, likeness, essentiality, ocean); 穎悟円覧 (intelligence, enlightenment, amicability, observation). Because the Monkey King was his tenth disciple, he obtained the tenth character *wu* 悟 (enlightenment or awareness). Since Xupudizushi was a specialist in the Dao 道 of *kong* 空, he bestowed upon him the combined designations of *wu* and *kong*.

Two other animal-spirit guardians of Sanzang have the character *wu* in their names as well. Zhu Bajie 猪八戒, which means "pig of eight restraints," also has the Buddhist name Zhu Wuneng 猪悟能, meaning "pig reincarnate who is aware of capability," a reference to the fact that he values himself so much as to forget his own grisly appearance. The third disciple of Sanzang, Sha Wujing 沙悟净, is a river monster. Guanyin 観音, the bodhisattva of compassion, came searching for powerful bodyguards in preparation for Sanzang's journey to the West. She recruited Sha Wujing in exchange for some relief from his suffering. She then converted him and gave him his current name, Sha Wujing. His surname "Sha" means "sand," while his Buddhist name Wujing means "Awakened to Purify."

The repeated emphasis on the word *wu* 悟 might remind some audiences of Xu Bing's earlier work, *Wu Street* (1993–1994, Figure 6.5).[39] The title of this work refers to the Chinese name for Fifth Avenue, the famous street in Manhattan where Xu Bing salvaged a group of abstract paintings from the garbage. Besides the number five, the word *wu* conveys several meanings in Chinese, including "misunderstanding" 誤 and "enlightenment" 悟. The dichotomy between understanding and misunderstanding languages is essential to the works *Wu Street* and *Shen Wai Shen*. In *Wu Street*, Xu Bing matched the found paintings from the street with a text written by an art critic describing the well-known abstract paintings of Jonathan Lasker.[40] The text so suitably described the paintings he salvaged that he edited it by substituting some of the identifiable content with fake names and the images of his salvaged works. Then, to demonstrate how the language employed in critiquing art can be arbitrary, he published a Chinese translation of the altered text (under the penname of Jason Jones) in the prestigious art magazine *Shijieyishu* 世界芸術 in 1993.[41] The translation from English to Chinese reinforced the ambiguity of the text, further illustrating his observation that culture and language are mere constructions rather than fixed repositories of truth.

Shen Wai Shen, on the other hand, experiments with the communicability among three languages that rely on Chinese-based

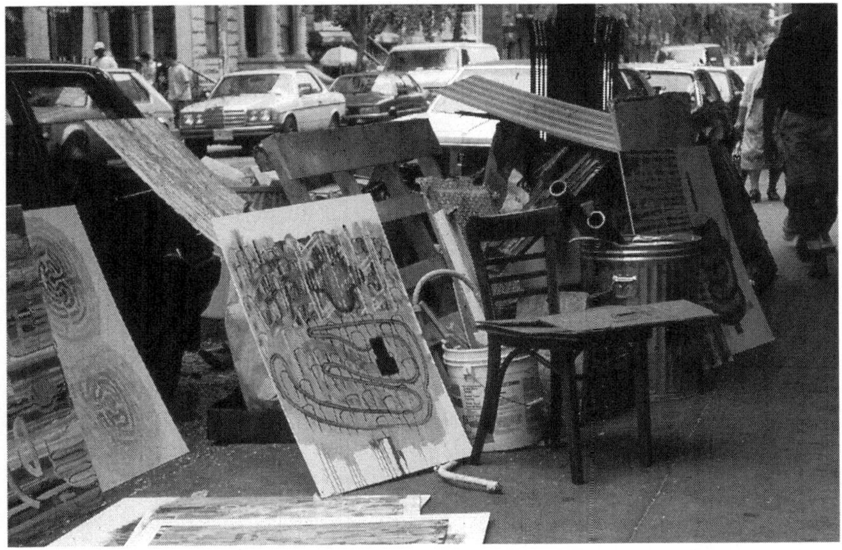

FIGURE 6.5. *Wu Street*, Xu Bing, mixed-media installation with found oil paintings and falsified magazine article, 1993–1994. (Courtesy of the artist.)

scripts. As a consequence of the random removal of sheets of paper, a block of multilingual text appears. This text produces a sense of discomfort when one makes an effort to understand the details of the story. Nevertheless, the fundamental content of the passage is comprehensible since all three languages share the common parent writing system, despite being mutually unintelligible in an oral sense. Thus, taken together, these languages are paradoxically communicable and incommunicable at the same time.

TOKUGAWA IDEOLOGY, POETRY, AND CALLIGRAPHY

Notably, Xu Bing's interests in the paradoxes of language transmission were also heated topics of discussion among eighteenth-century Tokugawa-era philosophers who developed different trends of Confucian-based ideologies. For the Japanese Confucians, composing *kanshi* 漢詩 (Chinese poetry) was an extremely important practice. To demonstrate the instability of linguistic and cultural identities, I would like to compare two examples of *kanshi*: one composed by Hayashi Razan 林羅山 (1583–1657), founder of the orthodox Hayashi Neo-Confucian School, and the other composed by Ogyū Sorai 荻生徂徠 (1666–1728), leader of the Kogaku-*ha* 古学派 School of Ancient Study.[42] This comparison will elucidate the position of Xu Bing, who criticizes the monopoly of art by elitist groups by reaching out to mass audiences.

Unable to pronounce the Chinese phonetic tones properly, Hayashi Razan relied on *shakubun* 釈文, a type of Japanese translation for Chinese classical writing 和習. Although the poem is written in Chinese characters, the Hayashi poets used *shakubun* to appreciate its sound and context.[43] Hayashi Razan's "Japanized" Chinese poetry functioned as a perfect vehicle to convey their Japanized Chinese philosophy, which propagated the Tokugawa political agenda.

When establishing the Shogunate in 1603, Tokugawa Ieyasu 徳川家康 (1543–1616) and his heirs sought to justify their right to rule through the Neo-Confucian teachings of Chinese philosopher Zhuzi 朱子 (1130–1200), whose primary concern was a doctrine of *li* 理, reason or principle. This teaching emphasized the proper conduct of human affairs as manifested in a strict hierarchy of classes and a loyalty to the lords. In this sense, it seemed well suited for the purposes of Japanese feudal rulers. However, Chinese ideology was not exactly workable in the Japanese sociopolitical system. The largest conflicts arising from an imposed Chinese ideology involved issues of militarism and heredity. In China, militarism was a subject of disdain, yet in Japan it was ranked highly in society.[44] China's governance was also conducted by scholar-officials recruited through an examination system while the Japanese *samurai* positions were strictly based on birthright, marriage, or adoption into families.

In order to solve this problem, the Tokugawa Shogunate officially appointed Hayashi Razan to modify Chinese teachings to fit the Japanese sociopolitical context. Razan justified the *samurai*'s ruling right by citing their status as military aristocrats who should cultivate the art of peace in the same manner as Chinese bureaucrats. At the same time, he encouraged the maintenance of hereditary rights by designating his own heirs as successors in the Orthodox Confucian Academy. His monopoly of power was manifested in his *shakubun* poetry, which was extremely difficult to comprehend for Japanese commoners who did not receive Hayashi education. This purposeful difficulty was intended to reinforce the hierarchical relationship between the elite *samurai* and the common people.

One of the poems by Razan is entitled *The Clear Moon of Musashino*:

武野晴月 (Chinese poetry)   武野の晴月 (Japanese translation)
武陵秋色月嬋娟   武陵の秋色は月嬋娟として
曠野平原晴快然   曠野も平原も晴れて快然たり
輾破青青無轍述   青青を輾破せるも轍述無く
一輪千里草連天   一輪千里草は天に連なれり⁴⁵

Takeno no Seigetsu (Japanese transliteration)
Buryō no aki'iro ha tsuki senken to shite
Kōya mo heigen mo harete kaizen tari
Seisei o tenha seru mo tetsujutsu naku
Ichi'rin senrisō ha ten ni tsura nareri

Clear Moon at Musashino (English translation)
Autumn color of Muling [Musashino] is shone by the clear moon,
There, the wild plain and open fields are clear and firm,
Without wheel track, distracts the fresh green grass,
Is the moonlight that reaches to the heaven.⁴⁶

This poem is based on that of the Tang poet Zheng Gu 鄭谷 (842–910). Razan chose the place-name Wuling 武陵, a reference to Tao Yuanming's 陶淵明 famous *Taohuayuanji* 桃花源記 poem. However, he replaced Chinese *wu* 武 with Japanese *mu* 武 since these two words are identical in script but distinct in sound. In so doing, he replaced Wuling 武陵 with Takeno 武野, another way of naming Musashino 武蔵野, which refers to the Tokugawa family's favorite hunting field near Edo 江戸, the political capital of the Tokugawa regime.⁴⁷ The letter *wu* 武 also refers to *bushi* 武士 or *samurai* class, so that Takeno 武野 could also be understood as a martial field. These methods show how Razan created a Japanized *kanshi* 漢詩.

In the same way that contemporary Chinese artists voice expressions of social criticism, the eighteenth-century Kogaku-*ha* Confucians were reacting against the Hayashi School philosophy. Just as Xu Bing crosses cultural boundaries by incorporating languages into the practice of visual art, so did Ogyū Sorai encourage his disciples to look back to ancient Chinese ideology before its Japanization in Hayashi hands. For instance, Ogyū Sorai cites the classical *Liujing* 六経 and the Confucian principle of "educability" to speak of everyone's ability to be educated and to contribute to a better society. With great idealism, he also shows his disdain for militarism while prioritizing cultural affairs.[48]

Ogyū Sorai also emphasized the importance of rhythm as expressed in the proper pronunciation of Chinese phonetic tones; rhythm symbolizes the balance between *yin* and *yang* from which emerges a harmonious universe. For this reason, he refused to use *shakubun*, which Hayashi Razan relied heavily on. Instead, he composed and read his poems using the original Chinese phonetic tones.

An example of his poem is entitled *Farewell at Autumn River*:

秋江送別 (Chinese poetry)　　　　秋江の送別 (Japanese translation)
白露青楓両岸秋　　　　　　　　　白露と青楓と両岸の秋に
無窮別恨満中流　　　　　　　　　窮り無し別れの恨み中流に満つ
何堪明月潮生早　　　　　　　　　何ぞ堪へん明月に潮の生ずること早きを
望断蓬莱仙子舟　　　　　　　　　望断ゆ蓬莱仙子の舟[49]

Farewell at Autumn River (English translation)
Autumn river runs between the white dew and green maple,
Loneliness filled in the middle of streams,
How can I bear the speed of current created by the bright moon?
Even the boat of Mt. Penglai seems hopeless.[50]

Earlier he used this *shakubun* (in the following, right side) to pronounce his poem, but then switched to omitting it in Chinese pronunciations (in the following, left side):

Qiuhong songbie　　　　　　*Shūko no sōbetsu*
(Chinese transliteration)　　　(Japanese transliteration)

Bai lou qing feng liang　　　　Hakuro to seifū ga ryōgan no
　　an qiu　　　　　　　　　　　akini
Wu qiong bie hen man　　　　kiwamari nashi wakare no urami
　　zhong liu　　　　　　　　　chūryū ni mitsu
He kan ming yue chao　　　　nanzo taen myōgetsu ni ushio
　　sheng zao　　　　　　　　　no shōzuru koto hayaki o
Wang duan peng lai xian　　　nozomi tachiyu hōrai senko no
　　zi zhou　　　　　　　　　　fune

Ogyū Sorai further theorized that pronouncing Chinese writing in Japanese phonetics might transmit the meaning *yi* 意, but not the word, *yu* 語.[51] Because *shakubun* does not transmit *yu*, it does not transmit cosmological messages from Heaven *tian* 天 and thus lacks the notion of *dao* 道, which provides the way of social improvement. Sorai suggests it is even better to translate Chinese texts using the Japanese vernacular than *shakubun*. Similarly, Xu Bing adheres to the socialist creed of "serving the people" and translates Chinese literature into the Japanese vernacular as another way to shorten the gap between art and the people. Sorai's concern for transmitting "messages" from Heaven relates to Xu Bing's statement here:

> Art has value because it is genuine, not false. If you create art, the material 'you' will mercilessly reveal you in all your complexity. Perhaps in life you can hide, but in art it is impossible. Regardless of whether you hope to hide or to flaunt an idea, it will all be recorded. What belongs to you is yours. You may wish to get rid of it, but you cannot. Then there are those things that do not belong to you and, regardless of your effort, will never belong to you. All of this is decided by fate. This might sound fatalistic, but it is what I have experienced. In reality, this 'fate' is what you experience: it is your cultural background and your life. It determines the inclination and style of your art. Your background is not of your own choosing; this is especially true for mainland Chinese artists. As far as I am concerned, artistic style and taste are not manmade; they are heaven-sent.[52]

Sorai attempted to articulate "proper Chinese pronunciation" through the "proper brushstroke" of calligraphy, and thus studied imported Chinese calligraphy models. By using brushstrokes that convey Chinese phonetic tones, he sought to articulate the balanced relationship between *yin* and *yang* and to express his ideals based on Confucian egalitarianism.

Ogyū Sorai's concern for social improvement was inherited by Yanagisawa Kien 柳沢淇園 (1704–1758), a well-born *samurai* and one of Sorai's disciples who sincerely practiced the way of calligraphy in the manner of Chinese masters. For example, Kien inscribed a Chinese poem in the style of Dong Qichang 董其昌 (1555–1636), the Ming literati painter/theorist/calligrapher. Dong Qichang's source of inspiration could also be traced back to the style of Mi Fu 米芾 (1051–1110), the Song Master. Their calligraphic styles conveyed political messages that criticized the corrupt conduct of their own government. Kien, following the discourse of Sorai, sought to improve social conditions by criticizing the Tokugawa Shogunate through adapting the calligraphy of Dong Qichang and Mi Fu.

The discourse of Ogyū Sorai was attacked by the Meiji administration and received severe criticism during the Second World War for three main reasons: (a) his direct disdain and disrespect for militarism; (b) his perception of the Tokugawa Shogunate as the ruling regime of Japan, instead of the Imperial Court; and (c) his recognition of China's superiority over Japan by his statement, "it is Heaven's command that Confucius (Kongzi 孔子) was born in China and *Liujing* was written in the Chinese, not in Japanese."[53] After Japan's declaration of unconditional surrender in 1945, Sorai's doctrines began to attract positive academic attention from the postwar generation, especially from those who desired to rebuild a peaceful environment without military forces.

The Kogaku-*ha* Confucian artists' attitude for social improvement aligns with Xu Bing's philosophy of making art for the sake of the people, a perspective shaped by the education he received during the socialist Cultural Revolution. Since his move to the United States in 1990, the Chinese government's past propaganda has become much less of a concern for Xu Bing. However, his belief and interest in the notion that "art should serve a social purpose" has not faded.[54] This approach is particularly evident in the way *Shen Wai Shen* reflects a notion of "equality" between the artwork and its viewers. As the Chinese text of the work is presented in simplified Chinese characters, the Japanese section of the same passage is presented in the vernacular. The Japanese vernacular is written in a combination of *kanji* and *hiragana* and Sorai encouraged Japanese scholars to use it for translating Chinese literature. Furthermore, *Shen Wai Shen* creates a space for viewers to participate in its final completion. In this sense, Xu Bing eradicates the boundary between art and audience, illustrating his view that art is a tool used for serving the people in order to improve social conditions.[55]

As an artist, Xu Bing declares that he definitely feels a sense of responsibility for social improvement. He rediscovers what is valuable in Chinese culture and finds ways to contribute the results to contemporary society. In so doing, he considers how his works will impact and engage the general public, taking into account whether or not it has any meaning or benefit to his audience. He hopes his works will reach "the broadest spectrum of people possible, everybody from the art expert to the average person."[56]

AFTERTHOUGHT ON *SHEN WAI SHEN*

Xu Bing's *Shen Wai Shen* is an installation that recontextualizes the issues around the political and ideological functions of Chinese-based writing systems. It may serve to forge bonds of friendship and trust among East Asian countries. Tsuno Umitarō 津野海太郎, editor-in-chief of The Book and Computer project, describes Sun Wukong's many cloned figures in his performance of *Shen Wai Shen* as being similar to the art of print media, which also generates numerous clones to transmit messages all over the world.[57] In the production of *Shen Wai Shen*, Xu Bing successfully exhibited the power of print technology, illustrating the instability of the three languages as well as the highly constructed nature of East Asian cultural identities. Tsuno also identifies Sun Wukong as a cultural and intellectual hero who might save the book and printing industry of this region from its current crisis.[58] Can Sun Wukong really save East Asia, as Tsuno suggested, when the credibility of words is largely questioned?

Although Xu Bing tends to deny any direct political implication in his works, he admits: "contemporary art is one of the most politically sensitive forms of public expression."[59] Several years have passed since the production of *Shen Wai Shen* took place, and while Sino-Japan relations have improved in an economic sense, the political relationship continues to struggle. Chinese vice-premier Wu Yi 吳儀 (1938–) cancelled her meeting with former Japanese Prime Minister Koizumi Jun'ichirō 小泉純一郎 (1942–), which was scheduled for May 28, 2005.[60] Citing the reasons for cancellation, China severely criticized Japan for not keeping its word on certain issues. Japan had previously submitted three written documents to China: the Sino-Japan Joint Statement 日中共同声明 (1972); the Sino-Japan Peace Friendship Treaty 日中平和友好条約 (1978); and the Sino-Japan Joint Declaration 日中共同宣言 (1998), in which Japan seemingly apologized and promised to make efforts towards a peaceful relationship between the two countries.[61] Unfortunately, Japan disappointed China by failing to keep these "promises."

When anger erupted in China over Japan's wartime atrocities, Chinese President Hu Jintao 胡錦濤 (1942–) and Koizumi decided to hold meetings on the sidelines of a summit in Jakarta on April 23, 2005. The high level of tension was reduced, but crucial questions regarding territory, energy, history textbooks

教科書問題, and, most of all, the issue of the Yasukuni Shrine 靖
国神社参拝 went unresolved. Koizumi shrugged off pressure from
Hu to address his controversial visits to the Yasukuni shrine, which
honored fallen soldiers and those considered "war criminals" by
the Chinese. Since taking office in April 2001, Koizumi has never
missed the annual pilgrimage to the Yasukuni shrine, which is
widely considered a symbol of Japan's militarism. The pilgrimages
have provoked strong protests in neighboring nations including
China, Taiwan, and North and South Korea. Nakasone Yasuhiro
中曽根康弘 (1918–) was the first prime minister to visit the Yasukuni Shrine in 1985, but he also wrote a letter to former Chinese
President Hu Yaobang 胡耀邦 (1915–1989) the so-called *Nakasone
shokan* 中曽根書簡, explaining his decision to ban the Japanese government's official visit to the Yasukuni Shine in 1986.[62] A survey
conducted by a popular TV show, *Sunday Projects*, reported that
support for Koizumi's visit to the Yasukuni Shrine dropped from
51 percent to 34 percent in 2005.[63]

Koizumi's pursuit of a showdown with Hu has proven to be
a diplomatic strategy as Japan seeks Asian support in its bid for a
permanent seat on the UN Security Council. According to Chinese
Premier Wen Jiabao 温家宝 (1942–), Japan should not be given the
veto power wielded by permanent members until it faces up to its
wartime past. Asian countries suffered greatly during Japan's milita-
ristic rise to power before and during the Second World War. Japan
must reflect deeply on the harm it has inflicted upon Asian nations
and fully atone for its past aggression. However, deeds speak louder
than words when it comes to such negotiations. The production of
Shen Wai Shen by Xu Bing is a deed that demonstrates a real effort
towards improving the relationships between East Asian countries.

There are many important issues that I have not touched upon
here and must be left to further research, including a discussion
of Korean language and culture, an important part of *Shen Wai
Shen* as well as The Book and Computer exhibition. I would like
to conclude this chapter by suggesting that the transmission of
meanings—achieved through the transformation of Chinese-based
scripts into other writing systems and guided by a common ideological interest in Confucian and Daoist cosmologies—could ultimately lead to a contemporary sociopolitical reconciliation among
East Asian countries. The establishment of a new allied power in
Asia may contribute to a balanced and complementary relationship
with Euro-American powers.

NOTES

1. The main source of information regarding *Shen Wai Shen* is located at Xu Bing's official website: http://www.xubing.com/.
2. Geographically, East Asia is a subregion of Asia covering about 6,640,000 km², or 15 percent of the Asian continent. Culturally, it embraces the societies that were heavily influenced by the Chinese language (including the traditional scripts), Confucianism, and Mahayana Buddhism. See http://en.wikipedia.org/wiki/East_Asia.
3. Erickson, *The Art of Xu Bing*, 33.
4. "In any society that is not totalitarian, certain cultural forms predominate over others, just as certain ideas are more influential than others; this form of cultural leadership is what Gramsci has identified as hegemony, an indispensable concept for any understanding of cultural life in the industrial West," (Edward Said, *Orientalism: Western Conceptions of the Orient* [Pantheon, 1978; revised edition Penguin, 1995], 7).
5. The GGG and The Book and Computer are supported by Dai Nippon Printing Co., Ltd., which is one of the leading corporations that represent Japan's printing industry. All the details of this exhibition, *Hon to konputaten* 本とコンピューター展「書物変容・アジアの時空」 December 4–22, 2000, are posted on the Saiyukiban 西遊記版 *Hon to konputa* (The Book and Computer) website version: http://www.honco.net/honcoten/.
6. The concepts of Near East, Far East, or Orient are strongly Euro-American constructions that serve to differentiate the Other and to maintain positions of privilege. The concept of the West or Occident is likewise a construction but is founded on more ambiguous and instable ideas. Said, *Orientalism*, 17.
7. Ahn's work is titled *Xiyouji—Words Diagram*「西遊記–文字図」, and Hirano's work is *Saiyuki—Volume 1, Chapter 1*『西遊記』一の一.
8. The story of a mythological monkey existed as oral folklore until it was written down; thus the authorship of *Journey to the West* still remains in dispute. Prior to the version written by Wu Cheng'en, there were many prototype versions of this story. Fragments of it were described, including the version written in the fourteenth-century Yuan dynasty period. After Wu Cheng'en, many different editions of the novel have appeared over the past four hundred years. The Chinese edition of 1955 was based on the earliest known edition; the Shidetang woodblock edition printed in Nanjing in the twentieth year of the Wanli reign (1592) in the Ming dynasty, and was further checked against six different editions from the Qing dynasty. See Wu Cheng'en and W.J.F. Jenner, trans., *Journey to the West* (Beijing: Foreign Languages Press, 1982); see also Ōta Tatsuo 太田辰夫 Saiyūki no kenkyū 西遊記の研究 (Tokyo: Kenbun Shuppan 研文出版, 1984), 97.

9. In this novel, the West (India), the land of Shakyamuni, metaphorically signifies the Western Paradise, the dwelling place of Amitabha Buddha, taught by the Pure Land sect Buddhism; see Ōta Tatsuo, Saiyūki no kenkyū, 132. (*Hirayama Ikuo to Genjō Sanzō hōshi monogatari, Bijutsu no mado* 平山郁夫と玄奘三蔵法師物語, Tokyo: 2001), 88.

10. Wu Cheng'en and Jenner, *Journey to the West*, 37.

11. Xu Bing often incorporates a transformational process as his artistic strategy in his works, such as *Tobacco Project* (2000) and *Silkworm Books* (2004–2005).

12. In the interview, Xu Bing himself mentions Cang Jie in "Shu Binshi, gikanji o tsukuru—kanji to arufabetto no aratanadeai 徐冰氏、偽漢字をつくる—漢字とアルファベットの新たな出会い," *kikan Hon to Konputa* 季刊本とコンピューター 9 (Summer 1999): 22–33. Also, Xu Bing has stated in his short essay that he has "created many works having to do with *shu* 書, but I am particularly wary of having to explain them. This is because I believe that if a work can be explained with words, then there can be no reason for it to exist. Each time I encounter a situation where I cannot avoid explaining one of my works, I always recall the legend of Cang Jie in *the Huai Nan Zi*." See "To Frighten Heaven and Earth and Make the Spirits Cry 天地を嚇し鬼神を泣かす," in *Baberu no toshokan—moji, shomotsu, media* バベルの図書館—文字・書物・メディア *The Library of Babel: Characters/Books/Media* (exhibition catalog), ed. Shinoda Takatoshi 篠田孝敏, 69 (Tokyo: NTT Intercommunication Center, 1998).

13. Cang Jie was the official recorder at the court of the legendary Huangdi 黄帝 the Yellow Emperor (2898–2679 BCE). See Charles Le Blanc, *Huai Nan Tzu: Philosophical Synthesis in Early Han Thought, The Idea of Resonance (Kan-Ying) with a Translation and Analysis of Chapter Six* (Hong Kong: Hong Kong University Press, 1985); and Harold D. Roth, *The Textual History of the Huai-Nan Tzu* (Michigan: The Association for Asian Studies, 1992), 12.

14. Chang, *Art, Myth and Ritual*, 81.

15. The Eight Trigrams are: *qian* 乾, *kan* 坎, *gen* 艮, *zhen* 震, *xun* 巽, *li* 离, *kun* 坤, and *dui*. Fu Shen, Glenn D. Lowry, and Ann Yonemura, *From Concept to Context: Approaches to Asian and Islamic Calligraphy* (Washington DC: Smithsonian Institution, Freer Gallery of Art, 1986), 16. The eight combinations represent heaven, earth, thunder, wind, water, fire, mountains, and river. Chiang Yee, *Chinese Calligraphy: An Introduction to Its Aesthetic and Technique* (Cambridge, MA: Harvard University Press, 1973), 18–20.

16. For instance, the first chapter of *Xiyouji* (when Sun Wukong performs the art of *Shen Wai Shen*) is related to *qian* 乾, the second chapter to *kun* 坤, the third to *tun* 屯, and so on. Nishi Kōjirō 西孝二郎, Saiyūki no kōzō『西遊記』の構造 (Tokyo: Shinfūsha 新風社, 1997).

17. Richard C. Kraus, *Brushes with Power: Modern Politics and the Chinese Art of Calligraphy* (Berkley, Los Angeles, and Oxford: University of California Press, 1991). Also see the article by Lau Guan Kim at http://bbs.chinadaily.com.cn/forumpost1.shtml?pid=47335.

18. Xu Bing, "The Living Word," trans. Ann L. Huss, in *The Art of Xu Bing*, 13.

19. The three scripts of calligraphy (regular, running, and cursive) were standardized by Wang Xizhi and his son Wang Xianzhi (344–388).

20. The original prose was considered such a fine work of calligraphy that the Tang dynasty Emperor Taizong (reigned 626–649) had it buried with him in his tomb in the mid-seventh century. This incident elevated prose/calligraphy, which was already highly respected, to an even higher status. The works surviving today in the form of ink rubbings, such as the Dingwu Version, are copied from stone tablets engraved during the Song dynasty period (960–1279). "Rantei jo: Five Versions by the Eastern Jin Dynasty Period Wang Xizhi," in *Chūgokuhō shosen Vol. 15* (Tokyo: Nigensha, 1988), 35.

21. However, Buddhist teachings were imported privately prior to this official introduction in 538.

22. *Treasures of a Sacred Mountain: Kukai and Mount Koya* (Kyoto: Kyoto National Museum, 2003), 200.

23. The Hossō sect is one of six Nara Buddhist sects, and was imported directly from China to Japan in 653 by the Japanese priest Dosho 道昭, who visited China and directly studied under the Tang priest Xuanzang 玄奘. The headquarters of the *Hossō* sect in Japan is located in Yakushiji 薬師寺, Nara. *Hirayama Ikuo to Genjōsanzōhōshi monogatari, Bijutsu no mado* (Seikatsu no tomosha, Tokyo: 2001), 2–3.

24. *Treasures of a Sacred Mountain*, 299–300.

25. See Nakata Yujiro and Alan Woodhull, trans., *The Art of Japanese Calligraphy* (New York: Weatherhill/Tokyo: Heibonsha, 1973), 125–127.

26. Chinese characters, or *Otokode*, were used for writing public, official documents; while *kana*, or *onnade*, were used for writing Japanese poetry by both men and women; so clearly the distinction was not attributable to a biological one. Chino Kaori, "Gender in Japanese Art," in *Gender and Power in the Japanese Visual Field*, ed. Joshua S. Mostow, Norman Bryson, and Maribeth Graybill, 25 (Honolulu: University of Hawai'i Press, 2003).

27. *Tsuzokusaiyūki*「通俗西遊記」was translated by the collective effort of authors, Kuchiki Sanjin 口木山人, Ishimaro Sanjin 石麻呂山人, Ogata Teisai 尾形貞斎, Gakutei Kyūzan 岳亭丘山; and *Gahonsaiyūki*「画本西遊記」was done by Kuchiki Sanjin, Yamaga Shishin 山珪士信, Gakutei Kyuzan. Both works were translated based on the Qing version, *Xiyouzhenzhu* 西遊真注, which was intended to entertain the masses, and was widely distributed. See Ota Tatsuo, 太田辰夫 *Saiyuki no kenkyu* 西遊記の研究, 187, 288.

28. Tezuka Osamu authored numerous classical *anime* series, including the *Astro Boy* (1963) aka *Tetsuwan Atom* and *Kimba the White Lion* (1965–1966) aka *Janguru Taitei*. *My Sun Wukong* was directed by Sugino Akio 杉野昭夫 and Yoshimura Fumihiro 吉村文宏 of the Tezuka Production. The film was released by Shochiku Film in July 2003. More information regarding the animated versions of Sun Wukong is posted on the official website of Tezuka Production: http://ja-f.tezuka.co.jp/home.html.

29. See Tokyopop website: http://www.tokyopop.com/dbpage.php?propertycode=SAI&categorycode=BMG&page=article.

30. See http://www.toei-anim.co.jp/tv/dragon/story.html.

31. Similar to the Heavens in *Journey to the West* with North, East, South, and West gates, the *Dragon Ball* galaxy is divided into four sections, each of which is controlled by a Kaiō 界王 king. See http://www.comic-ity.com/dbz/dbz.htm and http://www.toei-anim.co.jp/tv/dragonz/.

32. This story preludes the chaos that begins in *Tōgenkyō* 桃源郷, a paradise where humans and demons share their lives peacefully until the life of Gyūmaō 牛魔王, the super demon, returns. Gyūmaō is killed and buried in Tenjiku 天竺 by Nataku Taishi, one of the five gods who ruled the heaven some five hundred years ago. The familiar members Genjō Sanzō 玄奘三蔵, Son Gokū 孫悟空, Sha Gojyō 沙悟浄, and Cho Hakkai 猪八戒, are assigned to stop the turmoil. Shūeisha 集英社, Fuji TV production, Tōei 東映 Animation. See http://www.toei-anim.co.jp/tv/dragonz/.

33. When this *manga* was adapted by its TV series, aired between April 2000 and March 2001, its title was slightly modified as *Gensōmaden Saiyūki* 幻想魔伝最遊記. Further, the film version of same title was directed by Date Hayato 伊達勇登, from the Shochiku 松竹 Film Co., in the summer of 2001. *G-Fantasy* is published by Enikkusu, and *Zero-Sum* by 一賽舎. See http://pierrot.jp/title/saiyuki_reload/infomation.html.

34. Said, *Orientalism*; Linda Nochlin, *The Politics of Vision: Essays on 19th Century Art and Society, Women, Art and Power, and Realism* (Penguin, 1989).

35. Chino Kaori, "Gender in Japanese Art."

36. There were some female calligraphers involved in the production of *Thirty-Six Immortal Poets*, but most of the contributors were male.

37. *G-Fantasy Magazine*, http://www.geocities.com/Tokyo/Lights/7363/saiyuki.html.

38. According to the Yuan version, the name Sun Wuking was given to the Monkey King by Sanzang. Ota Tatsuo 太田辰夫, *Saiyuki no kenkyu* 西遊記の研究, 82.

39. See Erickson, *The Art of Xu Bing*, 52–53; the project process of *Wu Street* is recorded and posted on Xu Bing's official website at http://www.xubing.com/.

40. Ibid.

41. Ibid.

42. There are a several different ways of referring to the school of philosophy with which Ogyu Sorai is identified. Kobunjigaku 古文辞学, Fukkogaku 復古学, or Kogigaku 古義学 Yoshikawa Kōjirō 吉川幸次郎: *Jinsai/Sorai/Norinaga* 仁斎・徂来・宣長 (Tokyo: Iwanami shoten 岩波書店, 1975). Tahara Tuguo 田原嗣郎: *Soraigaku no sekai* 徂徠学の世界 (Tokyo: University of Tokyo Press 東京大学出版会, 1991).

43. See Nakamura Yukihiko 中村幸彦: *Kinsei no kanshi* 近世の漢詩 (Tokyo: Kumiko shoin 汲古書院, 1986); and also Yamagishi Tokubei 山岸徳平: *Kinsei Kanbungakushi* 近世漢文学史 (Tokyo: Kumiko shoin 汲古書院, 1987).

44. Yoshikawa Kojiro 吉川幸次郎, *Jinsai/ Sorai/ Norinaga* 仁斎・徂徠・宣長.

45. Yamagishi Tokubei 山岸徳平. *Kinsei Kanbungakushi* 近世漢文学史, 61.

46. Transcribed and translated by the author.

47. Ibid.

48. See, Yoshikawa Kojiro 吉川幸次郎, *Jinsai/Sorai/Norinaga* 仁斎・徂徠・宣長.

49. Yamagishi Tokubei 山岸徳平. *Kinsei Kanbungakushi* 近世漢文学史, 182.

50. Transcribed and translated by the author.

51. Ibid., 124.

52. Xu Bing, "The Living Word," in *The Art of Xu Bing*, 19.

53. Yoshikawa Kojiro 吉川幸次郎. *Jinsai/Sorai/Norinaga* 仁斎・徂徠・宣長, 98–99, 202–219, 276.

54. Erickson, *The Art of Xu Bing*, 67.

55. "Shū Binshi, gikanji o tsukuru—kanji to arufabetto no aratanadeai 徐冰氏、偽漢字をつくる―漢字とアルファベットの新たな出会い," *kikan Hon to Konputa* 季刊本とコンピューター 9 (Summer 1999): 32.

56. Erickson, *The Art of Xu Bing*, 69.

57. Tsuno Umitarō, *The Book and Computer* 14, no. 1 (December 2000): 209.

58. Ibid.

59. Xu Bing, in Liu, "An Interview with Xu Bing," 89.

60. *Asahi Dairy Newspaper*, May 30, 2005, 2.

61. Ibid.

62. This letter is published on http://www.cc.matsuyama-u.ac.jp/~tamura/nakasoneyokann.htm.

63. Aired on May 29, 2005.

CHAPTER SEVEN

The Space Between

Cross-Cultural Encounters in Contemporary Chinese Art

JEROME SILBERGELD

Xu Bing's *A Book from the Sky* (Figure I.1) deprives Chinese written characters of their ordinary linguistic significance, reduces them to their pure image state, and offers a new set of potential meanings derived not from content but from context. His *Square Word Calligraphy* provides meaning where none is suspected. These are matched by his *Reading Landscape*, which turns words into images, and his *Monkeys Grasp for the Moon*, which turns images into words. All of these establish a distinctive space between word and image, thinking and seeing, explicit and implicit, content and context, traditional and modern, Chinese and non-Chinese, politics and aesthetics, humor and seriousness, and never just one or the other of these, and never none.[1]

Zhang Hongtu operates with a similar sense of ironic humor and seriousness, simultaneously violating and extending the tradition-based values of Dong Qichang, creatively reinterpreting the canonical masters as Dong himself had done but also incorporating Western alternatives as Dong (presumably) had refused to do.[2] The game is Dong Qichang's but played on Zhang Hongtu's own terms, not just diachronic but now also cross-cultural. The result lies neither here nor there but here *and* there, a hybrid of two seeming irreconcilables not unlike Xu Bing's *Case Study of Transference* (Figure 4.6), or at least like the putative offspring of this animal miscegenation, and like Xu Bing's *Panda Zoo* with its painted New Hampshire pigs dressed up as Chinese bears in a mock Chinese landscape setting (Figure 7.1).[3]

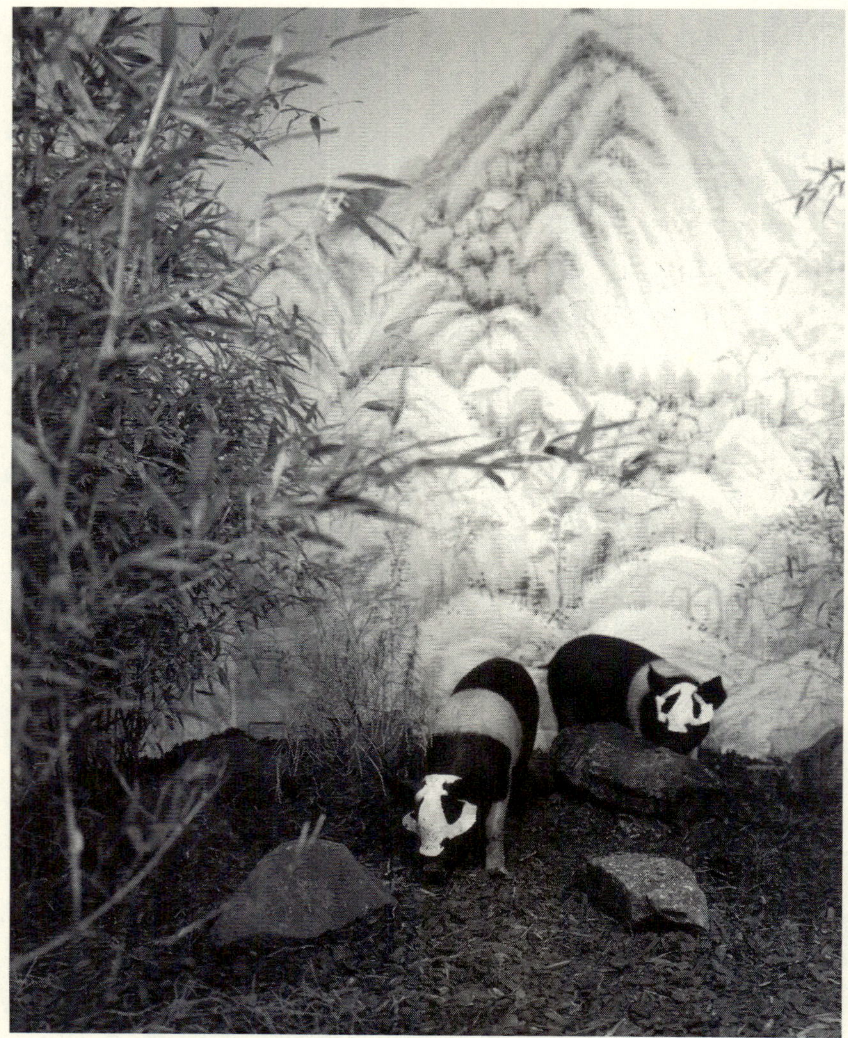

FIGURE 7.1. *Panda Zoo*, Xu Bing, performance and mixed-media installation of bamboo, New Hampshire pigs in masks, and classical Chinese paintings, 1998. (Courtesy of the artist.)

"Case study of transference" is a pretty fair descriptive term for these two artists, fellow expatriates and fellow New Yorkers, and for all of those—artists or not, diasporic or not—who are part of China's rapid transit between the nineteenth and twenty-first centuries, who recognize the myth of a stable monocultural past and express performatively the alternate reality of their destabilized, intercultural trajectory. Other theoretical terms apply equally well to these artists, whether referring to their "liminal" or "third space" or to their being "the other of the other," or whatever aspect of their condition one wishes to emphasize, not just theoretical, not quite real, not just describing, but a state of constantly becoming. Their condition is as much a challenge to their viewers as it is to themselves, and the function of their art is to make this so, to insist on it. They watch their watchers as much as their watchers watch them. Xu Bing loves to tell of the older scholars spending hours looking for an authentic, if impossibly obscure, character among the many made-up words in his *Book from the Sky*, and occasionally finding one. Zhang Hongtu, whose landscapes initially disturbed and disappointed Chinese and Western audiences alike, likes to tell how his *Last Supper*, with its all-Mao all-the-time lineup, its depiction of the Chairman betrayed by the Chairman himself, was sponsored by the United States Senate after Tiananmen as an endorsement of free speech principles, only to be shot down as sacrilegious by a particular liberal Catholic senator from Massachusetts, Edward Kennedy—an anticensorship exhibition censored. Zhang, now censored on two continents, withdrew from the exhibition rather than offer a substitute work, and he was followed by the withdrawal of most of the other original participants, thus scuttling the show and bringing a little bit of authentic Beijing "attitude" to Washington DC.

Three weeks after 9/11, I received a call from Zhang Hongtu asking if he could come down to Princeton for a visit. We walked the campus for a couple of hours. Distressed, he told me he hadn't been able to work since his adoptive hometown was savaged by Moslems—fellow Moslems, since Hongtu's reason for emigrating to New York was that as a Moslem, he was already fed up by 1982 with being a second-class Chinese in China. Now he was both ashamed of Islamic radicalism and afraid for his Moslem brothers back in China. At one point that afternoon, I asked him why, in all of his dissident art, he had never once referenced the Islamic issues so dear to his heart. He immediately slunk down onto a bench as if his legs had given way under him, and about a half minute later he answered that it had simply never occurred to him to do so. Zhang Hongtu, who is interested in "other" perspectives, in what we cannot see of ourselves (Figure 7.2), has yet to go there. Is he censoring himself? I doubt that he would have a very sympathetic audience on the issue of anti-Moslem discrimination, either in China or in Bush's America.

Regardless, Zhang Hongtu reminds us that the space between the artist's life and performative art is small to nonexistent. Zhang Hongtu has escaped Oriental tyranny only to run into Western hypocrisy. What "other" is there left for him to embrace, other than the alternatives he defines through his own art?

The space between cultures, native and adopted, is frequently dark, uncomfortable, or unexplored. Anthropologists refer to the enterprise of colonization as "civilizing projects," executed by militant powers under the guise of bringing the benefits of superior civilization to "lesser" cultures, whom the colonizers portray—and enlist in self-portrayal (or self-betrayal)—as mere primitives, as children or women, typically shown dancing, smiling, and festively costumed in naïve celebration of their native inferiority. Anthropologists also recognize that civilizing projects are not restricted to transnational encounters but occur as well within nations, between the governors and the governed. Just as some cultural critics write of an intercultural "liminal" or "third space," or of *differance*, anthropologists write, "In no case can we understand the entire project by looking from the perspective of only one side."[4] Everyone—those on both sides, those in the space between (hybridized, dissenting, co-opted), and likewise those who would prefer or pretend to

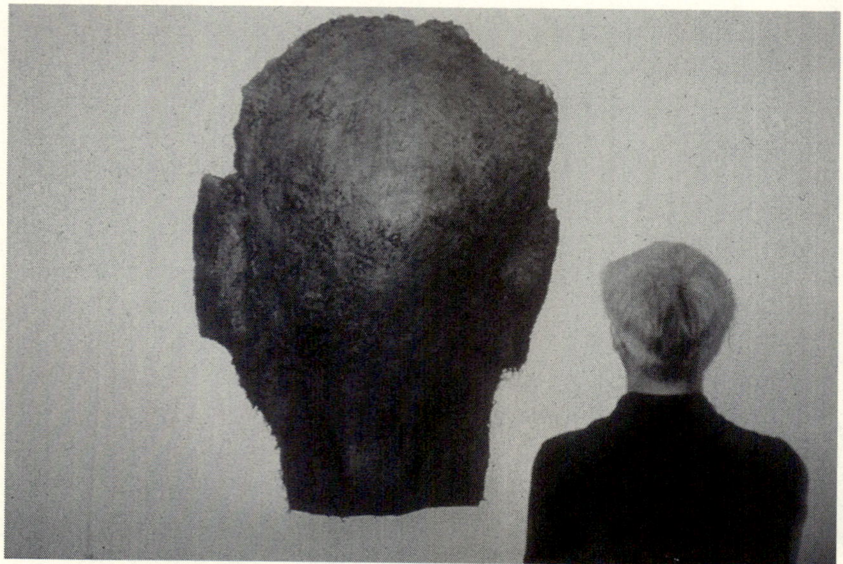

FIGURE 7.2. Zhang Hongtu, the artist and sculpture of the back of the artist's head. (Photograph by Jerome Silbergeld, 2006.)

merely observe and describe or "objectively" critique: everyone is changed by the colonial encounter and in cultural terms such that it does not always remain clear just who is colonizing whom. We learn about the encounter from behavioral responses in the colonizer as much as in the colonized, just as we learn a history of the arts from an observation of the audience as well as from the artist, not only from appreciative responses but also from expressions of discomfort and rejection or misunderstanding.

I have previously written about Rey Chow, who like Homi Bhabha refuses to assign China an "absolute difference" from the West and who locates her explorations "neither in the Chinese nor the Western but rather on a dialectic on which 'Chinese' and 'Western' is played."[5] And yet she writes that the "cinematic apparatus inherited from the West" is an alien medium to China ("mechanistic" and therefore inherently "fascistic"), and she describes much of the so-called Fifth Generation filmmakers' work as a "pornographic" play of "surfaces" that merely "fetishizes" the display of China's dirty laundry for "narcissistic" ends.[6] Uncomfortable with this highly visible cinematic eruption on a global stage, she prescribes what these Chinese artists should do and proscribes what they should not do, much like a "civilizer" addressing "her" primitives. While I cannot help but wonder why, for her, art in the age of mechanicity begins with Walter Benjamin and not with those Shang dynasty bronzes rolling off the assembly lines at Anyang in the thirteenth century BCE, still I don't simply reject Rey Chow's rejections: they tell a story; they are part of the story of those whom she rejects, part of the struggle of those who seek to define alternative spaces not dictated by those in power. For the artist, "those in power" include critics and art historians—aesthetic colonizers.

The "space between" is filled with collisions and hybrids, run-ins between all sorts of social norms, performed with all sorts of run-on styles, and featuring all sorts of "others." Zhi Lin's set of five fourteen-foot tall compositions on the theme of the *Five Capital Punishments in China* (Figure 7.5), painstakingly researched and produced over a fifteen-year period, from 1993 to 2007, could hardly have been conceived without encountering, conceptually, Li Peng and the Dalai Lama, the royal atelier at the court of Qianlong and the art of Caravaggio.[7]

Zhi Lin trained at the National Academy in Hangzhou and first came West in 1987. He was taking his MFA from the Slade School of Fine Art at the University of London when events of June 1989

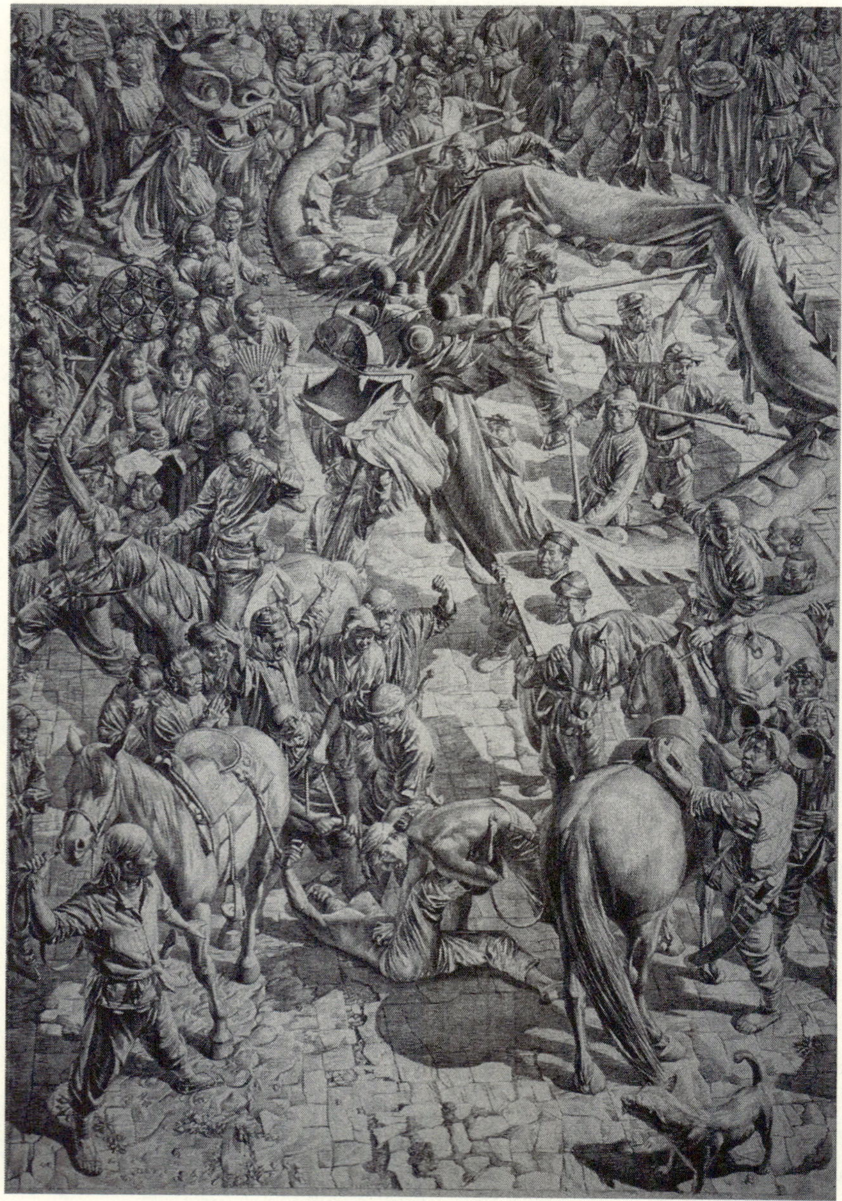

FIGURE 7.3. *Drawing-and-Quartering*, Zhi Lin, from the series *Five Capital Punishments in China*, 2003, Princeton University Art Museum. (Used courtesy of the artist.)

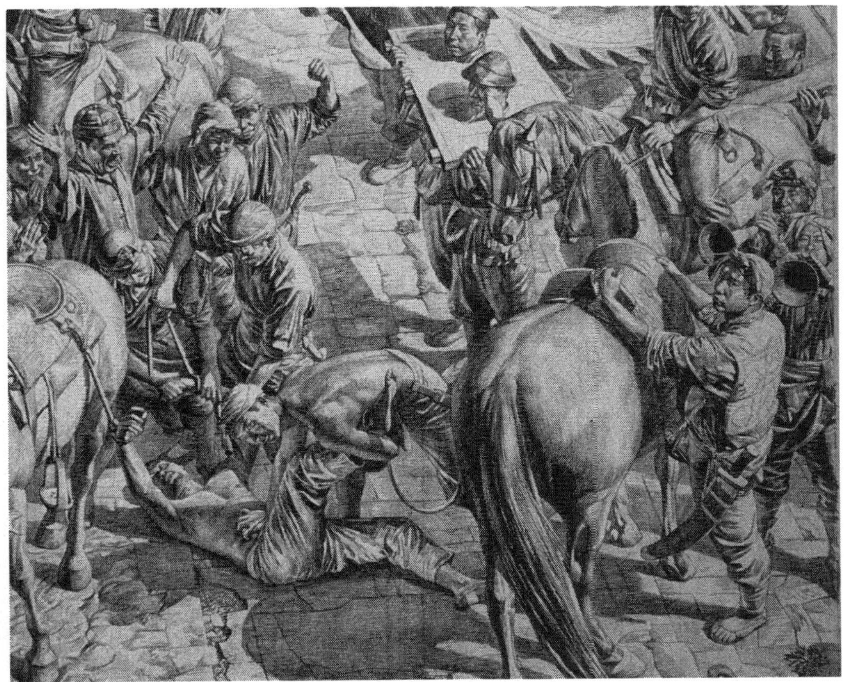

FIGURE 7.4. *Drawing-and-Quartering*, Zhi Lin, detail.

at Tiananmen convinced him that "art is not only for beauty and personal preference, but necessary for social change."[8] These events also closed the door on Zhi Lin's return to China and eventually led to his current professorship at the University of Washington, Seattle.

About the "five punishments" (*wu xing*) in China there is a great deal of traditional literature, from the *Shu jing* and the *Analects* down through the *Book of Filial Piety*, in the codes of law from Qin to Qing, and in twentieth-century fiction.[9] State-inflicted corporal punishment was directed against some three thousand offenses, according to Confucius, and none of these was more grave than the breach of filial piety, an offense against civilization itself, without retribution for which there would be "nothing lofty . . . no law . . . no relationships."[10] The "five" means by which civilization defended its prerogatives included, at various times, branding the forehead, cutting off noses or feet, strangulation, decapitation, drawing-and-quartering, cutting out the ribs of the still-living victim, and boiling in cauldrons of oil. Because of the extreme concern of Chinese people for preserving bodily integrity, death by starvation, slow and agonizing (though normally ending prematurely in strangulation within the constraining stocks), was typically favored over quicker methods that desecrated the body. For the more torturous methods, Chinese traditions of "mercy" saw to it that massive amounts of alcohol or drugs were administered to modify the suffering of the victim.

Zhi Lin's paintings are rooted in his intense study of Chinese material culture: the mechanical contrivances of death, late Qing security officers' uniforms, local foodstuffs, stone paving from the Beijing palace, nineteenth-century *yixing* teapots, and the observed details of daily behavior all come from research into ancient prints and museum collections. Yet these paintings are also no less Western, a mixing of cultures that map a path of artistic discovery leading backward in time from Jesuit painters and engravers at the Manchu court through the unusual color combinations of El Greco, Pontormo, and Rosso and compositional devices of Tintoretto and Caravaggio, back to Michelangelo and Titian's depictions of the saved and the damned and of Jesus Christ as the Ultimate Victim.

The undamned are just as important thematically as the condemned in Zhi Lin's works, gathered *en masse* in the upper registers, their colorful garb and their emotional disengagement all but mocking the tragedy of lives lost in their midst. Their outstretched arms and upward movement contribute to the celebration and sublimation embodied by flying and floating acrobats, the fluttering banner of a marketplace, a child's kite, a dragon dance, and these contrast sharply with the open space below in which the pitiable fall from grace of the damned is isolated and put on public display. But there is no pity: the starving are set in a food market (Figure 7.5); the beheaded are surrounded by slabs of slaughtered swine; a dog waits impatiently to devour the remains of the prisoner to be drawn-and-quartered; those to be shot meet their end in a mundane scene indicating the thorough regimentation of modern daily life. Most important to the artist, thematically, in all of these paintings is the docility of those who surround the victims, eating or watching holiday celebrations or traveling about with scarcely a sign of sympathy and not much more of curiosity. Without their silence, autocracy could hardly be maintained; through silence, they become complicit in the violence of their society. And yet, they too are victims, robbed not of their lives but of their humanity, their civilization. One looks for the exceptions: in a scene where the honking of horns (as a trope for "no protesting, no outcry") is forbidden, freedom of

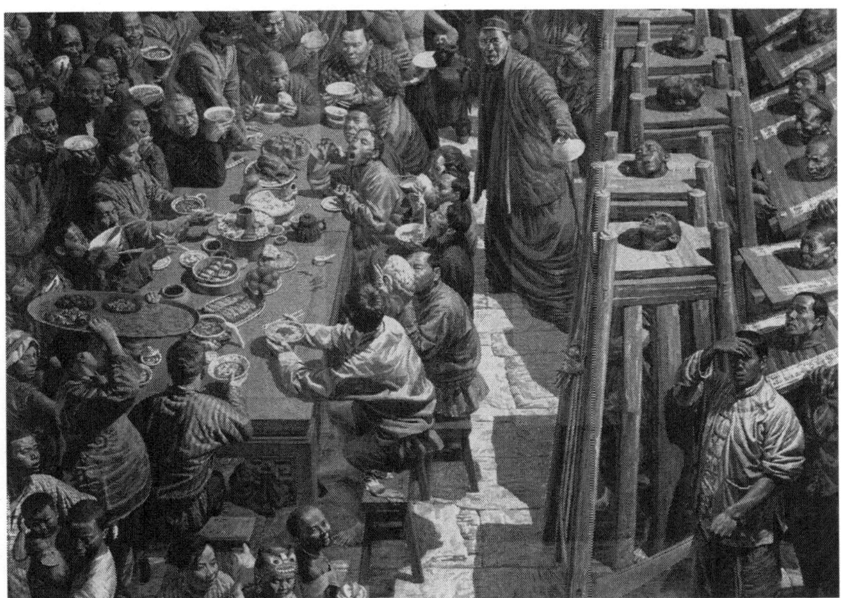

FIGURE 7.5. Detail from *Starvation*, Zhi Lin, from the series *Five Capital Punishments in China*, 1999. Collection of the artist.

movement is proscribed, perhaps we see the slightest turn of a head and a hint of sympathy from a young women, but she dares not express her feelings to others and perhaps not even to herself. In the name of stability there is only colonization, a force that doesn't civilize so much as it terrorizes its subject into a tame submission, "killing the chickens to scare the monkey." Thus, in the scene of drawing-and-quartering, the dragon's ritual pursuit of the pearl of wisdom lacks any real basis in wisdom or compassion.

Although the setting is China and in four out of five paintings the era is specifically Manchu, Zhi Lin does not intend to limit this topic to any single time or region or class, or even by implication to China. Today, it references Guantanamo and Darfur as much as it does the China of Tiananmen and Qin Shihuangdi. Thus, hybridity and the artist's embrace of Western stylistic traditions. Thus, a table set with foodstuffs from both north and south China (both hotpot and bamboo cookers), with ceramics from Yixing and Jingdezhen set side by side with lacquerware from Hunan. Thus, the presence of children to suggest the passing of these traditions of violence and passivity from generation to generation. Thus, the appearance of the artist himself in four of the paintings (as body model for all of the men slated for decapitation; as the foremost figure about to be executed by firing squad; three times over as a happy nonobserver in *Starvation*; and twice in *Drawing-and-Quartering*, once as a prisoner and once dispassionately fanning himself while enjoying the dragon dance), all of these appearances indicating the karmic uncertainty of remaining the bystander or becoming the victim of dispassion, and displaying the potential for being either caring or callous, feelings that Zhi Lin admits to having in himself.

Zhi Lin's East–West hybrid works are all mounted thanka-style, in reference to the Dalai Lama. The mounting also includes various images stenciled along the vertical margins: Confucius on Zhi Lin's *Execution by Flaying*, Guanyin on *Decapitation*, Sun Yat-sen and Mao Zedong on *Firing Squad*, Laozi on *Starvation*, Zhuangzi on *Drawing-and-Quartering*. On each but the drawn version of *Drawing-and-Quartering* is silkscreened in pale shades the silhouette of an ancient bronze ritual trident, a weapon symbolizing rule by force. Nearly five feet tall in the largest original examples excavated at Pingshan, Hebei province, from the royal tombs of the Zhongshan state including that of King Cuo (died ca. 308 BCE), Zhi Lin presents this as a "subliminal" message.[11] If one looks closely, it becomes apparent that Zhi Lin has depicted these silhouettes in reserve, lightly coloring the ground surrounding them rather than printing the outline of bronze figures themselves, and effectively *removing* them from the scene in an antiauthoritarian gesture. Transformed in this manner, they, like Zhi Lin himself, occupy the middle ground, a space between.

The hard-hitting, in-your-face style of director-writer-actor-producer Jiang Wen's cinematic masterpiece *Guizi laile, Devils on the Doorstep* (2000), seems reminiscent of films like Akira Kurosawa's *Rashomon* (1950) and Stanley Kubrick's *Dr. Strangelove*.[12] Placing Japanese- and American-backed colonizers on the same stage with communist subversives, whose presence is at best implicit and less significant than their conspicuous absence, it questions what room if any is left for an "authentic" Chinese experience, then in 1945 as now, when China seems so anxious to claim center stage for itself politically in East Asia at the same time as cultural diversity is being swept away by a wave of global sameness. In this cauldron of political conflict, *Devils* asks what is meant by "Chineseness" or "Japaneseness," or by that strange universal—"humanity"—that lies between but is constantly threatened with being squeezed out of existence.

Shot through with breakneck pacing and filmed on black-and-white stock with high-contrast lighting, *Devils on the Doorstep* is shown in extreme close-up and tightly framed in a way that reflects the forced intimacy of village life and the inability of helpless Chinese villagers to escape intruders from the outside (Figure 7.6). Like a densely wrought novel that has to be pondered while being read, *Devils* is a movie-house visualization of an intense dialogue in which each of the character-groups projects an imaginary, culturally

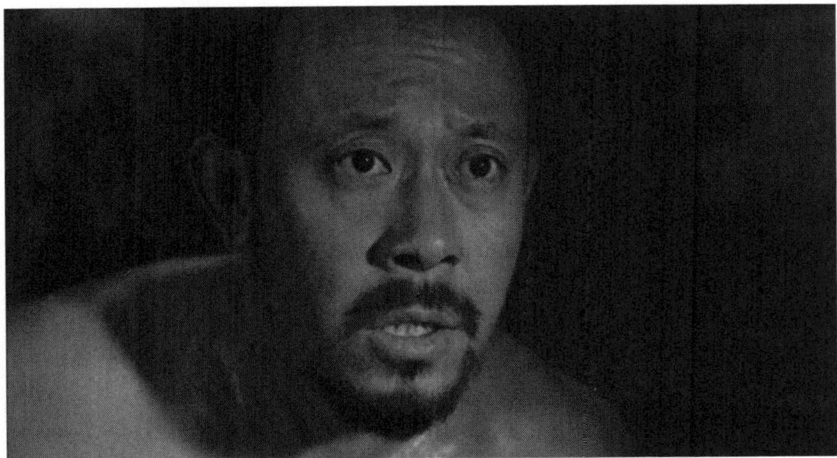

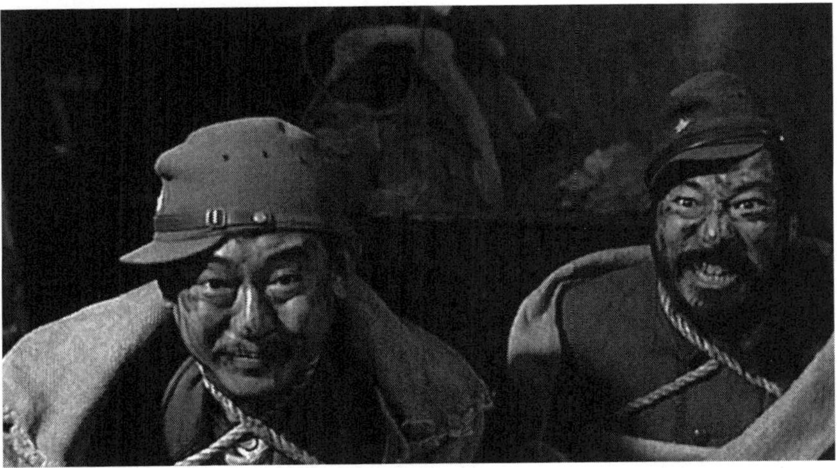

FIGURE 7.6. *Devils on the Doorstep* (Director Jiang Wen, 2000). (Top) Ma Dasan (actor Jiang Wen). (Bottom) Chinese translator Dong Hanchen (actor Yuan Ding), left; Japanese soldier Hanaya Kosaburo (actor Kagawa Teruyuki), right.

assigned role in the colonizing process while openly pondering the reality and the unreality of these roles and the various possible trajectories, outcomes, and escapes from the process if these roles can adequately be manipulated or successfully abandoned. But the forced pace of the film prevents much of the needed pondering and sets the audience in the same quandary as the film characters, who never have enough time to think their predicament through before they are obliged to act.

Set in the last months of the war against Japan, it begins with the unexpected delivery by an unseen, presumably communist, cadre to an ordinary Chinese peasant of two war captives, bound and gagged inside of burlap bags. Interrupted in the act of making love, the peasant Ma Dasan's attention is forcibly turned from typical peasant escapism to an unintended confrontation with worldly realities. Played by director-scriptwriter Jiang Wen himself, Ma Dasan is faced with the obvious expectation that he help the villagers avenge themselves for Japan's brutal colonization of their village. But as the heir to two thousand years of self-contained and essentially subservient village attitudes, this peace-loving protagonist innately tends away from mimicking the Japanese model of militancy. In the midst of pitched battle, where choice is narrowed to the question of which-side-are-you-on, colonizer or resistor, he becomes caught up in a philosophical tug-of-war. In the process, he is exposed to all the stereotypes of what differentiates Chinese (undisciplined, dirty) and Japanese (militant, cruel) behavior (Figure 7.7), but he also manages to discover and briefly embrace the values that bind these people together as real, civilized human beings, in contrast to mere animals. He rejects the rejection of Japanese by Chinese and of Chinese by Japanese. He insists on protecting the space between. In the end, however, every situation offers far greater complications than expected, and after virtually every permutation of every possible resolution has been explored, imagined, or put into practice, he is left with the realization that different men can aspire to entirely different virtues and that differences of circumstance can justify their behaving like dogs and donkeys. Civilization proves too thin, and Ma Dasan's "primitive" urge to reconcile the contradictions between others, along with the twists and turns of fate that he runs into and the untamed flaws in his own character, all prove so damnably frustrating that by the end he has simply seen too much of real life, run out of options, and a quick death (the Great Other) becomes preferable to a lingering existence in this world.

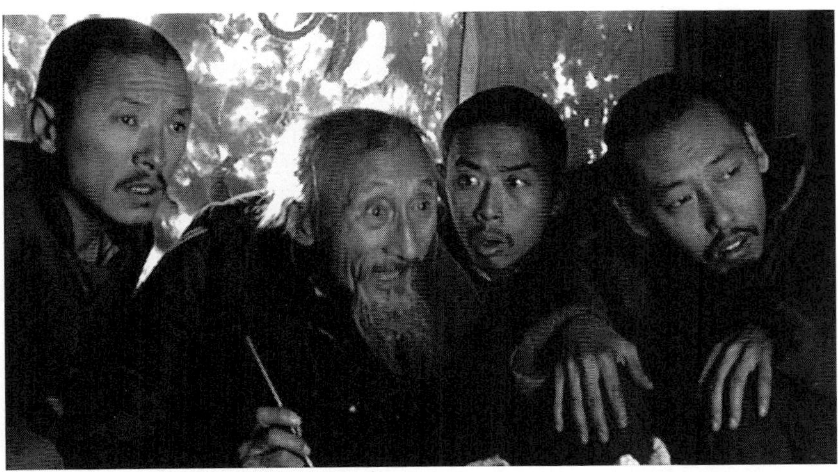

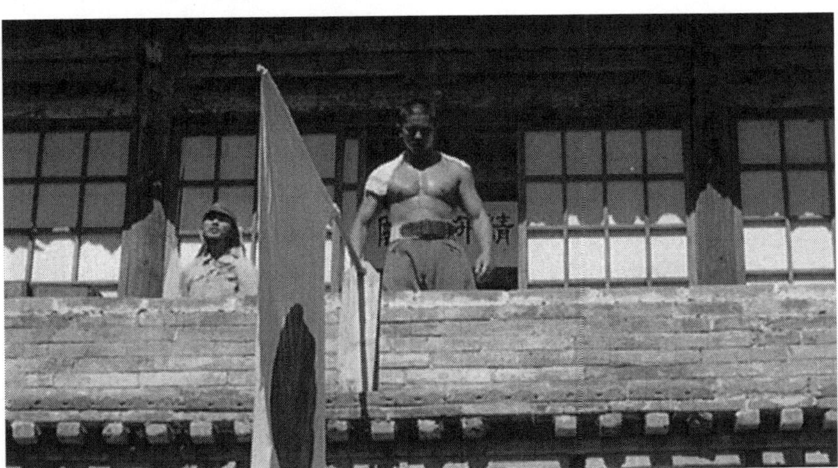

FIGURE 7.7. *Devils on the Doorstep.* (Top) Chinese villagers (actor Xi Zi as village elder, second from left). (Bottom) Japanese Captain Sakatsuka Inokichi (actor Sawada Kenya).

Like Don Quixote, Ma Dasan finds himself involved in an impossible quest for justice in an unjust world and is caught up in a tragicomedy of confused words and images. But unlike Quixote, he bears no weapons, wishes to assault no enemies, seeks no drama, and operates less through his own volition than through fate thrust upon him. It turns out that only one of his two prisoners is Japanese while the other is Chinese, a collaborator who translates. It is a shock to the villagers' assumptions of "difference," and yet the two captives could not be more different. The Chinese naturally aspires to longevity and fears for his life; he seeks security, practices inaction, while the Japanese fears only for his honor and struggles for a way to commit suicide rather than suffer the dishonor of imprisonment or death at the hand of enemy peasants. Radically opposed Chinese and Japanese attitudes toward the body are fully played out here. The translator, Dong Hanchen, introduces himself to the villagers saying, "I turn Japanese into Chinese and Chinese into Japanese," but he doesn't. Trying to protect the Japanese Hanaya Kosaburo from his own Japaneseness, Dong Hanchen constantly *mis*translates. The opening encounter reads something like this:

> Village head: "So, what's his name. Have him tell us himself"
> Hanaya Kosaburo (in Japanese): "Shoot me! Kill me! If you've got the guts. Cowards!"
> Villagers: "How come his name's so long?"
> Village head: "Has he killed Chinese men? Violated Chinese women?"
> Hanaya (in Japanese): "Of course. That's what I came to China for."
> Dong Hanchen ("translating" this): "He's new to China. Hasn't seen any women yet. He's killed no one. He's a cook." Then, to Hanaya: "Why are you doing this?"
> Hanaya (in Japanese, to Hanchen): "I want to anger these cowards! I won't cooperate with swine!"
> Dong Hanchen: "He begs you not to kill him!"

Failing at suicide, then tied up so that he can no longer keep trying, Hanaya decides to starve himself to death and spits his food in Ma Dasan's face when fed.

> Hanaya: "Bastard! Humiliating an Imperial soldier! I'll kill you! Chinese pig!"
> Ma Dasan: "What's he want?"
> Dong Hanchen "translates": "White flour."

So Ma Dasan goes looking for white flour, a precious commodity at that time, while Hanaya says to his translator: "Dong. Teach me some Chinese . . . I want to swear at them. Infuriate them and they'll have to kill me. Chinese hate people who curse their ancestors. . . . I want to turn the curses you teach me into bullets to fire at them." When Dasan and his mistress return, actually bearing some white-flour dumplings for him, Hanaya leers at them, sneers at them, cursing them with the phrases Dong has taught him (Figure 7.8):

> "Brother and sister-in-law, happy new year! You're my granddad, I'm your son."
> Yu'er, the mistress, looking puzzled: "The words are nice. Why does he sound so angry?"
> Ma Dasan: "Japs sound the same whether they're happy or angry. Why d'ya think we call them devils?"

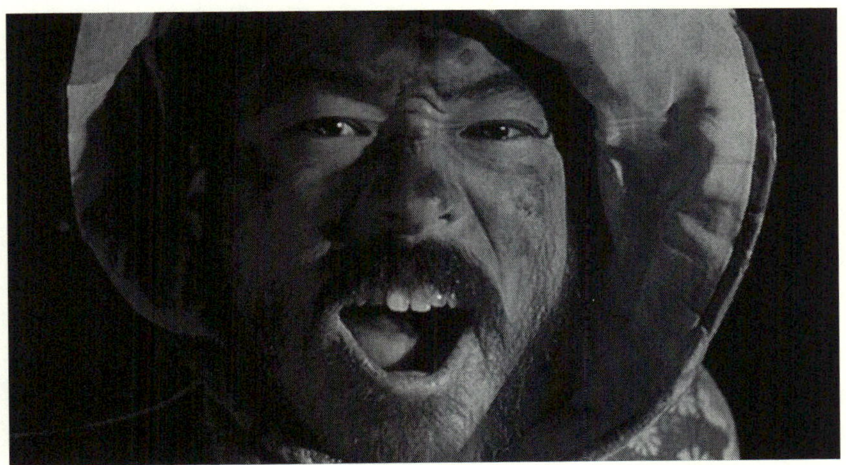

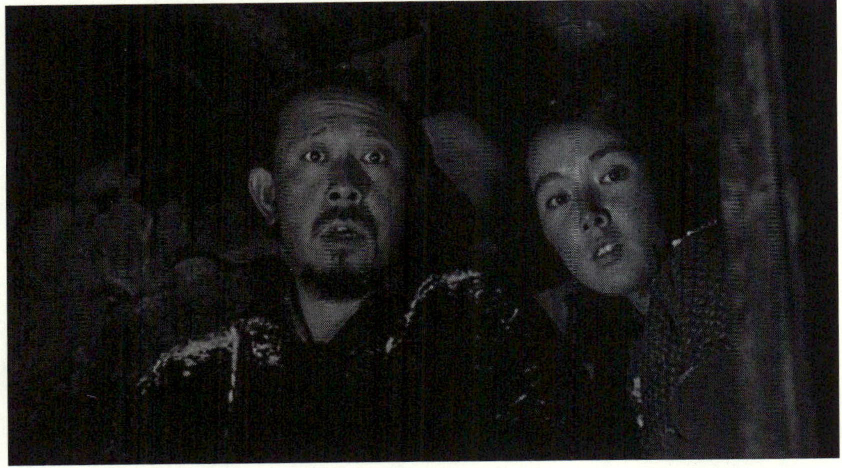

FIGURE 7.8. *Devils on the Doorstep.* (Top) Hanaya Kosaburo. (Bottom) Ma Dasan and Yu'er (actress Jiang Hongbo).

> Hanaya, looking puzzled by the failure of his insults to produce
>   the intended effect, asks his translator: "Why aren't they
>   angry?"
> Dong Hanchen: "Japanese are always cursing them. They're used
>   to it."
> Ma Dasan, now planning to release his prisoners to the Japanese
>   for a reward: "Now eat up. It's your last chance. By tonight,
>   you'll be on the road."
> Hanaya, looking at the white flour Dasan has scrounged: "Hoard-
>   ers. I'll kill you for sure."
> Dong Hanchen: "No chance of that."
> Hanaya: "Why not?
> Dong Hanchen: "'On the road' means 'to die' in Chinese. This
>   is our last meal. We're goners."
> Hanaya: "Why don't they act like they're going to kill us?"
> Dong Hanchen: "Even when a Chinese kills someone, his expres-
>   sion never changes."
> Village head, to an increasingly distressed looking Dong Hanchen:
>   "You'll be on the road soon, and whatever happens, happens.
>   Enjoy your dumplings."
> Dong Hanchen, sure now that he's about to be killed: "All right. I
>   will. And then I'll 'go on the road.' I lived by my mouth. Now
>   I'll die by it. If only I hadn't learned Japanese! In my next life
>   I'll come back a mute."

Obviously, the two captives are as much caught in a space between conflicting norms as are Ma Dasan and the villagers. When it begins to dawn on them that they really aren't going to die, Hanaya begins to cry, his honorable death once again deferred:

> Village head: "What now?"
> Dong Hanchen, much relieved for his own sake: "The Japs are
>   like this. They love to cry. They love to sing."

Throughout much of the film, tragedy is preceded by this kind of comedy as Jiang Wen plays with these stereotypes and dismisses them only to have his characters resurrect them all over again in new forms and contexts and turn them, in the end, into reality.

Progress toward transnational reconciliation is made among this small experimental group, aided by the discovery that Hanaya is no *samurai* at all but just a lowly villager like his Chinese captors. He happens to come from the same village as his Japanese commander and derives his militancy from him, but now becomes demilitarized and recolonized, class trumping nationality. But after Hanaya befriends the Chinese peasants and is returned unharmed by them, he is beaten brutally for surviving by his commander, who has already reported his noble death in battle and had him installed in the notorious Yasukuni Shrine. And an even worse fate still awaits the villagers, more horrible than anyone has foreseen. On the night of the Japanese military surrender, August 15, 1945, the Japanese commander (a true militant, feeling betrayed by his own emperor and now more loyal to the culture of colonization than to the cult of personality) first fetes and then slaughters the entire village.

The suddenly victorious Nationalist Chinese troops led by Colonel Gao now arrive with a band of jeep-driving, gum-chewing American bodyguards to establish a new political order within the community. The colonel's first act is to use the translator Dong Hanchen as a model victim upon whom to build his authority, and he has him shot as a collaborator. Ma Dasan, having struggled to protect Hanchen and strained to maintain the "space between," seeing all postwar hope for a new, elevated order of justice disintegrate around him, goes berserk. Slaughtering unarmed Japanese soldiers as they had once slaughtered his fellow villagers, he is subdued and condemned by the Nationalist colonel to be decapitated. The stereotypes of difference and the "space between," an alternative order to nationalism and demonization, collapse, and no one is the better for it.

As a final agonizing twist, based on old, unchanging values, the colonel insists that the task of executing Ma Dasan be carried out by Japanese because Ma Dasan, having lowered himself to the status of an animal, shouldn't pollute the hands of a Chinese soldier with his blood—the Chinese now adopting all the colonial arrogance of the Japanese. The Japanese soldier designated to carry out this deed is none other than Hanaya, who helped to land Dasan in this cycle of events to begin with, whose life Dasan repeatedly risked his own to spare, and who by destroying this Chinese life recovers his Japanese "dignity." Ma Dasan dies: his head rolls across the execution ground nine times and stops, with three blinks and a smile, happy at last to exchange his crazy life on earth for peace in Heaven (Figure 7.10).

As Chinese theories of justice would have it, in violating the official order of things one offends against civilization itself, abandons

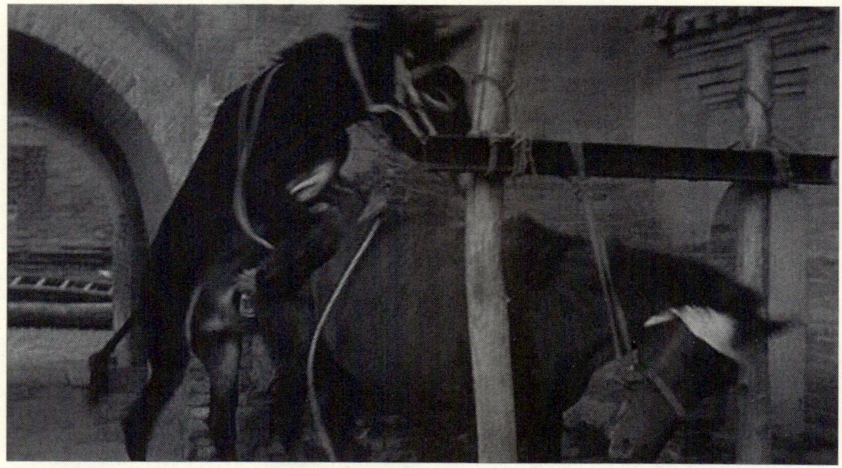

FIGURE 7.9. *Devils on the Doorstep.* Chinese mule violates Japanese horse.

one's humanity, and deserves no more mercy than an animal (for whom the Chinese have traditionally had little functional empathy). Like Zhi Lin's victims, they occupy a unique space. Having wandered into an ambivalent "third space," somewhere between the native passivity of the Chinese peasantry and the uniformly militant and unforgiving codes of the Japanese imperialists, Chinese communists, and Chinese Nationalists, Dasan has unwittingly become to all others something of a barnyard beast, like Xu Bing's cross-cultural pigs and trans-speciated "pandas." The film offers constant reminders of species-transference through a verbal barrage of Japanese references to the Chinese as pigs and dogs. The film's ongoing punctuation by a series of barnyard images offers a more subtle cinematic version of the same: the Japanese commander's horse lowers its head in shame when Hanaya makes his unwelcome return to ranks; sharing the villagers delight at trading their unwanted captives for six cartloads of Japanese grain, a celebratory Chinese donkey attempts to hump the Japanese commander's horse, with no evident respect for superior genetics, a comi-tragic turning point that signals the futility of Chinese–Japanese reconciliation (Figure 7.9).

Surrendering Japanese troops are herded into the city square side by side with a flock of docile sheep; on the execution ground, a marauding pig rides off with a startled Nationalist soldier on

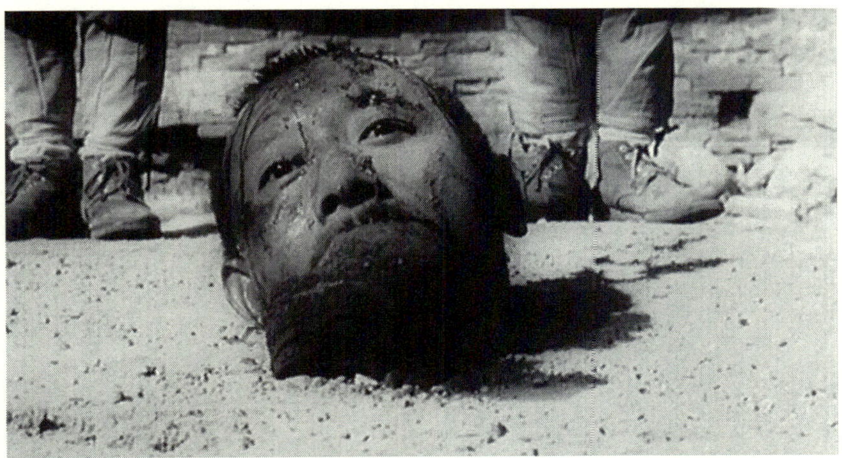

FIGURE 7.10. *Devils on the Doorstep.* The head of Ma Dasan.

his back, making a laughingstock of the Chinese colonel's poor attempt to install a new moral order; an irritated donkey mare digs a hoof into her own innocently nursing foal, kicking it aside just as the Chinese officer condemns his own fellow countryman, Ma Dasan, to death; another donkey suddenly wanders into view behind Dasan just at the moment he is allowed to make a final statement but instead brays to heaven like an inarticulate beast (Figure 7.11).

In the film world, production of *Devils on the Doorstep* earned director Jiang Wen a space of his own: an indefinite ban on future film direction. And *Devils*, winner of the Jury Grand Prize at Cannes but never sanctioned for viewing in China, has only been visible abroad. Jiang moved to France, where he acquired a French bride, acting in a number of successful Chinese films but refusing to direct another film until he could make it in China.[13]

All four of the artists discussed here—Xu Bing, Zhang Hongtu, Zhi Lin, Jiang Wen—are dissident, antiauthoritarian. All four have developed signature styles based on borrowings from China and the West, transforming these into something neither East nor West, not just Chinese, not not Chinese. Their art creates and operates in a world of its own, in a space between. What impact it might have on the world of "Others" is open to question. Art is shaped by society in ways that can be measured in the art itself. But how does one

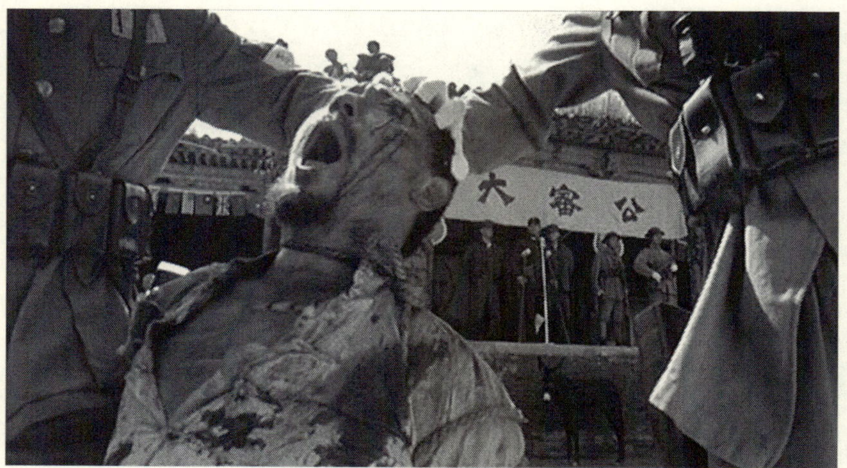

FIGURE 7.11. *Devils on the Doorstep*. Ma Dasan brays to Heaven.

measure whether art, in turn, changes society? Zhi Lin believes it must and it will. Near the time of this symposium, I met the Chinese-American writer Ha Jin, who fits the "in between" description of these other four artists and who raised the same question. He answered this with a laugh and a question of his own: "Do you think Lu Xun has changed the soul of China?"

NOTES

1. For the most recent of many studies on Xu Bing, see Jerome Silbergeld and Dora Ching, eds., *Persistence/Transformation: Text as Image in the Art of Xu Bing* (Princeton, NJ: Princeton University Press, 2005), including essays from a multidisciplinary variety of Chinese and non-Chinese viewpoints by Xu Bing, Hal Foster, Robert Harrist, Perry Link, and Gennifer Weisenfeld, and a bibliography of other publications.

2. On the question of Dong Qichang and Western influence, see James Cahill, *The Compelling Image: Nature and Style in Seventeenth-Century Painting* (Cambridge, MA: Harvard University Press, 1982), especially chapters 1 and 2, and the review of this by Wen Fong in *Art Bulletin* 68.3 (September 1986): 504–508.

3. Jerome Silbergeld, "Zhang Hongtu's Alternative History of Painting," in *Zhang Hongtu: An On-Going Painting Project* (New York: On-Going Publications, 2000); Jerome Silbergeld, "Zhang Hongtu: The Art of Straddling Boundaries," in *Zhang Hongtu* (Taipei and Beijing: Lin and Keng Gallery, 2007), viii–xxv.

4. Stevan Harrell, "Introduction," in *Cultural Encounters on China's Ethnic Frontiers*, ed. S. Harrell, 4 (Seattle and London: University of Washington Press, 1995).

5. Rey Chow, *Women and Chinese Modernity: The Politics of Reading between East and West* (Minneapolis: University of Minnesota Press, 1991), xvii.

6. "Zhang [Yimou] is building one semiotic system on another, in such a manner as always to bracket the denotative meaning of the 'raw' first level of signification. . . . What is displayed [in his films] is not so much woman or even feudal China per se as the act of displaying, of making visible. What Zhang 'fetishizes' is primarily cinematography itself. If we speak of a narcissism here, it is a repeated playing with 'the self' that is the visuality intrinsic to film. This play is the sexuality of Zhang's works. . . . Accordingly the seduction of Zhang's films—the appeal of his visual ethnography—is that they keep crossing boundaries and shifting into new spheres of circulation. The wish to 'liberate' Chinese women, which seems to be the 'content,' shifts into the liberation of 'China,' which shifts into the liberation of the 'image' of China on films, which shifts into the liberation of 'China' on film in the international culture market, and so on." Chow is writing here of Zhang's films *Red Sorghum* (1987), *Judou* (1990), and *Raise the Red Lantern* (1991). See Rey Chow, *Primitive Passions: Visuality, Sexuality, Ethnography, and Contemporary Chinese Cinema* (New York: Columbia University Press, 1995), 149. See my reponses to this in Jerome Silbergeld, *China into Film: Frames of Reference in Contemporary Chinese Cinema* (London: Reaktion Books, 1999).

7. Zhi Lin produced two versions of the final composition, the first a completed drawing, finished in 2003, and a painted version of this completed in 2007. For the first five finished works, see Jan Schall et al., *Zhi Lin: Crossing History/Crossing Cultures* (Seattle: Frye Art Museum, 2003).

8. Schall et al., *Zhi Lin*, 8.

9. For a review of early twentieth-century fiction on this subject, see David Der-wei Wang, *The Monster That Is History: History, Violence, and Fictional Writing in Twentieth-Century China* (Berkeley: University of California Press, 2004).

10. *Xiao Jing, The Book of Filial Piety*; cf. translation by James Legge, *The Sacred Books of China: The Texts of Confucianism* (Oxford: Clarendon Press, 1899), vol. I, *The Hsiao King*, 481.

11. For an illustration of this, see Yang Xiaoneng, ed., *The Golden Age of Chinese Architecture: Celebrated Discoveries from the People's Republic of China* (New Haven, CT: Yale University Press, 1999), 355–356.

12. *Devils on the Doorstep (Guizi laile, The Devils Have Come)*. Director, Jiang Wen. Screenplay, Jiang Wen, Shu Ping, also Liu Xing, Shi

Jianquan, Li Haiying. Original text, You Fengwei, novella *Shengcun* (*Survival*). Cinematography, Gu Changwei. Film editing, Folmer Wiesinger, Zhang Yifan. Original music, Cui Jian, Li Haiying, Liu Xing. Art direction, Cai Weidong. Producers, Dong Ping, Jiang Wen, Zheng Quangang. Studio, Asia Union Film & Entertainment, China Film Coproduction Corporation. Black-and-white and color. 139 minutes. *Devils on the Doorstep* and Jiang Wen's earlier film, *In the Heat of the Sun* (*Yangguang canlan de rizi*, 1994) are the subject of my book *Body in Question: Image and Illusion in Two Chinese Films by Director Jiang Wen* (Princeton, NJ: Princeton University Press, 2008).

13. *Devils on the Doorstep*, long unavailable for viewing in America as well as in China, was finally released with English subtitles on DVD in April 2005, by Home Vision Entertainment. In 2005, after a five-year hiatus, Jiang Wen began directing a new film, *The Sun Also Rises* (*Taiyang zaici shengqi*), which was released in 2007.

Bibliography on Xu Bing and Related Issues in Contemporary Chinese Art

ZOE LI

Abe, Stanley K. "No Questions, No Answers: China and *A Book from the Sky*." *Boundary* 225, no. 3 (Autumn 1998): 169–192.

Allott, Robin. "Language and the Origin of Semiosis." In *Origins of Semiosis: Sign Evolution in Nature and Culture*, edited by Winfried Noth, 255–268. Berlin and New York: Mouton de Gruyter, 1994.

Ames, Roger T. "*Li* and the A-theistic Religiousness of Classical Confucianism." In *Confucian Spirituality*, edited by Tu Wei-ming and Mary Evelyn Tucker, 174. New York: The Crossroad Publishing Company, 2003.

Ames, Roger T., and David L. Hall. *Focusing the Familiar: A Translation and Philosophical Interpretation of the* Zhongyong. Honolulu: University of Hawai'i Press, 2001.

———. *Dao De Jing: "Making This Life Significant": A Philosophical Translation*. New York: Ballantine Books, 2003.

Ames, Roger T., and Henry Rosemont, Jr. *The Analects of Confucius: A Philosophical Translation*. New York: Ballantine Books, 1998.

Arac, Jonathan. "Chinese Postmodernism: Toward a Global Context." *Boundary* 224, no. 3 (Fall 1997): 262–275.

Baker, Steve. *The Postmodern Animal*. London: Reaktion Books, 2000.

Bal, Mieke. *Travelling Concepts in the Humanities: A Rough Guide*. Toronto: University of Toronto Press, 2002.

Barme, Geremie. "Exploit, Export, Expropriate: Artful Marketing From China, 1989–93." In *New Art from China, 1989–93*, edited by Johnson Chang, 47–51. Hong Kong: Hanart, 1993.

Barthes, Roland. "The Death of the Author." In *The Death and Resurrection of the Author?*, edited by W. Irwin, 3–9. London: Greenwood Press, 2002.

Benjamin, Walter. *Reflections.* Edited by Peter Demetz. Translated by Edmund Jephcott. New York: Harcourt Brace Jovanovich, 1978.

Berger, Patricia. "Pun Intended: A Response to Stanley Abe, 'Reading the Sky.'" In *Cross-Cultural Readings of Chineseness: Narratives, Images, and Interpretations of the 1990's*, edited by Yeh Wenhsin, 80–100. Berkeley: Institute of East Asian Studies, UC Berkeley, 2000.

Berger, Peter, and Samuel P. Huntington. *Many Globalizations: Cultural Diversity in the Contemporary World.* Oxford and New York: Oxford University Press, 2002.

Berthrong, John H. *Concerning Creativity: A Comparison of Chu Hsi, Whitehead, and Neville.* Albany: State University of New York Press, 1998.

Bhabha, Homi K. *The Location of Culture.* New York: Routledge, 2002.

Boardman, Andrew. "Xu Bing's Square Words and the Fragility of Language." In *Around Us, Inside Us—Continents Boras Konsmuseum*, 18–22. Sweden: Boras Konsmuseum, 1997.

Bolter, Jay David. *Writing Space: The Computer, Hypertext and the History of Writing.* Mahwah, NJ: Lawrence Erlbaum Associates, 1991.

Byram, M. *Cultural Studies in Foreign Language Education.* Clevedon, UK: Multilingual Matters, 1989.

Cahill, James. *The Compelling Image: Nature and Style in Seventeenth-Century Painting.* Cambridge, MA: Harvard University Press, 1982.

Chan, Wing-tsit. *A Source Book of Chinese Philosophy.* Princeton, NJ: Princeton University Press, 1963.

Chang, K.C. *Art, Myth and Ritual: The Path to Political Authority in Ancient China.* Cambridge, MA: Harvard University Press, 1983.

Chang, Tsong-Zung. "Beyond the Middle Kingdom: An Insider's View." In *Inside Out: New Chinese Art*, edited by Gao Minglu, 67–75. Berkeley and Los Angeles: University of California Press, 1998.

———, ed. *Xingxing shinian (The Stars: 10 Years).* Hong Kong: Hanart 2 Gallery, 1989.

Cheek, Tim. "Where Do Correct Ideas Come From? Xu Jilin and the Search for a Theory of Practice among Contemporary Chinese Intellectuals." University of British Columbia. Article draft for the China Studies Group, Centre for Chinese Research, IAR/UBC, August 2004.

Chino Kaori. "Gender in Japanese Art." In *Gender and Power in the Japanese Visual Field*, edited by Joshua S. Mostow, Norman Bryson, and Maribeth Graybill, 25. Honolulu: University of Hawai'i Press, 2003.

Chow, Rey. *Primitive Passions: Visuality, Sexuality, Ethnography, and Contemporary Chinese Cinema.* New York: Columbia University Press, 1995.

———. *Women and Chinese Modernity: The Politics of Reading between East and West.* Minneapolis: University of Minnesota Press, 1991.

Ciyuan Dictionary. Beijing: Dictionary Press, 1988.

Clark, John, ed. *Modernity in Asian Art.* Australia: Wild Peony, 1993.

Clarke, J.J. *The Tao of the West: Western Transformations of Taoist Thought*. London and New York: Routledge, 2000.

Cleary, Thomas, trans. *The Sutra of Hui-Neng Grand Master of Zen with Hui-neng's Commentary on the Diamond Sutra*. Boston: Shambala, 1998.

Cohen, J.L. *The New Chinese Painting, 1949–1986*. New York: H.N. Abrams, 1987.

Coleman, James W. *The New Buddhism: The Western Transformation of an Ancient Tradition*. Oxford: Oxford University Press, 2001.

Dai, Jinhua. "Imagined Nostalgia." *Boundary* 224, no. 3 (Fall 1997): 143–161.

Davidson, Donald. "A Nice Derangement of Epitaphs." In *Truth, Language, and History*. New York and Oxford, 1986.

———. "What Metaphors Mean." In *Inquiries into Truth and Interpretation*. New York: Oxford University Press, 1984.

Davies, Gloria. "Anticipating Community, Producing Dissent: The Politics of Recent Chinese Intellectual Praxis." *China Review* 2, no. 2 (Fall 2002).

Der-wei Wang, David. *The Monster That Is History: History, Violence, and Fictional Writing in Twentieth-Century China*. Berkeley: University of California Press, 2004.

Deutsch, Eliot. *Persons and Valuable Worlds: A Global Philosophy*. Lanham: Rowman and Littlefield Publishers, 2002.

Dewey, John. *Early Works, 1892–98*. 5 vols. Edited by Jo Ann Boydston. Carbondale: Southern Illinois University, 1969–1972.

———."Having an Experience." In *The Philosophy of John Dewey*, edited by John J. McDermott. Chicago: University of Chicago Press, 1973.

———. *Human Nature and Conduct*. Mineola, NY: Dover Publications, Inc., 2002.

———. "Religion versus the Religious." In *The Later Works. Vol. 9*, edited by Jo Ann Boydston. Carbondale and Edwardsville: Southern Illinois University Press, 1986.

———. "Time and Individuality." In *The Later Works. Vol. 14*, edited by Jo Ann Boydston, 99–102. Carbondale and Edwardsville: Southern Illinois University Press, 1988.

Dumoulin, Heinrich. *Zen Buddhism: A History*. Translated by James Heisig and Paul Knitter. New York: Macmillan, 1988.

Erickson, Britta. *The Art of Xu Bing: Words without Meaning, Meaning without Words*. Seattle and London: University of Washington Press, 2001.

———. *Three Installations by Xu Bing*. Madison, WI: Elvehjem Museum of Art, 1991.

Fibicher, Bernhard. "Cultural Partnerships, Maybe More: On the Reception of Contemporary Chinese Art in the West." In *Mahjong: Contemporary Chinese Art from the Sigg Collection*, edited by Bernhard

Fibicher and Matthias Frehner, 41–48. Ostfildern-Ruit, Germany: Hatje Cantz Verlag, 2005.

Fields, Rick. *How the Swans Came to the Lake*. Boulder, CO: Shambala, 1992.

Finn, John. *Natural Law and Natural Rights*. Oxford: Oxford University Press, 1980.

Foster, Hal. "The Artist as Ethnographer." In *The Return of the Real*. Cambridge: MIT Press, 1996.

Fu Shen, Glenn D. Lowry, and Ann Yonemura. *From Concept to Context: Approaches to Asian and Islamic Calligraphy*. Washington DC: Smithsonian Institution, Freer Gallery of Art, 1986.

Gadamer, Hans-Georg. *Truth and Method*. New York: Crossroad Publishing Company, 1985.

Gao Minglu, ed. *Inside Out: New Chinese Art*. San Francisco: Museum of Modern Art, 1998.

———. "Toward a Transnational Modernity." In *Inside Out: New Chinese Art*, edited by Gao Minglu. Berkeley and Los Angeles: University of California Press, 1998.

Gargain, Aldo. "Religious Experience as Event and Interpretation." In *Religion*, edited by Jacques Derrida and Gianni Vattimo. Stanford: Stanford University Press, 1998.

Goodman, Jonathan. "Bing Xu: 4,000 Characters in Search of a Meaning." *Art News. New York* 93, no. 7 (September 1994): 99–101.

———. "Chinese Character." *World Art, New York* 14 (1997).

Graham, A.C. *Chuang-tzu: The Inner Chapters*. Indianapolis: Hackett Publishing Company, 2001.

Green, Charles. "Beyond the Future: The Third Asia-Pacific Triennial." *Art Journal* 58, no. 4 (Winter 1999): 81–87.

Gu, Xiong, ed. *Gu Xiong and Xu Bing: Here Is What I Mean*. London: Museum of London, 2004.

Harrell, Stevan. "Introduction." In *Cultural Encounters on China's Ethnic Frontiers*, edited by S. Harrell, 4. Seattle and London: University of Washington Press, 1995.

Heidegger, Martin. *On the Way to Language*. New York: HarperCollins Publishers, 1982.

Hershock, Peter D. *Chan Buddhism*. Honolulu: University of Hawai'i Press, 2005.

Hobsbawm, E., and T. Ranger, eds. *Invented Traditions*. Cambridge: Cambridge University Press, 1983.

"Hon to konputaten [Shomotsu henyo/Asia no jiku] 本とコンピューター展—書物変容・アジアの時空." *Kikan Hon to Konputa* 季刊本とコンピューター 14 (Autumn 2000).

Hope Mason, John. *The Value of Creativity: The Origins and Emergence of a Modern Belief*. Aldershot: Ashgate, 2003.

Hou, Hanru, and Gao Minglu. "Strategies of Survival in the Third Space: A Conversation on the Situation of Overseas Chinese Artists." In *Inside Out: New Chinese Art*, edited by Gao Minglu. Berkeley and Los Angeles: University of California Press, 1998.

Huang, Yongping. "Xiamen Dada-yizhong xianhoudai?" In *Xiamen Xin dada yishuzhan*. 1986.

Hui, Neng. Thomas Cleary, trans. *The Sutra of Hui-Neng Grand Master of Zen with Huineng's Commentary on the Diamond Sutra*. Boston: Shambala, 1998.

Jameson, Frederic. "Globalization and Political Strategy." *New Left Review* 4 (July–August 2000): 49–68.

———. *Postmodernism and Cultural Theories: Lectures in China (Houxiandaizhuyi he Wenhualilun)*. Xi'an: Shaanxi Teacher's University, 1987.

———. "Postmodernism, or the Cultural Logic of Late Capitalism." *New Left Review* 146 (July–August 1984).

Jullien, Francois. Sophie Hawkes, trans. *Detour and Access*. New York: Zone Books, 2000.

Kao Mayching, ed. *Twentieth-Century Chinese Painting*. Hong Kong: Oxford University Press, 1988.

Karetzky, Patricia. "A Modern Literati: The Art of Xu Bing." *Oriental Art* xlvii, no. 4 (2001): 41–52.

Koppel-Yang, Martina. *Semiotic Warfare: The Chinese Avant Garde 1979–1989. A Semiotic Analysis*. Shenzhen: Timezone 8, 2004.

Kovács, János Mátyás. "Rival Temptations and Passive Resistance: Cultural Globalization in Hungary." In *Many Globalizations: Cultural Diversity in the Contemporary World*, edited by Peter Berger, 146–182. Oxford: Oxford University Press, 2002.

Kraus, Richard C. *Brushes with Power: Modern Politics and the Chinese Art of Calligraphy*. Berkeley, Los Angeles, and Oxford: University of California Press, 1991.

Lacan, Jacques. *The Line and Light*. Oxford: Oxford University Press, 1989.

Lakoff, George. *Woman, Fire, and Dangerous Things: What Categories Reveal about the Mind*. Chicago: University of Chicago Press, 1987.

Lakoff, George and Mark Johnson. *Metaphors We Live By*. Chicago: University of Chicago Press, 1980.

Lavrijsen, Ria, ed. *Global Encounters in the World of Art: Collisions of Tradition and Modernity*. Amsterdam: Royal Tropical Institute, 1998.

Laycock, Steven W. "The Dialectics of Nothingness: A Reexamination of Shen-hsiu and Huineng." *Journal of Chinese Philosophy* 24 (1997): 19–41.

Le Blanc, Charles. *Huai Nan Tzu: Philosophical Synthesis in Early Han Thought, The Idea of Resonance (Kan-Ying) with a Translation and Analysis of Chapter Six*. Hong Kong: Hong Kong University Press, 1985.

Legge, James. *The Sacred Books of China: The Texts of Confucianism.* Oxford: Clarendon Press, 1899.

Leung, Simon, Janet A. Kaplan, Gu Wenda, Xu Bing, and Jonathan Hay. "Pseudo-Languages: A Conversation with Wenda Gu, Xu Bing, and Jonathan Hay." *Art Journal* 58, no. 3 (Autumn 1999): 86–99.

Li Feng-mao. "Seriousness and Playfulness: Daoist San-yuan Festival and Customs of Tang Dynasty." In *Anthology of the Tenth Annual Conference of Institute of Chinese Literature and Philosophy.* Taipei: Academia Sinica Press, 2001.

Ling, L.H.M. *Postcolonial International Relations: Conquest and Desire between Asia and the West.* New York: Palgrave, 2002.

Little, Stephen, ed. *Taoism and the Arts of China.* Chicago: The Art Institute, 2000.

Liu, April. "An Interview with Xu Bing: Nonsensical Spaces and Cultural Tatoos." *Yishu Journal of Contemporary Chinese Art* (December 2005): 88–95.

Martin, Jean-Hubert, et al., eds. *Magiciens de la terre.* Paris: Editions du Centre Pompidou, 1989.

Marx, Karl, and Friedrich Engels. *Manifesto of the Communist Party.* Signet Classics, 1998.

Meech-Pekarik, Julia. "Disguised Scripts and Hidden Poems in an Illustrated Heian Sutra: Ashide and Uta-e in the Heike Nogyo." *Archives of Asian Art* 31 (1977–1978): 53–78.

Nakamura Yukihiko 中村幸彦: *Kinsei no kanshi* 近世の漢詩. Tokyo: Kumiko shoin 汲古書院, 1986.

Nishi Kojiro 西孝二郎. Saiyuki no kozo『西遊記』の構造. Tokyo: Shinfu-sha 新風社, 1997.

Nochlin, Linda. *The Politics of Vision: Essays on 19th Century Art and Society, Women, Art and Power, and Realism.* Penguin, 1989.

Norman, J., and T. Mei. "The Austroasiatics in Ancient South China: Some Lexical Evidence." *Monumenta Serica* 32 (1976): 274–301.

Okutsu, Hijiri. "Gengo no kouzo toshiteno shikakugeijutsu—Shu Bin no baai. 言語の構造としての視覚芸術−徐冰の場合." *Yamaguchi daigaku tetsugakukenkyu* 山口大学哲学研究 11 (2002): 2752.

Oshita, Sanae 大下さなえ. "Mishiranu moji to 'Meiku' 見知らぬ文字と「明空」." *Meiku* 明空 2 (1998).

Ota Tatsuo 太田辰夫. *Saiyuki no kenkyu* 西遊記の研究. Tokyo: Kenbunsh-uppan 研文出版, 1984.

Otto, Rudolf. *The Idea of the Holy: An Inquiry into the Non-Rational Factor in the Idea of the Divine and Its Relation to the Rational.* London: Oxford University Press, 1958.

Palmer, Richard E. *Hermeneutics.* Evanston, IL: Northwestern University Press, 1969.

Papastergiadis, Nikos. "The Limits of Cultural Translation." In *Over Here: International Perspectives on Art and Culture*, edited by Gerardo Mosquera and Jean Fisher, 330–347. Cambridge and London: MIT Press, 2005.

Pepper, Stephen. *Concept and Quality: A World Hypothesis*. La Salle, IL: Open Court, 1967.

———. *World Hypotheses: A Study in Evidence*. Berkeley: University of California Press, 1967.

Peterson, Willard J. "Making Connections: 'Commentary on the Attached Verbalizations' of the *Book of Change*." *Harvard Journal of Asiatic Studies* 42, no. 1: 67.

Pinker, Steven. *The Language Instinct: The New Science of Language and Mind*. New York: Morrow, 1994.

Richard, Nelly. "Postmodern Decentredness and Cultural Periphery: The Disalignments and Realignments of Cultural Power." In *Beyond the Fantastic: Contemporary Art from Latin America*, edited by Gerardo Mosquera, 260–270. Boston: MIT Press, 1996.

Roth, Harold D. "The Inner Cultivation Tradition of Early Daoism." In *Religions of China in Practice*, edited by Donald S. Lopez, Jr. Princeton, NJ: Princeton University Press, 1996.

———. *The Textual History of the Huai-Nan Tzu*. Michigan: The Association for Asian Studies, 1992.

Rowe, Peter G., and Seng Kuan. *Architectural Encounters with Essence and Form in Modern China*. Cambridge, MA: MIT Press, 2002.

Said, Edward. *Orientalism: Western Conceptions of the Orient*. Pantheon, 1978. Revised edition Penguin, 1995.

Saussy, Haun. "*China Illustrata*: The Universe in a Cup of Tea." In *The Great Art of Knowing: The Baroque Encyclopedia of Athanasius Kircher*, edited by Daniel Stolzenberg, 111–112. Stanford, CA: Stanford University Libraries, 2001.

Schall, Jan, et al. *Zhi Lin: Crossing History/Crossing Cultures*. Seattle: Frye Art Museum, 2003.

Schell, Orville, and Shambaugh, David. *The China Reader: The Reform Era*. Toronto and New York: Vintage, 1999.

Sebeok, Thomas A. "Goals and Limitations of the Study of Animal Communication." In *Perspectives in Zoosemiotics*. The Hague: Mouton and Co., 1972.

Shaughnessy, Edward L., trans. *I Ching: The Classic of Changes*. New York: Ballantine, 1997.

Shepard, Paul. *Thinking Animals: Animals and the Development of Human Intelligence*. Athens: University of Georgia Press, 1998.

Shinoda, Takatoshi 篠田孝敏, ed. *Baberu no toshokan—moji, shomotsu, media* バベルの図書館―文字・書物・メディア *(The Library of Babel: Characters/Books/Media)*. Tokyo: NTT Intercommunication Center, 1998.

"Shu Binshi, gikanji o tsukuru—kanji to arufabetto no aratanadeai 徐冰氏、偽漢字をつくる—漢字とアルファベットの新たな 会い." *kikan Hon to Konputa* 季刊本とコンピューター 9 (Summer 1999): 22–33.

Silbergeld, Jerome. *Body in Question: Image and Illusion in Two Chinese Films by Director Jiang Wen.* Princeton, NJ: Princeton University Press, 2008.

———. *China into Film: Frames of Reference in Contemporary Chinese Cinema.* London: Reaktion Books, 1999.

———. "Zhang Hongtu's Alternative History of Painting." In *Zhang Hongtu: An On-Going Painting Project.* New York: On-Going Publications, 2000.

———. "Zhang Hongtu: The Art of Straddling Boundaries." In *Zhang Hongtu.* Taipei and Beijing: Lin and Keng Gallery, 2007.

Silbergeld, Jerome, and Dora Ching, eds. *Persistence/Transformation: Text as Image in the Art of Xu Bing.* Princeton, NJ: Princeton University Press, 2005.

Solomon, Andrew. "Their Irony, Humor (and Art) Can Save China." *New York Times Sunday Magazine*, December 19, 1993.

Spender, Stephen. *China Diary.* New York: Harry N. Abrams, Inc., 1982.

Steele, David Ramsey, ed. *Genius in Their Own Words.* Chicago: Open Court, 2002.

Suzuki, D.T. *The Zen Doctrine of No Mind.* London: Rider and Company, 1969.

Swetz, Frank J. "Leibniz, the Yijing, and the Religious Conversion of the Chinese." *Mathematics Magazine* (October 2003).

Tabarroni, Andrea. "Mental Signs and the Theory of Representation in Ockham." In *On the Medieval Theory of Signs*, edited by Umberto Eco and Costantino Marmo, 195–224. Amsterdam and Philadelphia: John Benjamins Publishing Company, 1989.

Tahara Tuguo 田原嗣郎: *Soraigaku no sekai* 徂徠学の世界. Tokyo: University of Tokyo Press 東京大学出版会, 1991.

Tang, Junyi. *Complete Works Vol 11.* Taipei: Xuesheng shuju, 1988.

Teiser, Stephen F. "The Spirits of Chinese Religion." In *Religions of China in Practice*, edited by Donald S. Lopez, Jr., 33. Princeton, NJ: Princeton University Press, 1996.

Treasures of a Sacred Mountain: Kukai and Mount Koya. Kyoto: Kyoto National Museum, 2003.

Tsuno Umitarō. *The Book and Computer* 14, no. 1 (December 2000): 209.

Tu Wei-ming. *Centrality and Commonality: An Essay on Confucian Religiousness.* Albany: State University of New York Press, 1989.

———. "Chinese Philosophy: A Synopsis." In *A Companion to World Philosophies,* edited by Eliot Deutsch and Ron Bontekoe. Oxford: Blackwell, 1997.

Vattimo, Gianni. *After Christianity*. Translated by Luca D'Isanto. New York: Columbia University Press, 2002.

Wang, Ning. "The Mapping of Chinese Postmodernity." *Boundary* 224, no. 3 (Fall 1997): 19–40.

Wang, Yichuan, Dao Zi, Zhang Yiwu, Lei Yi, Feng Boyi, Bai Quianshen, and John R. Finlay. "Seven Critics Discuss 'Elementary New English Calligraphy' by Xu Bing." *Artscircle, Guang Xi, China* 129 (February 1997): 21–24.

Wang Youru. *Linguistic Strategies in Daoist Zhuangzi and Chan Buddhism: The Other Way of Speaking*. London and New York: Routledge Curzon, 2003.

Wang Zhaowen. *One Is Good as Ten* 一 以当十. Beijing: Zhaohua meishu Press, 1956.

Weintraub, Linda. "Allegorical Personal." In *Animal. Anima. Animus*, 43–49. Pori, Finland: Pori Art Museum, 1998.

Wen Fong. *Art Bulletin* 68.3 (September 1986): 504–508.

Wen Fong, et al., eds. *Images of the Mind: Selections from the Edward L. Elliott Family and John B. Elliott Collections of Chinese Calligraphy and Painting at The Art Museum, Princeton, University*. Princeton, NJ: The Art Museum, 1984.

Whitehead, A.N. *Process and Reality: An Essay in Cosmology*. Donald Sherbourne corrected edition. New York: Free Press, 1979.

Wilhelm, Richard, and Cary F. Baynes. *I Ching or Book of Changes*. Princeton, NJ: Princeton University Press, 1967.

Wilkins, David G., Bernard Schultz, and Katheryn M. Linduff. *Art Past Art Present*. 4th ed. Upper Saddle River, NJ: Prentice Hall, 2001.

Wu Cheng'en, and W.J.F. Jenner, trans. *Journey to the West*. Beijing: Foreign Languages Press, 1982.

Wu Hung. "A 'Ghost Rebellion': Notes on Xu Bing's 'Nonsense Writing' and Other Works." *Public Culture* 6, no. 2 (Winter 1994): 411.

———. *Transience: Chinese Experimental Art at the End of the Twentieth Century*. Chicago: Smart Museum of Art, 1999.

———. "'Vernacular' Post-Modern: The Art of Song Dong and Yin Xiuzhen." In *Chopstick*, edited by C. Mao, Y. Xiuzhen, and S. Dong. Chambers Fine Art, 2002.

Wu, Hung, Wang Huansheng, and Feng Boyi, eds. *The First Guangzhou Triennial: A Decade of Experimental Chinese Art (1990–2000)*. Guangzhou: Guangdong Museum of Art, 2002.

Wu, Hung, and Christopher Phillips, eds. *Between Past and Future: New Photography and Video from China*. Chicago: Smart Museum of Art, 2004.

Wu Shanzhuan. "About the Red Humor." *Meishu Sichao (Art Waves)* 1 (1987).

Xu Bing. "To Frighten Heaven and Earth and Make the Spirits Cry 天地を嚇し鬼神を泣かす." In *Baberu no toshokan—moji, shomotsu, media* バベルの図書館—文字・書物・メディア *The Library of Babel: Characters/ Books/Media*, edited by Shinoda Takatoshi 篠田孝敏, 69. Tokyo: NTT Intercommunication Center, 1998.

———. "Looking for Something Different in a Quiet Place." *Beijing Qingnian Bao* (Beijing Youth Newspaper), February 10, 1989.

———. "Shu Binshi, gikanji o tsukuru—kanji to arufabetto no aratanadeai 徐冰氏、偽漢字をつくる—漢字とアルファベットの新たな出会い." *kikan Hon to Konputa* 季刊本とコンピューター 9 (Summer 1999): 22–33.

Xu, Zitong. "Xungen wenxue zhong de Jia Pingwa he Ah Cheng" [Jia Pingwa and Ah Cheng in Root-Searching Literature]. *Bulletin of Chinese Studies* 3 (1996): 81–91.

Yamagishi Tokubei 山岸徳平: *Kinsei Kanbungakushi* 近世漢文学史. Tokyo: Kumiko shoin 汲古書院, 1987.

Yang, Alice. *Why Asia?: Contemporary Asian and Asian American Art.* New York: New York University Press, 1998.

Yang Chengying. "Xu Bing de Yishu: Behind the Success." *Zhongguo Meishu Bao* 中国美术报 [*Chinese Art Weekly*] 22 (1989).

Yang Xiaoneng, ed. *The Golden Age of Chinese Architecture: Celebrated Discoveries from the People's Republic of China.* New Haven, CT: Yale University Press, 1999.

Yee, Chiang. *Chinese Calligraphy: An Introduction to Its Aesthetic and Technique.* Cambridge, MA: Harvard University Press, 1973.

Yoshikawa Kojiro 吉川幸次郎: *Jinsai/Sorai/Norinaga* 仁斎・徂来・宣長. Tokyo: Iwanami shoten 岩波書店, 1975.

Zhang, Xudong. "Modernity as Cultural Politics: Jameson and China." In *Frederic Jameson: A Critical Reader*, edited by Douglas Kellner and Sean Homer. New York: Palgrave Macmillan, 2004.

Zhao Li and Yu Ding, eds. *1542–2000: Documenting Chinese Oil Painting.* Changsha: Hunan Art Press, 2002.

Zito, Angela. *Of Body and Brush: Grand Sacrifice as Text/Performance in Eighteen-Century China.* Chicago: University of Chicago Press, 1997.

INTERNET SOURCES

http://news.bbc.co.uk/1/hi/wales/3577285.stm
http://www.asia.si.edu/exhibitions/online/xubing/default.html
http://www.echinaart.com/Advisor/adv_xubing_gallery.htm
http://www.xubing.com/

ADDITIONAL WEB RESOURCES

"Artist Talk" Fukuoka Asia Cultural Forum, no. 14, 2003. http://blog. readymade.jp/tiao/archives/000284.html.

Hon to konputa (The Book and The Computer) website version, *Saiyukiban Hon to konputaten* 西遊記版 本とコンピューター展, December 2000. http://www.honco.net/honcoten/.

The Library of Babel バベルの図書館 http://www.ntticc.or.jp/Archive/1998/The_Library_of_Babel/preface_j.html.

Moji no izumai 文字のいずまい, no. 5. http://www.gei-shin.co.jp/comunity/03/05_2.html.

Sendai Media Talk 仙台メディア・トーク. http://www.smt.jp/opening/exhibition2/exhibition2_8.html.

Sherrill, Martha. "The American Yen for Zen." *Slate*. http://slate.msn.com/id/105946/ January 2005.

Usuda, Shoji 臼田捷治. "On the Enigmatic: 'Proliferating Books' and Their Verso, the 'Signifying Power of Writing'" 「拡散する書物」と、その裏返しの「文字の表徴力」の不可思議さをめぐって *ICC*.

List of Important Events between 1979 and 2005

SUSAN CHANG

YEAR	CHINA	TAIWAN
1979	—Beijing and Washington announce full diplomatic relations.	—The US terminates formal diplomatic ties with the Republic of China in Taiwan.
	—*The New Spring Exhibition* (Xinchun huahui zhanlan 新春繪畫展覽) opens in Beijing featuring some 40 artists from different generations.	—The performance work *Cage Piece* (ziqiu 自囚) by Taiwanese artist Hsieh Te-ching 谢德庆 in New York provokes controversy.
	—Yuan Yunsheng's 袁运生 mural painting at the Beijing International Airport *Water-Splashing Festival: Ode to Life*, (Poshuijie: shengming de zange 泼水节: 生命的赞歌) includes nude female figures which triggers a serious debate.	—*Retrospective Exhibition of Taiwan Art during Japanese Colonization* (Guangfu qian Taiwan meishu huiguzhan 光复前台湾美术回顾展) opens.
	—*Twelve Artists Show* (Shierren huazhan 十二人画展) opens in Shanghai featuring Impressionist and Postimpressionist works.	—Li Chung-sheng 李仲生, mentor to the Eastern Painting Group, holds his first and only solo exhibition.
	—Scar Painting (Shanghen huihua 伤痕绘画) and the Stars Group (Xing xing Meizhan 星星美展) emerge as the two most important art movements of 1979 which aim at criticizing the realities of contemporary China.	—A demonstration organized by oppositional politicians and the *Formosa Magazine* staff aimed at advocating democracy ends in confrontation. The government closes the magazine and arrests its staff and supporters. This event comes to be known as the Formosa Incident (美丽岛事件 Meilidao shijian).
1980	—Month-long trial of the "Gang of Four" (Siren Bang 四人帮).	—Nativist movement that started in 1975 continues.

YEAR	CHINA	TAIWAN
1980 (*cont.*)	—*Art Monthly* (Meishu 美术) publishes an article by Qu Leilei 曲磊磊, a member of the Stars Group, proclaiming art should be for the sake of self-expression. —Stars Group's show that criticizes the authority, especially Wang Keping's 王克平 wooden sculpture of Mao as Buddha, arouses controversy. —The trend of Rustic Realism (Xiantu sieshi 乡土写实) becomes prominent. Artists depict Cultural Revolution's impact on ordinary people in rural and border regions, such as Chen Danqing's 陈丹青 *Tibetan Series* and Luo Zhongli's 罗中立 *Father*.	—Nativist movement that started in 1975 continues to flourish. —Many art groups are established promoting experiment and avant-garde art. —Artists promoting the Modernist movement in the 1950s and '60s as well as members of the Eastern (Dongfang 东方) and Fifth Moon (Wuyue 五月) Painting Groups who had went abroad return to Taiwan. —Government revenue and private money is devoted to the arts, including building county cultural centers, art museums and setting up private galleries.
1981	—Hu Yaobang 胡耀邦 replaces Hua Guofeng 华国锋 as the chairman of the China Communist Party. —Deng Xiaoping 邓小平 becomes chairman of the Central Committee's military commission. —*The Exhibition of Liu Kuo-sung's* 刘国松 *Paintings* opens. —Several Modernist shows open around the country.	—Hsi Te-chin 席德进, a watercolorist who combines modernist and native idioms, passes away. —Zao Wou-ki 赵无极 visits Taiwan. —The conceptual artist Chung Pu 庄普 returns to Taiwan. —Installation and mixed-media work become popular among younger artists.
1982	—Chinese Government launches the Anti-Spiritual Pollution Campaign (Fanjingshen wuran yundong 清除精神污染运动). It condemns three westernizing trends in art after the Cultural Revolution: individualist values, art for art's sake and abstraction. —An exhibition of the Boston Museum of Fine Arts' collection opens in Beijing.	—The 101 Contemporary Artist Group is founded, including Lu Tian-yan 卢天炎, Wu Tien-chang 吴天章, Yang Mao-lin 杨茂林 who advocate a grassroots sensibility. —*Lion Art* (Xiongshi meishu 雄狮美术) and *Artist Magazine* (Yishujia 艺术家) begin to report art developments in China.
1983	—The editorial team in *Art Monthly* is replaced because the magazine publishes articles about abstract art.	—The Taipei Fine Arts Museum (TFAM) opens, which is the first museum in Taiwan to focus specifically on modern and contemporary art.

YEAR	CHINA	TAIWAN

1983
(*cont.*) —Exhibitions of Italian Renaissance art, the works of Picasso and Munch, and French contemporary oil painting are held in Beijing.

1984 —Deng Xiaoping proposes a 'one country, two systems' solution for settling problems of Hong Kong and Taiwan.

—*Five-Person Exhibition of Modern Artists* in Xiaman 厦门 (Xiamen wuren xiandai yishu-zuopin zhan 厦门五人现代艺术作品展) features conceptual arts and readymade objects.

—*The Experimental Painting Exhibition: The Stage 1983* (Basannian jieduan: Huihua shiyan zhanlan 八三年阶段: 绘画实验展览) in Shanghai is forced to close soon after the opening.

[TAIWAN]

—The Taipei Painting Group (Taipei Huapei 台北画派) is established, advocating art that reflects political and social realities. Its members include Lu Tian-yan and Wu Tien-chang.

—*Retrospective Exhibition of the Development of Taiwan Art* (Taiwan diqu meishu fazhan huiguzhan 台湾地区美术发展回顾展) is organized by The Council for Cultural Affairs (文化建设委员会).

—*Exhibition of Modern Art in Korea* (韩国现代美术展) opens at Taipei Fine Art Museum.

1985 —Jiang Zemin 江泽民 becomes mayor of Shanghai and oversees the economic development of the city.

—The Anti-Spiritual Pollution Campaign ends. Released from the restraints of the previous three years, avant-gardism flourishes across the arts, a phenomenon named as the '85 Movement. More than 80 art groups appear across the country during 1985–87. They sponsor some 150 events during 1985–86, involving at least 2,250 artists. They champion individualism, freedom of expression, and western modern and postmodern styles. The leading artists include Wang Guangyi 王广义, Zhang Peili 张培力, Geng Jianyi 耿建翌, Huang Yongping 黄永平, Gu Wenda 谷文达 and Wu Shanzhuan 吴山专.

—*A Retrospective Exhibition of Robert Rauschenbert's Works* opens at the National Gallery Beijing.

[TAIWAN]

—Over a thousand art events are held this year and more private galleries are opened.

—Activities in the Taipei Fine Arts Museum are the focus of the media.

—Broad range of concerns are addressed by artists, among them, environmental issues.

—Lee Tsai-chien's 李再钤 star-shaped red sculpture, *Minimal Infinite* (Dixiande wuxian 低限的无限), exhibited at Taipei Fine Art Museum causes concern that it might be misunderstood as a Communist red star. Therefore, the sculpture is painted grey by the Museum without artist's permission. It raises issues of freedom of expression.

YEAR	CHINA	TAIWAN
1986	—*The Last Exhibition '86 No. 1* ('86 zuihou zhanlan yi hao 八六最后展览一号) opens at the Zhejiang Art Gallery featuring works with ready-made objects and performance.	—Taiwan's first opposition party, the Democratic Progressive Party (DPP, Minzhu jinbu dang 民主进步党), is formed.
	—Wu Shanzhuan and fellow artists hold private exhibitions of installation in Hangzhou.	—Lee Tsai-chien's star-shaped sculpture is painted red again.
	—*Festival of Youth Art* in Hubei opens, including 50 small groups of artists with 2,000 works. Their works fuse vernacular culture with contemporary style.	—*Exhibition of Modern Art in Germany* (德国现代美术展) opens at Taipei Fine Art Museum.
	—A Symposium on the '85 Movement and the Chinese avant-garde is organized in Zhuhai and Guangdong and is attended by critics, editors, and artists from across the country.	—The Studio of Contemporary Art (Xiandai yishu gongzuoshi 现代艺术工作室) is founded by artist June Lai 赖纯纯.
	—An exhibition of Xiamen Dada group led by Huang Yongping opens, advocating the synthesis of Dada and Chan Buddhism.	—The first solo exhibition of self-taught Chinese ink painter Yu Cheng-yao 余承尧 at the age of 88 is well received.
	—The Pool Society, including artists Zhang Peili and Geng Jiangyi creates a series called *Yangshi Taichi No. 1* (Taiji xilie yihao 太极系列一号).	
	—The Chinese Modern Art Research Committee is founded in Beijing by about 30 critics.	
	—The authorities launch a campaign against bourgeois liberalism (Fan Zichanjieji Ziyouhua 反资产阶级自由化), targeting new political and cultural thought, which hamper the activities of the avant-garde.	
1987	—Hu Yaobang, Communist China's main reformer, is forced to resign and replaced by Zhao Ziyang 赵紫阳.	—The Martial Law is lifted. The government announces that residents of Taiwan are officially allowed to visit relatives on the mainland. It also lifts the restriction on newspapers and publishing.
	—A plan for a nationwide exhibition of avant-garde art is halted by the government.	

YEAR	CHINA	TAIWAN

1987 (*cont.*)

—Some avant-garde groups continue their activities. However, the avant-garde movement is weakened by government directed antibourgeois campaign and pressure to produce commercial art.

—Some important artists begin to move overseas, such as Gu Wenda who settles in New York.

1988

—The campaign against bourgeois liberalism ends and some avant-garde activities resume.

—Xu Bing's 徐冰 installation *Book from the Sky* (Tianshu 天书) arouses much discussion.

—*1988 Chinese Modern Art Convention* (1988 Dangdai yishu yantaohui 1988 当代艺术研讨会) opens, and is attended by 100 artists and critics from across China. They aim at revitalizing the avant-garde movement and organizing a national exhibition.

—President Chaing Ching-kuo 蒋经国 dies and is succeeded by vice-president, Lee Teng-hui 李登辉. Lee is the first native-born president.

—The Provincial Art Museum opens in Tai-chung.

—*Artist Magazine* in Taiwan and Mainland journal *Fine Arts in China* begin editorial exchanges.

1989

—The first nationwide avant-garde art exhibition opens at the National Gallery, Beijing. Organized by Li Xianting 栗宪廷 and Gao Minglu 高名潞, *the China/Avant-Garde* (Zhongguo xiandai yishuzhan 中国现代艺术展) displays a total of 293 paintings, sculptures, videos, and installations by 186 artists, including Wang Guangyi, Xu Bing, Wu Shanzhuan, Huang Yongping, and Gu Wenda .The show is closed twice by authorities during its two-week run.

—Students join in a pro-democracy protest in the Tiananmen Square of Beijing, but was cracked down by troops and tanks with several hundred killed—known as Tiananmen Square incident.

—Taipei Fine Arts Museum opens its basement display area for regular experimental art exhibitions.

—National Taiwan University establishes a Graduate School of Art History.

—Alternative art spaces, IT Park Gallery (I-tong Gonyuan 伊通公园) and Apartment No. 2 (Erhao gongyu 二号公寓) start to operate.

—An exhibition of the Taipei Painting Group opens at Taipei Fine Art Museum. Wu Tien-chang's paintings *Five Periods of Ching Ching-kuo* (Ching Ching-kuo de Wuge shidai 蒋经国的五个时代), a series of large satiric paintings of the late president, attract the most attention.

YEAR	CHINA	TAIWAN
1989 (*cont.*)	—Gu Dexin 顾德新, Huang Yong-ping, Yang Jiechang 杨诘昌 partici-pate in *Les Magiciens de la terre*, an exhibition organized by the Pom-pidou Centre in Paris. After the show Huang Yongping remains in Paris.	
1990	—As a result of the post-Tianan-men censorship, as well as ongo-ing commercial pressures, idealist avant-garde activity in China declines drastically. —The art journal *Fine Arts in China* (Zhongguo meishu Bao 中國美術報), which played an impor-tant role in the avant-garde move-ment, is closed by authorities. —*Art Monthly*, which had devoted considerable attention to the '85 Movement, is re-staffed with conservatives. —Cynical Realism (Wanshi xian-shi zhuyi 玩世写实主义) leads the trend of paintings in the early 90s. —An exhibition of eight women artists *The World of Women Paint-ers* (Nuhuajia de shijie 女画家的世界) opens. —Xu Bing finishes his installa-tion project, *Ghosts Pounding the Wall* (Guidaqiang 鬼打墙. After this project, Xu Bing moves to the United States. —Fei Dawei 费大为curates the largest exhibition of modern Chinese art to date in a western country, *Chine: Demain pour hier* in France.	—The National Unification Committee and the Foundation for Cross-Straits Relations are founded. —A new avant-grarde group, Tai-wan Archives Workshop (Taiwan Danganshi 台湾档案室), organizes an exhibition *A Celebration of President Lee Teng-hui's Inaugura-tion*, criticizing ruling party Kong-mintang's (KMT 国民党, Nationalist Party) political policy. —Women's Awareness Association (Funu xinzhi 妇女新知) sponsors Wowen's Art Week (Nuxing yishu-zhou 女性艺术周) with an exhibition and symposium. —*Taiwan Art: 300 Years* (Tai-wan meishu sanbai nian 台湾美术三百年展) opens at the Provincial Museum at Tai-chung. —*A Retrospective of Western-influ-enced Art in Taiwan, 1895–1945* (Taiwan zaoqi xiyang meishu huiqu zhan 台湾早期西洋美术回顾展, 1895–1945) opens at Taipei Fine Art Museum. —The Association of Museums in Taiwan is founded.
1991	—China joins the Asia-Pacific Economic Cooperation (APEC).	—The Research Committee on the February 28 Incident was established. —All the senior legislators in the Taiwan's National Assembly retired.

YEAR	CHINA	TAIWAN

1991
(*cont.*)

CHINA:

—An exhibit *"I Don't Want to Play Cards with Cézanne" and Other Works: Selections from the Chinese "New Wave" and "Avant-Garde" Art of the Eighties* is held in the Pacific Asia Museum in Pasadena California, including artworks of Geng Jianyi, He Duoling 何多苓, Xu Bing, Yu Hong 喻红, Zhang Peili, and Zhang Xiaogang 张晓刚 and others.

—*The Exceptional Passage* is held at the Fukuoka Museum in Japan. Participating artists include Gu Wenda, Huang Yongping, Cai Guoqiang 蔡国强, Yang Jiecang, and Wang Luyan 王鲁炎.

TAIWAN:

—A private-owned museum, Hung-hsi (鸿禧) museum, opens.

—*China Times* sponsors *The Fantastic World of Miro* at Taipei Fine Art Museum.

—*Taipei-New York: Encountering Modernism* is held at Taipei Fine Art Museum.

—Art critic Ni Tsai-chin's 倪再沁 articles endorsing Nativism art generate fierce debate.

1992

CHINA:

—The first nationwide avant-garde exhibition since the Tiananmen Incident, *Guangzhou First Oil Painting Biennial* (Guangzhou diyijie youhua shuangnianzhan 广州第一届油画双年展), opens in Guangzhou. The show is developed under official policies to increase the value of Chinese avant-garde art in both domestic and international markets. The focus in the exhibt is Political Pop art (Zhengzhi popu 政治波普), which combines socialist realist or imagery in the Cultural Revolution with the style of American Pop Art.

—Artists Ni Haifeng 倪海峰, Sun Liang 孙良, Chou Deshu 仇德树, Wang Youshen 王友身, Li Shan 李山, Cai Guoqiang 蔡国强 and Lu Shengzhong 吕胜中 participate the exhibition *K-18: Encountering the Other*, in Kassel, Germany.

TAIWAN:

—The Art Gallery Association of Taiwan is founded and organizes the first International Art fair.

—Huang Hai-ming 黄海鸣 curates, *Dis/Continuity: Religion, Shamanism, Nature* (Yanxu yu duanlie: Zongjiao, wushu, ziran 延续与断裂—宗教、巫术、自然) with the conference *Eastern Aesthetics and Modern Art* (Dongfang meixue yu xiandai meishu yantaohui 东方美术与现代艺术研讨会) at TFAM.

—*The First Taipei Biennial of Contemporary Art* is held at TFAM.

—TFAM purchase Hans Arp's works marking its first collection of foreign artwork.

—Artists Chou Pang-ling 周邦玲, Ho Huai-shuo 何怀硕, Huang Chin-ho 黄进河, Kuo Jen-chang 郭振昌, Grace Yang-tze Tong 董阳孜, Wu Tien-chang 吴天章, and Yu Peng 于澎 participate the exhibition *K-18: Encountering the Other*, in Kassel, Germany.

1993

CHINA:

—Jiang Zemin is appointed president of Communist China.

TAIWAN:

—Taiwan's foreign reserve reaches US$ 8.31 billion, ranked the highest in the world.

YEAR	CHINA	TAIWAN
1993 (*cont.*)	—The Chinese avant-garde artists such as members in the New History Group (Xinlishi 新历史) and the Long-tailed Elephant Group (Dweixing 大尾象) begin producing works that address problems of consumerism and materialism in China. —The exhibit, *China's New Art, Post-1989*, opens at the Hong Kong Arts Centre in January and then travels to Australia. The exhibition includes more than 200 works by 50 artists, including paintings, sculptures, and installations. Political Pop and Cynical Realist works are predominant style in the show. —Thirteen artists from the *China's New Art* show are invited to participate in the 45th Venice Biennale. —*Fragmented Memory: The Chinese Avant-Garde in Exile* opens at Columbia, Ohio and exhibit works by Gu Wenda, Huang Yongping, Wu Shanzhuan and Xu Bing.	—The policy Detailed Measures for the Sponsorship of Cultural Events goes into effect. This policy requires the developers of any publicly-owned building to put aside 1% of total construction cost for the purchase of art works. —Artist magazine begins a special monthly column on feminist art. —Lee Ming-sheng 李铭盛 is invited to participate the 45th Venice Biennale. —TFAM organizes an exhibition for Auguste Rodin's Sculpture. —National Museum of History organizes an exhibition for artist Li Keran 李可染 in China. —Mountain Arts, Culture, and Education Foundation (山艺术文教基金会) works with Kaohsiung municipal government to organize *Love River Art Festival* (Aihe Yishujie 爱河艺术节).
1994	—Communist China's gross domestic product grows at an average annual rate of about 10%, the highest in the world, between 1994 and 2000. —Ma Liuming 马六明, Zhu Min 朱冥and other young artists stage performance in private space. —Zhu Jinshi 朱金, Wang Gongxin 王功新 and Lin Tian-miao 林天苗 organizes art activities in his own apartments. —*The Com-Art Show: China, Korea and Japan '94* opens in the Capital Normal University, Beijing, presenting modern paintings and installation works.	—Community cultural development projects are promoted by various townships. —Provincial Art Museum in Taichung organizes the exhibition *Contemporary Chinese Ink Painting* (Zhongguo xiandai shuimohua dazhan 中国现代水墨画大展). Over a hundred artists from the Mainland, Hong Kong, and Taiwan participate, representing the largest cross-straits assembly of artists since 1945. —*The 1994 Taipei Biennial of Contemporary Art* (Taibei xiandai meishu shuangnianzhan), held at TFAM.

YEAR	CHINA	TAIWAN
1994 (*cont.*)	—Political Pop artists Li Shan李山, Yu Youhan 余尤含, Wang Guangyi, Liu Wei 刘韡, Fang Lijun 方力钧, and Zhang Xiaogang 张晓刚 participate in *The 22nd International Sao Paulo Bienal*.	—Kaohsiung Museum of Art organizes *A Retrospective Exhibition for Cobra's Karel Appel*. Appel comes to hold the opening. —*A Retrospective Exhibition for Andy Warhol* is opened at TFAM. —Swen-yi 顺益 Taiwan Aboriginal museum opens, the first museum in Taiwan dedicated to indigenous culture.
1995	—Capital Normal University sponsors a series of solo exhibition for avant-garde artists and organizes *Beijing-Berlin art Exchange* (Beijing-Bolin yishu jiaoliuzhan 北京柏林艺术交流展). —Chinese avant-garde art show, *Avantguardes art stiques xinese*, opens at Centre d'Art Santa Monica, Barcelona.	—Taipei Fine Arts Museum participates in the Venice Biennial for the first time. Art Taiwan is planned with works by artists Lien Te-cheng 连德诚, Wu Ma-li 吴玛俐, Huang Chi-ho 黄进河, Hou chung-ming 侯俊明 and Huang Chih-yang 黄志阳. —Dimensions Art Foundation collaborates with the Louvre Museum to hold an exhibition of Louvre's 71 paintings at the National Palace Museum.
1996	—*Reality, Today and Tomorrow: An Exhibition of Contemporary Chinese Art* (Xianshi, jintain yu mingtian 现实，今天与明天) opens at Beijing, organized by a new generation of art critics presenting a new generation of artists' works. —Chinese avant-garde art exhibit, *China: Zeitgenössische Malerei* opens at Kunstmuseums Bonn.	—The first direct presidential election is held. Incumbent president and KMT candidate Lee Teng-hui is elected. —Accompanying the *Taipei Biennial of Contemporary Art*, a symposium on the identity of Taiwan art is organized by TFAM, which arouses debate widely. —New York Metropolitan Museum and the National Palace Museum in Taipei arrange a US tour of 475 works from the Palace Museum. It prompts a protest among citizens who concerns the fragile condition of some works. The museum eliminates 7 most sensitive works from the show.

YEAR	CHINA	TAIWAN
1997	—Deng Xiaoping dies. —Britain cedes Hong Kong back to China. —Jiang Zemin legalizes private enterprise and unveils a plan to privatize Communist China's state-owned enterprises. —Several exhibits on Chinese avant-garde art opens such as, *Quotation Marks* at Singapore Museum, *Against the Tide* at New York, and *Cities on the Move* at Vienna.	—*Sadness Transformed: The February 28 Commemorative Exhibition* (Beiqing shenghua 2.28 meizhan 悲情升华：二二八美展) is held at TFAM. —An exhibition of 60 Impressionist paintings from Musee d'Orsay opens in Taipei and Kaohsiung. —With the effort of artists and art critics, Huashan Art and Culture District (Huashan Yiwen tequ 华山艺文特区) in downtown Taipei is established.
1998	—Zhu Rongji (朱镕基) is appointed prime minister. He introduced a sweeping program to privatize state-run businesses and further liberalize the nation's economy. —*A Century—Female Art Exhibition* (Shiji Nuxing yishuzhan世纪·女性艺术展) opens in Beijing. —Gao Minglu organizes the exhibition *Inside Out: New Chinese Art* in New York (1998–1999). The exhibition features work by artists from mainland China, Hong Kong and Taiwan as well as those living abroad, consisting of nearly 90 works created in the years 1985–1998.	—*The Taipei Biennial: Site of Desire* (Yuwang Changyu 欲望场域) marks the first time a foreign curator was invited to curate an exhibition in Taiwan. Artworks include those from Taiwan, Japan, South Korea and China. Taiwanese artists in the Biennial includes Mei Dean-e 梅丁衍, Chen Chieh-jen 陈界仁, Wu Ma-li and Huang Chi-ho etc. Works of Cai Guoqiang 蔡国强 and Xubing 徐冰 from China attract much attention. —*Symposium of Worldwide Chinese Curator* opens at the Provincial Museum at Tai-chung. Participants include Lin Hsin-yueh 林惺岳, Li Jun-hsian 李俊贤 Ni Tsai-chin 倪再沁, Huang Hai-ming 黄海鸣, Shi Rui-ren 石瑞仁, Kao Chien-hui 高千惠, Li Xianting 栗宪廷, Fei Dawei 费大为, Gao Minglu 高名潞, and Liao Wen 廖雯.
1999	—China rounds up thousands of members of the Falun Gong sect 法轮功. —The exhibition *Rainbow Across the Century: Vulgar Art* (Kua shiji caihong: yansu yishu 跨世纪彩虹—艳俗艺术) opens at Tianjin.	—On September 21st a strong earthquake shocks Taiwan. 2070 people die. —Wang Chun-chieh's 王俊杰 sarcastic work—a serious of virtual products—critique consumerism. —Juming 朱铭 Museum opens.

YEAR	CHINA	TAIWAN
1999 (*cont.*)		—Huang Hai-ming curate *The Heart of History—Exhibition of Installation Art* at a small historical town, Lugang 鹿港.
2000	—*Shanghai Biennial 2000* (2000 上海双年展) opens in the Shanghai Art Gallery in November, through to January 2001. This exhibit offers contemporary Chinese artists to exhibit their works under the auspices of the government for the first time. This exhibition includes oil painting, traditional Chinese painting, wood carving, sculpture, photography, interior decor and video art. A dozen artists from 18 countries have been invited to participate in the exhibition. —The *Exhibition of Salvador Dali's Art* is held in Beijing.	—Democratic Progressive Party candidate Chen Shui-bian (陈水扁) is elected president of the Republic of China in Taiwan. —Many art activities are held to raise fund for victims of 921 earthquake. —*2000 Taipei Biennial: The Sky is the Limit* opens. Young artist Lin Ming-hong's 林明宏 huge installation featuring vernacular cloth is one of the focuses. —No. 20 Storehouse (Ershihao Cangku 二十号仓库), an unused space at Taichung Railway station, re-opens as exhibition space for artists.
2001	—China joins the World Trade Organization. —The debut of exhibition dedicated to abstract art *Metaphysics 2001: Shanghai Abstract Art Exhibition* opens. —Ministry of Culture issues a notice requesting artists to stop performance with bloodiness, violence, sex or dirty scene in the name of action art. —The art magazine *Meishu* 美术 includes articles discussing Action art.	—Taipei lifts a 50-year ban on direct trade and investment with China. —Museum of Contemporary Art, Taipei (MOCA) opens, the first museum in Taiwan featuring contemporary art. —Fubon Art Foundation 富邦藝術基金會 organizes exhibition *Very Fun Park* 粉樂町 in which artworks are displayed and installed outdoors in Taipei's eastern neighborhoods. —The debut of Kaohsiung International Container Art Festival 高雄國際貨櫃藝術節, a biennial cultural event in Kaohsiung, in which artists around world are invited to express their ideas on urban ecology by transforming empty containers to artworks. —The exhibition *From Poussin to Cezanne: 300 YEARS OF FRENCH PAINTING* 從普桑到塞尚: 法國繪畫三百年 is held in National Palace Museum, Taipei.

YEAR	CHINA	TAIWAN
2002	—Hu Jintao 胡景濤 becomes the head of the ruing Communist party. —The Guangzhou Contemporary Art Triennial opens with exhibition *Reinterpretation: A Decade of Experimental Chinese Art (1990–2000)* 重新解读：中国实验艺术十年 (1990–2000), organized by Wu Hung 吳鴻. —*2002 Shanghai Biennial* 2002 上海雙年展 is held at Shanghai Art Museum with theme on urban developments in China and their consequences for society. It shows about 300 works by more than 60 artists and architects from 26 countries.	—Taiwan officially enters the World Trade Organization. —Taishin Arts Awards 臺新藝術獎 set up by Taishin Bank Foundation for Arts and Culture 台新銀行文化藝術基金會 draws many attentions with its high award. —A group of art students, with money they earn from part-time job, set up Taipei Biennale Awards 台北雙年獎 to challenge the authority of art awards. —Art critic Li Xianting 栗憲庭 and artist Liu Xiaodong 劉小東 from China teach at the Department of Fine Arts in Tonghai University as visiting professors. —Lin Man-Li 林曼麗, Huang Hai-ming 黃海鳴, Shi Juijen 石瑞仁, Tsai-chin 倪再沁, Chen Zuei-wen 陳瑞文 and Lin Chi-Ming 林志明 initiate the exhibition *CO2—Taiwan Avant Garde Documenta* involving most of avant-garde artists and art groups in Taiwan.
2003	—China was rocked by the Sars virus. —Lost for 143 years since the Qing dynasty, four of the bronze animal statues (pig, ox, tiger, & monkey) from the Yuanmingyuan park were returned to China to be exhibited publicly. —The Bejing International Art Biennial opens. 577 works from 45 countries are showcased. Text and Subtext : Female Art Exhibition of Asia 主題與副題—亞洲女藝術家作品展 opens in Beijing. The theme of the exhibitions focuses on women's role in the world.	—Dramatic rise in cases of the pneumonia-like Sars virus. —The exhibition *Ilha Formosa: The Emergence of Taiwan on the World Scene in the 17th Century* 福爾摩沙—十七世紀的台灣.荷蘭與東亞 opens in the National Palace Museum, Taipei. —Huang Ming-chuan 黃明川 received the first Visual Arts Award of Taishin Arts Awards. —*The First International Women's Art Festival in Taiwan* 台灣國際女性藝術節 opens in Kaohsiung. —Taiwan government promotes investment in Taiwan's Culture and Creative Industries 文化創意產業.

YEAR	CHINA	TAIWAN

CHINA

—Hou Hanru 侯瀚如 curates *Zone of Urgency* in the 50th International Art Exhibition of the Venice Biennale concerning the explosive expansion of today's megalopolises, primarily in the Asia-Pacific region

TAIWAN

—Guggenheim Museum's plans to open a new location in Taichung of middle Taiwan fires up heated debates with pros and cons of various types.

2004

CHINA

—The exhibition *Well Then, China?* opens at the Centre Pompidou, in Paris. It is the first officially sponsored exhibition of avant-garde Chinese art abroad. More than 50 well-known artists' works in various media are shown, including painting, photograph, video, sculpture, installation, film and architecture etc.

—*The Dashanzi International Art Festival* 大山子国际艺术节 debuts at Beijing's 798 Art District showing experimental art.

—The *International Character Expo 2004* 2004 動漫形象博覽會 opens in Shanghai exhibiting comics and animations together with cosplay performance.

—The exhibition *Impressionism Treasures from the National Collection of France* 法國印象派繪畫珍品展 is held in Beijing, Shanghai and Hong Kong.

TAIWAN

—President Chen Shui-bian wins a second term by a slender margin.

—Twenty-four volumes of *Taiwan Contemporary Art Series* 台灣當代美術大系 are published by the Artist Publishing.

—Mei Dean-e 梅丁衍 received the Visual Arts Award of Taishin Arts Awards for his exhibition *Mei's Interpretation* 梅氏解讀玩, in which he criticizes Taiwan's politic situations with sarcastic irony.

—The exhibition *Fiction. Love—Ultra New Vision in Contemporary Art* 虛擬的愛: 當代新異術 opens at Taipei, featuring videos and digital images, as well as comics and animation.

—*Bunker Museum of Contemporary Art—18 Solo Exhibitions* 金門碉堡藝術館—18 個個展 curated by Cai Guogiang 蔡國強 opens in Kinmen 金門 island, a once military reserve. Involving artists/art groups from both Taiwan and China, this show features 18 unused eighteen bunkers transformed into art museums/objects.

2005

CHINA

—The first direct flight between China and Taiwan since 1949 was inaugurated.

—*Songzhoang Cultural Art Festival* opens at the art village near Beijing. For five days, 300 artists show more than 600 works in 50 studios.

TAIWAN

—National Party (KMT) leader Lien Chan 連戰 visits China for the first meeting between Nationalist and Communist Party leaders since 1949.

—Kaohsiung Children's Museum of Art, the first public museum for children in Taiwan, opens.

YEAR	CHINA	TAIWAN
2005 (*cont.*)	—Highlighting Piccaso's 265 pieces of prints, drawings and watercolors, the exhibition *Picasso—Forbidden City* 畢加索—紫禁城 opens in Beijing. —Jin Shangy's 靳尚誼 first solo exhibition is held at National Art Museum of China after he engages at painting for 50 years. It showcases 160 oil paintings from different periods of his life.	—Plan for National Palace Museum Southern Branch in Jayi positions the branch for exhibiting Asian culture. —Chia Chi Jason Wang 王嘉驥 curates *The Spectre of Freedom* in the 51st International Art Exhibition of the Venice Biennale, conveying the concept of freedom as an illusive spectre to reveal the contemporary human condition. The exhibition showcases four artists from Taiwan, including Kao Chung-li 高重黎, Kuo I-chen 郭奕臣, Hsin-i Eva Lin 林欣怡, and Tsui Kuang-yu 崔廣宇.

Contributors

ROGER T. AMES is Professor of Philosophy and editor of *Philosophy East & West*. His recent publications include translations of Chinese classics, most recently the *Classic of Family Reverence: A Philosophical Translation of the* Xiaojing (with H. Rosemont). He has also authored many interpretative studies of Chinese philosophy and culture: *Thinking Through Confucius* (1987), *Anticipating China: Thinking through the Narratives of Chinese and Western Culture* (1995), and *Thinking from the Han: Self, Truth, and Transcendence in Chinese and Western Culture* (1997) (all with D.L. Hall). He has most recently been engaged in compiling the new *Blackwell Sourcebook of Chinese Philosophy*, and in writing articles promoting a conversation between American pragmatism and Confucianism.

KUAN-HUNG CHEN is a senior PhD candidate in the Philosophy Department at the University of Hawai'i working on a dissertation entitled "Knowledge and Conduct: Reexamining the Epistemic and Ethical Stances of Xunzi" that aims to reexamine the epistemic framework of the "modern self" through the application of Chinese assumptions about the nature and function of knowledge and moral values.

KAZUKO KAMEDA-MADAR is a PhD candidate of the Department of Art History, Visual Arts, and Theory at University of British Columbia. After working for three years in a fine arts gallery in Japan, she began her study of art history and received her BA in 1997 and MA in 2002 at the University of Hawai'i. She did further study at Kyoto University in 2003. Her special interest is the paintings of the Tokugawa period in general, and the "Orchid Pavilion Gathering" theme in particular. She explores the arts as they reflect Sino-Japan cultural relations, and is also researching issues concerning contemporary Chinese art.

APRIL LIU is a doctoral student in Chinese Art History at the University of British Columbia in Vancouver, Canada. She is completing a dissertation on nineteenth-century Chinese woodblock prints and the production of locality in rural China. Liu holds an MFA in Sculpture from Michigan State University and has exhibited and curated exhibitions in the United States, China, and Austria. Her research interests include late imperial Chinese print culture, contemporary Chinese art, and Buddhist visual culture.

JEROME SILBERGELD is the P.Y. and Kinmay W. Tang Professor of Chinese Art History and Director of the Tang Center for East Asian Art at Princeton University. He was previously the chair of Art History and director of the School of Art at the University of Washington, where he taught for twenty-five years. He teaches and publishes in the areas of Chinese painting history, both traditional and contemporary, Chinese cinema and photography, and Chinese architecture and gardens. He is the author of more than forty articles and book chapters, as well as seven books and three coedited volumes, including *Chinese Painting Style* (1982), *Contradictions: Artistic Life, the Socialist State, and the Chinese Painter Li Hua-sheng* (1993), *China Into Film* (1999), *Hitchcock with a Chinese Face* (2004), *Body in Question: Image and Illusion in Two Chinese Films by Director Jiang Wen* (2008), and *Outside In: Chinese x American x Contemporary x Art* (2009).

HSINGYUAN TSAO is an assistant professor in the Department of Art History, Visual Art, and Theory at University of British Columbia in Vancouver. She holds a PhD in Art History from Stanford University. Her area of special interest is the art of China's Middle Period (the tenth to twelfth centuries), the ruling period of the Liao and Song dynasties. She is also interested in contemporary art and film.

RICHARD VINOGRAD is the Christensen Fund Professor in Asian Art in the Department of Art and Art History at Stanford University, where he has taught since 1989. He is the author of *Boundaries of the Self: Chinese Portraits, 1600–1900* (1992), coeditor of the *New Understandings of Ming and Qing Painting* exhibition and catalogue (1994), and coauthor of *Chinese Art & Culture* (2001). Professor Vinograd has also written numerous journal articles, as well as anthology, conference, and catalogue essays on research interests that include Chinese portraiture, landscape painting, urban cultural spaces, painting aesthetics and theory, print culture and media studies, on topics ranging from tenth-century landscape painting to contemporary transnational arts.

Index